ROUTLEDGE LIBRARY EDITIONS: LIBRARY AND INFORMATION SCIENCE

Volume 23

COORDINATING COOPERATIVE COLLECTION DEVELOPMENT

COORDINATING COOPERATIVE COLLECTION DEVELOPMENT
A National Perspective

Edited by
WILSON LUQUIRE

Routledge
Taylor & Francis Group
LONDON AND NEW YORK

First published in 1986 by The Haworth Press, Inc.

This edition first published in 2020
by Routledge
2 Park Square, Milton Park, Abingdon, Oxon OX14 4RN

and by Routledge
52 Vanderbilt Avenue, New York, NY 10017

Routledge is an imprint of the Taylor & Francis Group, an informa business

© 1986 The Haworth Press, Inc.

All rights reserved. No part of this book may be reprinted or reproduced or utilised in any form or by any electronic, mechanical, or other means, now known or hereafter invented, including photocopying and recording, or in any information storage or retrieval system, without permission in writing from the publishers.

Trademark notice: Product or corporate names may be trademarks or registered trademarks, and are used only for identification and explanation without intent to infringe.

British Library Cataloguing in Publication Data
A catalogue record for this book is available from the British Library

ISBN: 978-0-367-34616-4 (Set)
ISBN: 978-0-429-34352-0 (Set) (ebk)
ISBN: 978-0-367-37684-0 (Volume 23) (hbk)
ISBN: 978-0-367-40365-2 (Volume 23) (pbk)
ISBN: 978-0-429-35568-4 (Volume 23) (ebk)

Publisher's Note
The publisher has gone to great lengths to ensure the quality of this reprint but points out that some imperfections in the original copies may be apparent.

Disclaimer
The publisher has made every effort to trace copyright holders and would welcome correspondence from those they have been unable to trace.

Coordinating Cooperative Collection Development: A National Perspective

Wilson Luquire
Editor

The Haworth Press
New York • London

Coordinating Cooperative Collection Development: A National Perspective has also been published as *Resource Sharing and Information Networks*, Volume 2, Numbers 3/4, Spring/Summer 1985.

© 1986 by The Haworth Press, Inc. All rights reserved. No part of this book may be reproduced or utilized in any form or by any means, electronic or mechanical including photocopying, microfilm, and recording, or by any information storage and retrieval system without permission in writing from the publisher. Printed in the United States of America.

The Haworth Press, Inc., 28 East 22 Street, New York, NY 10010-6194
EUROSPAN/Haworth, 3 Henrietta Street, London WC2E 8LU England

Library of Congress Cataloging-in-Publication Data
Main entry under title:

Coordinating cooperative collection development.

    Proceedings of the Conference on "Coordinating Cooperative Collection Development: a National Perspective," Chicago, Apr. 1-2, 1985, sponsored by the Eastern Illinois University and the Illinois Board of Higher Education.
    Includes bibliographies.
    1. Collection development (Libraries)—United States—Congresses. 2. Library cooperation—United States—Congresses. I. Luquire, Wilson. II. Conference on "Coordinating Cooperative Collection Development : a National Perspective" (1985 : Chicago, Ill.) III. Eastern Illinois University. IV. Illinois. Board of Higher Education.
Z687.C68   1986   025.2'0973   85-24847
ISBN 0-86656-543-4

Coordinating Cooperative Collection Development: A National Perspective

Resource Sharing and Information Networks
Volume 2, Numbers 3/4

CONTENTS

Foreword   1
    Geri Schmidt, Independent Consultant,
    Oglesby, Illinois

Preface   5
    Jutta Reed-Scott,
    Collection Development Specialist,
    Association of Research Libraries,
    Office of Management Studies

Introduction   7
    Glenn R. Scharfenorth, Associate
    Vice President for Academic Affairs,
    DePaul University,
    Chicago, Illinois

Library Resource Sharing: The Illinois Experience   11
    Robert Wallhaus, Deputy Director,
    Academic Affairs, The Illinois Board
    of Higher Education,
    Springfield, Illinois

  Libraries Are Inventory Problems   14
  The Illinois Experience   15
  Future Directions   18

A National Scheme for Collaboration in Collection Development: The RLG-NCIP Effort   21
    Paul H. Mosher

The Myth of the "Self-Sufficient Collection"   21
Toward a New Mythology: "Collaborative" Collection
   Development   24
Collaboration and Cooperation in Collection
   Development   26
The RLG Conspectus   28
Uses of the RLG Conspectus   30
The NCIP Project   31

The North American Collections Inventory Project (NCIP): 1984 Phase II Results in Indiana   37
    David Farrell,
    Indiana University

The Common Framework   37
Definitions   39
Elements of the Cooperative Environment in Indiana   40
Coordinating Collection Management in Indiana:
   Phase II Results   42
NCIP Phase II Results   47

A System Level Coordinated Cooperative Collection Development Model for Illinois   49
    Karen Krueger

Cooperative Collection Development Among Research Libraries: The Colorado Experience   65
    Joel Rutstein, Assistant Director
    for Collection Services, The Libraries,
    Colorado State University
    Johannah Sherrer, Director of Public
    Services, Michener Library,
    University of Northern Colorado

Part I: Development of COLA as a Cooperative
   Acquisitions Group   65
Part II: Movement Towards a Broader Cooperative Base   67
Part III: The Focus on Policy Statements   69

Part IV: The Workshops	71
Part V: Anatomy of a Collection Policy Statement— Master List of Disciplines	72
Narrative Descriptions	74
Conspectus Reporting Form	76
Intensity Codes	76
Conclusion: A Look to the Future	77

Indiana, Colorado, and Illinois—Comments on Three Approaches to Coordinated Cooperative Collection Development (CCCD) — 81

Terry L. Weech, Associate Professor, Graduate School of Library and Information Science, University of Illinois, Champaign-Urbana, Illinois

Comments on David Farrell's Paper	81
Comments on Karen Krueger's Paper	83
Comments on Joel Rutstein's Paper	85
Overview of All Three Papers	86

Discussion #1 — 91

Discussion Leader, Terry L. Weech

Cooperative Acquisitions Within a System: The University of California Shared Purchase Program — 99

Marion L. Buzzard, Head, Collection Development and Acquisitions, Main Library, University of California

Program Goals and Background	100
Governance	101
Funding	101
Expansion of the Program	102
Operation of the Program	103
Types of Materials Acquired	104
Bibliographic Access	105
Delivery	106
Location and Ownership	107
Strengths and Weaknesses	109
New Developments	111

The New York State Experience with Coordinated Collection Development: Funding the Stimulus 115
    Joan Neumann, Executive Director,
    New York Metropolitan Reference
    and Research Library Agency

Goals	116
Time in Operation	117
Governance	118
Financing	118
Coordinating	119
Make up: Participants	120
Make up: The Coordinated Collection Development Plan	120
Bibliographic Access	122
Delivery System	124
Resource-Sharing Existant	124
What Would You Do Differently?	125

Discussion Summary of the California and New York State Plans 129
    Mary Alice Moulton, Associate Director,
    Government Relations,
    Illinois Board of Higher Education,
    Springfield, Illinois

Discussion #2 133
    Discussion Leader, Mary Alice Moulton

Cooperative Collection Development Programs of the Triangle Research Libraries Network 139
    Joe A. Hewitt, Associate University
    Librarian for Technical Services,
    University of North Carolina, Chapel Hill

HILC at Thirty-Four: A View from Within 151
    Billie Rae Bozone, College Librarian,
    Smith College

Response to the Paper HILC at Thirty-Four: A View from Within	**161**
Susan M. Maltese, Coordinator of Library Services, Oakton Community College, Des Plaines, Illinois	
Response to the Paper Cooperative Collection Development in the Triangle Research Libraries Network	163
Discussion #3	**167**
Discussion Leader, Susan Maltese	
A Stitch in Time: The Alaska Cooperative Collection Development Project	**173**
Dennis Stephens, Associate Professor of Library Science, Collection Development Officer, Rasmuson Library	
The Pacific Northwest Collection Assessment Project	**185**
Anne Haley, Director of the Walla Walla Public Library, President of the Washington Library Association Douglas K. Ferguson, Director of the Library and Information Resources for the Northwest Program of the Fred Meyer Charitable Trust	
New Ways of Managing Collections	185
The Regional Context	186
A Foundation Initiative	186
Designing the Assessment	188
Assessment Training	190
The Pacific Northwest Conspectus Database	192
Expecting Timing of Events	192
Assessment Participation	193
Directory of Special Collections	193

Information Delivery Demonstration	194
Cooperative Acquisition Agreements	194
Financial Obligations	194
Outcomes and Continuation	195
Conclusion	196

Commentary on the Stephens and Haley Papers — 199
Scott Bennett, Assistant University Librarian for Collection Management, Northwestern University, Evanston, Illinois

Discussion #4 — 203
Discussion Leader, Scott Bennett

A Model Criterion for a Statewide Plan/Process/System — 215
Carl W. Deal, Director of Library Collections, University Library, University of Illinois at Urbana-Champaign

Introduction	215
Model Criteria for Coordinating Cooperative Collection Development Among Academic Libraries	217

Panel Discussion — 233
Moderator, Carl W. Deal

Foreword

Geri Schmidt

Independent Consultant
Oglesby, Illinois

Cooperative Collection Development is not a new concept. It is an activity libraries have been participating in with noted progress for a number of years. However, it is interesting to note how various groups of libraries have interpreted the term, cooperative collection development, and to note the unique types of activities that have emerged in the guise of cooperative collection development.

The contributors to this issue bring to our attention issues associated with cooperative collection development. Is it an activity most suitable for large research libraries or is it possible for all sizes and types of libraries to participate? Must aspects of management, preservation, storage and discarding be addressed or does the term simply imply cooperative acquisitions? Is collection assessment intrinsic to the process and, if so, what method of assessment is best? What role must bibliographic access and delivery play in a cooperative collection development project? Is access to resources equal to ownership of resources? Will cooperative collection development projects result in a decrease of expenditures or more efficient use of dollars?

Robert Wallhaus examines some of these issues using as an example the inventory of non-library resources. His presentation clarifies the objectives of any inventory/resource sharing project and outlines common considerations.

Paul Mosher tells us that what libraries need today goes beyond cooperative collection development; the goal we must strive for is *collaborative* collection development, a process beyond cooperation. He details the "grandfather" of cooperative collection devel-

---

Geri Schmidt is an independent consultant working with cooperative collection development projects. P.O. Box 158, Oglesby, IL 61348.

© 1986 by The Haworth Press, Inc. All rights reserved.

opment projects, The Research Libraries Group (RLG) Collection Management and Development Projects; as well as identifies the term conspectus and describes its use.

The North American Collections Inventory Project (NCIP) builds on the base developed by The Research Libraries Group and, using a common framework, allows additional libraries to contribute information about their collections. David Farrel provides insight into the pilot NCIP project in Indiana.

With the assistance of the Illinois State Library, a methodology was developed for System Level Coordinated Cooperative Development in Illinois. This method differentiates between client-centered assessment and collection-centered assessment. Collection-centered assessment "treats a collection as a resource irrespective of actual demand use. It focused on the intellectual breadth and depth of the collection and responds to the concept that a research collection's value is intrinsically related to the unknown needs of future scholars." The Illinois Model described is a client-centered assessment which "focuses on the actual utility of the collection to its current users."

Cooperative collection development among research libraries in Colorado began with cooperative purchasing. However, uniform collection policy statements and a conspectus which serves as a mechanism for identifying collection strengths in research libraries within the state are end-products of the effort.

The University of California also began cooperative collection development activities with a cooperative acquisitions project. The Shared Purchase Program, now in its ninth year, was implemented to prevent unnecessary duplication of expensive, low-use materials among the nine campus libraries.

Funding was the stimulus for the New York State experience with Coordinated Collection Development. This program is intended to augment collection strength and encourage regional resource sharing. The New York State program began in 1981 and provides funds to libraries involved in resource sharing. It is a sharp contrast to the Cooperative Collection Development Program of the Triangle Research Libraries Network in North Carolina which began informally over fifty years ago and has survived without the aid of additional funding. The Hampshire Inter-library Center (HILC) located in Massachusettes is a non-profit organization which pursues cooperative collection development by coordinating serials, cataloging, and maintaining a joint data base for its five member institutions. Thirty-four years of library experience has proven that HILC is able to provide better library services to their users through cooperation than they are able to provide alone.

It is encouraging to note that two of the newest cooperative collection development projects, The Alaska Statewide Cooperative Collection Development Project and the Pacific Northwest Collection Assessment Project, are able to benefit and build from some of the pioneering efforts in cooperative collection development. Both projects use a conspectus as developed by the RLG to map collection strengths and serve as the bases for coordinated collection development, but have modified the program so all types and sizes of libraries may participate.

These papers provide a series of practical seminars on how libraries have attempted cooperative collection development projects. In statewide, regional, interstate, and national programs we see a trend toward compatability. Compatability of terminology and methodology is important so the information we gather about our collections is comparable among not only different sizes and types of libraries, but also by libraries regardless of the location.

Rarely are libraries given the opportunity to learn and build on the cooperative experiences of others for the benefit of all. Each of these papers has contributed to the collective experience in cooperative collection development/management. With serious consideration of these programs we can meet our common objective: to serve the needs of library users as completely, efficiently and economically as possible.

Preface

Jutta Reed-Scott

Collection Development Specialist
Association of Research Libraries
Office of Management Studies

The conference on "Coordinating Cooperative Collection Development: A National Perspective," sponsored by Eastern Illinois University and the Illinois Board of Higher Education, took place in Chicago on April 1-2, 1985.

The conference had a dual purpose. One was to provide a comprehensive, state-of-the-art review of present cooperative collection development programs. The other objective was to develop model criteria for a statewide plan for coordinated collection development in Illinois.

The conference brought together representatives from a wide spectrum of cooperative programs, including statewide projects in Colorado, Illinois, Alaska and New York, the University of California Shared Purchase Program, the Hampshire Inter-Library Center, the Triangle Research Libraries Network, the Pacific Northwest Collection Assessment Project, and the North American Collections Inventory Project.

Taken together the proceedings of the conference provide critical perspectives on coordinated collection development and offer thoughtful assessments of the challenges of implementing effective programs. The value of the papers lies in the fact that the speakers moved beyond the description of the specific programs and analyzed successes and limitations. Several speakers concluded that critical preconditions contributing to effective programs are online bibliographic access to member holdings, rapid delivery of materials, formal agreements on shared responsibility for collection development, and a long-range timeframe.

The conference underscored the complexity and difficulty of designing organizational structures that support decision making for substantive cooperation without limiting individual libraries' autonomy. But the conference also highlighted the significant benefits of coordinated collection development programs. The most significant outcome is a set of criteria for building a model state plan which integrates the most successful components of present programs.

Introduction

Glenn R. Scharfenorth

Associate Vice President for Academic Affairs
DePaul University
Chicago, Illinois

I'd like to welcome you to a beautiful spring day in Chicago. We planned it on April's Fool's Day and we were fooled. My name is Glenn Scharfenorth. I'm the Associate Vice President for Academic Affairs at DePaul University formerly Librarian at DePaul—and at heart, still a librarian—welcoming you to this conference which is run jointly by the various groups that are listed in your program. As you know the theme of the conference is "Coordinating Cooperative Collection Development: A National Perspective." As we can see by the attendance, this is a very popular subject at this point in academic libraries. We have representation from 32 states, and enrollment to date (at the moment) is 174. We are very pleased with this turnout and hope that all of you will benefit from the conference. Our work here in Illinois has shown a need for a conference such as this and we hope it will benefit us as well as those attending.

The proceedings of the conference will be available in printed form. You can order your copy by talking to the people at the registration desk in the lobby, if you wish to do it ahead of time; if not, I'm sure it will be published in the literature. It is published through the facilities at Eastern Illinois University.

A few housekeeping details: We ask that none of you sit—and you are not sitting there now—at the back tables. They are reserved for lunch and if you could, please, remain sitting in this area including the coffee break, and not sit at those tables because they will be setting them up for lunch.

I will also ask that the speakers and moderators join me at the front table in the cycles in which they are speaking, using the coffee breaks and lunches as the dividing points. Also, we will take photographs of the speakers at 1:45 today here at the podium.

© 1986 by The Haworth Press, Inc. All rights reserved.

Photograph by: Maurice C. Libbey and Gene W. Scholes, Eastern Illinois University.

To give you a brief background of how we arrived at the conference—I'm chairing a committee in Illinois sponsored by the Illinois Association of College and Research Libraries and the Illinois

Board of Higher Education. One of our charges was to look at what can happen with cooperative collection development. Many projects had started in Illinois on a large scale and small scale: some successful and some not. Our task was to look at the various things both in Illinois and nationally that are shaping our future in cooperative collection development and/or management.

In doing our research, we discovered there really is no central place for information or answer to the problem. Thus, we arrived at the concept of this conference to gather together as many people as we could, nationally and locally, to discuss the issues relating to cooperative collection management and development. And therefore, we have done that here today. We hope.

We will be moving through it in cycles, beginning with an introduction in Illinois from the Board of Higher Education, moving into the National Perspective, and then talking about the various State Plans that have evolved. It is our anticipation at the end that those discussion leaders within each cycle will summarize, and we will attempt to develop a Model Plan that we might experiment with.

Library Resource Sharing: The Illinois Experience

Robert Wallhaus

Deputy Director, Academic Affairs
The Illinois Board of Higher Education
Springfield, Illinois

I'm an industrial engineer—at least by academic background. Since you're going to be spending a day and a half talking about library matters, I thought I'd talk a few minutes about industrial engineering, specifically about a classical industrial engineering problem—the inventory problem.

Chart A is a graphical representation of the single product inventory problem. As you can see from that chart, "cost" is plotted on one axis and "the quantity of inventory" on the other axis. We find that one type of cost increases with the quantity of inventory maintained. This is typically called the "holding cost." For example, as inventory expands it's necessary to spend more money on such things as the space to store the inventory, insurance on the inventory, the utilities associated with space, and so forth. Also, as we spend more money on inventory, that capital can not be used to generate earnings through some other kind of investment. This is called the "foregone earnings cost," and could be considered another component of the "holding cost."

On the other hand, there's a cost that decreases as we increase the amount of inventory acquired. This cost is typically called "the shortage cost." This cost is a bit more difficult to quantify. It reflects the avoidance of lost profits because we don't have inventory available to sell. It also reflects the cost of having dissatisfied customers when the product they want to buy is not available. These so-called shortage costs can be reduced by maintaining very large inventories.

If we add these two different kinds of costs together to obtain a

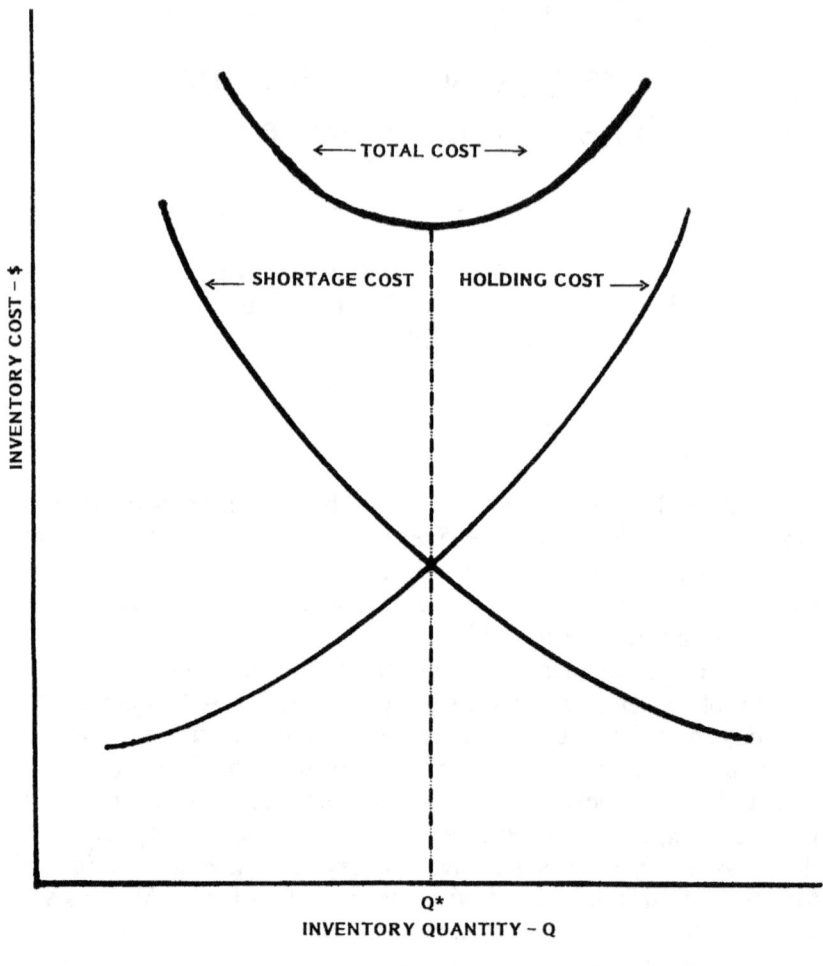

CHART A

total cost is appears as a bowl shaped curve in Chart A. You can see from the graph that the total cost is high for small quantities of inventory. Then it reaches a minimum, and finally increases again for large quantities of inventory. The objective in solving the inventory problem is to find that point on the curve where the cost is minimized. I've denoted that point with a "Q^*".

I won't go into the details of how one solves such problems mathematically. Just let me assure you that they can be solved—at least in the simple cases—such as the single product case just as I've described. However, it is absolutely essential to have data about historical customer demand for the product in question if one is going to analyze the inventory problem.

Therefore, the first principle in solving inventory problems is: in order to effectively manage inventories it's necessary to develop a data base which reflects the history of inventory transactions, and to continually analyze these data in order to gain insight into how well customer demands are being met. I'll refer to this as *The Analytical Problem.*

What I have described up to this point is the relatively simple case of a single product inventory. In the real world, inventory problems are much more complex. They involve multiple products that are interrelated. There's usually stochastic demand (that is, a probability function describes customer orders) and often, inventory is maintained at hierarchical levels within an organization.

This latter type of inventory problem is sometimes referred to in the literature as the multi-echelon inventory problem. I'll use a rather familiar example to illustrate a multi-echelon problem: the maintenance of yellow paper pads. The central office supply storerooms on your campuses typically order these yellow pads in carload lots in order to obtain better prices (i.e., price breaks), academic units periodically check out quantities of those yellow pads and store them in their departmental supply storerooms; and faculty and staff often go to the storeroom and pick up three or four yellow pads and put them in their top desk drawer for their personal convenience. These practices virtually maximize the amount of yellow pads on campus and usually result in very high "holding costs."

So, what can we do if we're trying to minimize total cost as shown in Chart A? One option is to ask that each time a faculty member needs another yellow pad, that he or she take a trip over to the central office supply storeroom and requisition one. This would eliminate all the excess yellow pads stored in desk drawers and departmental storage cabinets across the campus. But, it would also result in an outcry that would rival a proposal to reassign faculty parking spaces. And, for good reason! The cost of wasted faculty time would far outweigh the "holding cost" savings that would accrue by optimizing the mathematical model. Yet, it's precisely the kind of proposal that a naive and detached industrial engineer is likely to make.

This leads me to state a second principle: in order to effectively manage inventories, it is necessary to be aware of the subtle costs such as the cost of inconvenience and the cost of negative morale. Further, it is necessary to consult with those who have first hand insights relative to those intangible costs. I'll refer to this as *The Organizational Problem.* It has various subcomponents such as seeking expert advice; creating positive incentives; and encouraging the acceptance of change.

Lead time is another important consideration in inventory problems. It's defined as the time lag between when a customer perceives the need for a product and when the customer receives the product. For example, assume we could develop a system whereby whenever a faculty member pressed a button on his or her desk a new yellow pad would instantaneously appear. If we could technologically do this we would cut the lead time to zero. Furthermore, where the yellow pad came from would be transparent to the faculty member. Over some period of time he or she would care less whether yellow pads were in the top desk drawer, in the departmental storage cabinet, or for that matter in the central campus storeroom. Most important, all the other inventory problems I've described—reducing holding costs, the organizational problems, and so forth—would also tend to disappear.

This leads me to the statement of the third principle: in order to make the most effective use of inventories, it is important to make their physical location transparent to the customers, in other words, to reduce the lead time. I'll refer to this as *The Lead Time Problem.*

Having said all that, there are probably many of you who are wondering why I spent the precious few minutes that the planners of this symposium allotted to me discussing the technicalities of inventory problems. I suspect that there are also a number of you who see the relevance of some of the principles I have described to the objectives of this symposium.

LIBRARIES ARE INVENTORY PROBLEMS

The bottom line is: libraries are inventory problems in disguise. In order to set directions for the future, particularly in the area of coordinated collection development, it will be necessary to address the three inventory challenges that I have described. I'll henceforth refer to them not as 'problems,' but as 'challenges,' and these are: *The Analytical Challenge; The Organizational Challenge,* including

Seeking Expert Advice, Creating Positive Incentives, Encourage the Acceptance of Change; and *The Lead Time Challenge.*

THE ILLINOIS EXPERIENCE

How has Illinois addressed those challenges? Over eight years ago a liaison committee representing librarians from all types of Illinois colleges and universities, the Illinois Board of Higher Education staff, and the Illinois State Library was established. This committee continues to meet on a regular basis and its role has become increasingly effective and influential. The committee is called The Illinois Board of Higher Education/Illinois Association of College and Research Libraries Liaison Committee. Its charge is: To advise the Illinois Board of Higher Education on opportunities for more effectively developing and utilizing our library resources. It has addressed such topics as: collection conservation, advising the Board as to priorities for libraries in annual budgets, library computer systems, library space utilization, cooperative collection development, and opportunities for utilizing emerging communication technologies for transmitting information. In summary, its charge is broad.

In the context of the challenges I have described, this committee, its subcommittees, and its linkages to library groups, professional organizations and to internal campus structures have addressed the organizational challenge in two significant ways:

1. It has provided expert advise and direction. It has prevented industrial engineers, and in my case bureaucrats, from overlooking the subtleties and intangibilities involved in complex developments related to libraries, and
2. It has provided leadership for change.

If there were one message above all that I would leave with you from my perspective in Illinois, it would be: Address the organizational challenges at the outset—the political, administrative, and process challenges—and give them priority attention from that point on!

A second major development in Illinois has been the implementation of the Library Computer System (LCS). This system has been in operation since about 1978, over 5 years ago. LCS is an online, computer-based, access and circulation system that currently serves libraries in 25 colleges and universities including all Illinois public universities, 3 community colleges, and 10 ten private colleges and universities. LCS is administered by the University of Illinois, and advised by a policy council and an operations council representing the LCS participating institutions.

LCS is based upon computer software developed at Ohio State University in the late 1960's. It is *not* a technological marvel. In fact, there are online circulation systems being utilized on individual campuses and consortia of institutions that are more sophisticated than the LCS. LCS's main contribution is not that it's on the leading edge of the state-of-the-art.

However, the distinguishing characteristic of LCS in Illinois is its magnitude and its growth. By the end of last year, the LCS holdings count passed thirteen million volumes. The LCS computerized data base includes 9.8 million monograph volumes representing 7.7 million monograph titles, and 3.4 million serials volumes representing 400,000 serials titles. Last year, LCS users initiated 33 million transactions. This represents a workload of more than twice that of three years ago. LCS processes as many as 15,000 transactions per hour during peak times. Two hundred and seventy-five thousand interlibrary circulation transactions were initiatied last year, which was an increase of 36 percent over the preceding year. Approximately 600 computer terminals are supported by LCS. LCS is the third largest computer-based library system in the country. Only OCLC and the Research Libraries Information Network support more terminals. It is the largest computer-based statewide library system and it has the largest resource sharing pool of currently held materials of any state in the Union.

What's the significance of LCS in terms of the three challenges I have outlined? LCS addresses two of those challenges. First, it addresses the lead time challenge. Users are gradually realizing that through LCS they have reasonably good access to a broader range of library resources than ever before. Second, LCS provides the basis for addressing what I have called the analytical challenge. The LCS data base is a computerized inventory of library resources which can be analyzed by subject classifications and physical locations. Further, historical demand data in the form of user transactions is being captured in a machine readable form on a day by day basis. In summary, while LCS is being used, it is generating the basic data that will be needed to carry out the analytical studies

Photograph by: Maurice C. Libbey and Gene W. Scholes, Eastern Illinois University.

which will inform future collection development policies and decisions.

Finally, Illinois has taken another significant step to address the lead time challenge. The Illinois State Library, utilizing State resources and Library Service and Construction Act monies totalling over $350,000 per year, has supported the Intersystems Library Delivery Service. This delivery service serves both LCS institutions and public libraries on a statewide basis, and links to regional library delivery systems. Even as I talk, vans are moving up and down and across this State delivering library materials from one location to another.

Our objective is to assure that library materials are in the hands of the requesting user within two days, independent of their physical location in the State. Our longer range objective is to substantially reduce this lead time by capitalizing upon communication technologies as they become available.

FUTURE DIRECTIONS

From my perspective, our future direction is simply stated (and perhaps 50 percent of this audience—that is, the 50 percent from Illinois—would say it's simple-minded). It follows the approach that one would utilize to address all other inventory problems.

1. First, we will, on a continuing basis, seek to understand the characteristics of our complex, multi-product, multi-echelon, shared inventory. That is, to analyze the strengths and weaknesses of our statewide library holdings; and to analyze the user demand for our statewide library holdings. Then, we will direct new and reallocated dollars based on these studies. Then, we will do more studies, and direct resources to address the priorities that those studies indicate are most useful in serving our citizens, faculty and students. By virtue of LCS data base, I believe, we are well positioned in Illinois to do this.
2. Second, we will support enhancements of LCS, such as expanding it to include full bibliographic records. We will work toward the development of an integrated network of regional sub-systems in cooperation with the State Library and the public library systems.
3. Third, we will strive to cut library lead times by capitalizing on opportunities to employ new communication technologies as they become feasible.
4. Fourth, and most important, we will continue to call upon our libraries to provide counsel relative to the subtleties and intangibles that analytical efforts alone can not provide. We will continue to rely upon their leadership in overcoming resistance to change. We will ask that they respond positively as dollars, both new and reallocated, are directed toward better managing and developing a shared resource. And, we will hope that they prevent the simple ideas of bureaucrats from becoming attractive when they are simple-minded.

Again, I believe Illinois is well positioned to meet this all important "organizational challenge," based on my experience in working with the leadership in our library systems.

In conclusion, I welcome you to Illinois. I have, by no means, done justice to the topic of my presentation—"The Illinois Experience." Karen Krueger, Carl Deal, and others will portray a more complete and accurate picture of the Illinois scene as this conference unfolds.

On behalf of Wilson Luquire, his co-workers in organizing this conference, and my colleagues in Illinois libraries, I express our appreciation for your coming to our State; and most of all, for helping to enlighten us in regard to our common goal—that is, the preservation, development, and effective utilization of our inventory of knowledge.

A National Scheme for Collaboration in Collection Development: The RLG-NCIP Effort

Paul H. Mosher

THE MYTH OF THE "SELF-SUFFICIENT COLLECTION"

Every year, some 700,000 new book titles are produced around the world—perhaps a little less than that now since the publishing rate, at least for a time, has leveled or even declined in a number of countries in recent years. To these may be added unnumbered additional millions of less controllable bibliographic items, such as pamphlets, newspapers, printed documents, technical reports, videotapes, maps, data tapes and bases and so forth. These serve to swell the ocean of 70 million or more titles published in the past. Adequate access to this sea of resources for scholars and other library patrons is the ultimate concern of this paper, and so to the centrality, I think, of the whole discussion. How can we get them to all of this material?

In the past, research libraries were often relatively isolated from each other, without suitable communication or delivery links to allow rapid exchange of bibliographic records or items among libraries. And the collections of many libraries were inadequate to support new, growing and diversifying research programs. While the National Union Catalog and the national interlibrary loan system were extraordinary and useful innovations for their time, and linked libraries and their collections more closely than had ever before been the case, these tools proved insufficient to sustain the ambitious new patterns of growth and demand or ambitious resource sharing schemes. Hence the development of the myth of the self-sufficient, or "comprehensive" collection intended to serve all reasonable

© 1986 by The Haworth Press, Inc. All rights reserved.

needs of patrons with only minimal recourse to the collections of other libraries. It was a *useful* myth in its time—a goal to enable the development of quality local collections to support quality local research.

While we have expended vast human and financial effort over the years to build and maintain very considerable library collections to support the work of our scholarly communities, we have been defeated in developing the independent, self-sufficient collections that were often the goal of our faculty and bibliographers.

Former Harvard University Librarian Douglas Bryant wrote, in 1976, that,

> A dozen years ago I said that 'research interests have become so broad and the quantity of printed materials useful to research has increased so greatly that the Harvard University Library today, with its 7 million volumes, is more frequently reminded of its inadequacies than it was 60 years ago when it had only 1 million'. We have added to the Harvard Library more than 2 million volumes since 1963, when I made that confession, but the reminders of inadequacy continue to increase in frequency.[1]

Many of us decided that we would have to abandon our former adherence to the advice of Polonius, to be neither a borrower nor a lender. Instead we decided to devise some new schemes to provide for the needs of research in an environment that would continue to be characterized by cost pressures. As Pat Battin has written, "The siren song of institutional autonomy and self-sufficient collection standards obscured those earlier recognitions that the process of scholarship and its demand for information cannot be confined to one building, to one institution, to one region, or even to one political jurisdiction."[2]

The myth of the self-sufficient collection has also been punctured by a series of collection overlap studies published in the library literature. The conclusion of recent studies is unavoidable: there is a surprising amount of unique material distributed among the libraries of a state or a region of the United States or even among research libraries of Great Britain. Indeed, the distribution of materials among groups of libraries tested argues strongly for the potential benefits of cooperative or distributed library functions, such as collection development, shared storage and pruning activity, preservation, and cataloging. Judicious use of findings from overlap study may result in less redundant and more effective use of local resources. On what findings is this hypothesis based?

A 1975 study of overlap among University of California System libraries revealed that 75% of Berkeley's holdings were unique among the northern libraries and 45% of UCLA's titles were unique in the south. Fifty-three percent of the collections at Berkeley and UCLA were duplicated at the other library.[3] Eighty-seven percent of titles held by SUNY libraries and Cornell were cataloged by one library only.[4] In the state of Wisconsin, 82% of all titles added in the University System libraries during a 2-year period (1977-1979) were held by just one library; only 18% of the titles were held by two or more libraries. When only recent acquisition of current imprints is compared, unique titles dropped to 68%—still very significant.[5]

Similar results come from Great Britain in the findings of Arms (1973)[6] that about 50% of titles held by British research libraries were unique, and, from an American multitype library system, in the findings of McGrath and Simon that 83% of the titles acquired by libraries in the state of Louisiana over an 18-month period were acquired by only one library.[7] Potter, summarizing these and other findings, found that uniquely held titles in a consortium or region varied between 50 and 86% . . . .[8]

In another recent study, Scrimgeour et al. found that among 82 theological and religious libraries in the American Theological Library Association, 22% of the titles held by all libraries are held by one library only.[9] The intent of the study was to determine the smallest number of collections required to provide 100% of titles; 60% of the titles were held by one library, whereas 100% were held by 39 of the 82 libraries."[10]

All the important books in all fields of scholarly research, in other words, are not held by any single library, not even the largest. As the comparative overlap ("verification") studies of the RLG Conspectus Project have shown, holdings are distributed among libraries in fascinating—and not always predictable—patterns. Even the Library of Congress, with its 19 million volumes, is exceeded by university libraries in holdings in certain disciplines, such as agricultural economics. In some fields, such as French literature, no library—including the Library of Congress—held more than 62% of the scholarly titles cited by the study. On the other hand, four large university libraries together possessed 83%.

This data supports Pat Battin's argument that:

> if we are to acknowledge openly our heretofore implicit acceptance of the responsibility for the health of national scholarship, we must channel our energies into the design and development of effective cooperative activities at the national level, which will then enable us to discharge our obligations to our regional and local colleagues.[11]

And these cooperative efforts must involve collaboration and distribution of effort among research libraries.

In this new environment, many of us have recognized, with Ms. Battin, that libraries no longer need seek the unattainable goal of self-sufficiency. We have recognized that circumstances call for cooperation—for ways to optimize each library's capacity to serve its constituency with basic, core materials, and link with other libraries in consortia or networks that will allow access to the collective research resources of all participants. We also understand that this would usually allow many libraries to serve their patrons and programs better, as they would come to feel less collection driven and become more patron and program driven.

Illinois has been a leader in this effort. The Cooperative Collection Development Subcommittee produced, in 1977, a thoughtful report entitled "Toward Cooperative Collection Development in the Illinois Library and Information Network."[12] This study recommended fostering the concept of local core collections, recognized the absence of collection development policies at most libraries, called for a means of mapping collection strengths and weaknesses, recommended rationalizing the research and information resources of the state, and called both for cooperative development of the state's knowledge and information resources and improved methods of bibliographic access and delivery to make the state's library resources optimally available to all citizens of the state.

TOWARD A NEW MYTHOLOGY: "COLLABORATIVE" COLLECTION DEVELOPMENT

Times, then, have changed, and old myths become less useful, are challenged and abandoned. New mythologies are created and replace old ones to serve as goals and ideals for new generations and

Photograph by: Maurice C. Libbey and Gene W. Scholes, Eastern Illinois University.

changed circumstances. Such is the case with the myth of the self-sufficient collection. Shopworn and battered, it has been largely discarded. The number of research libraries has increased enormously during the past forty years, as has the number of libraries of all kinds, and the environment in which our libraries do business is being transformed by the electronic revolution as well as improved methods for delivering or transmitting library materials and the information they contain.

What is called for is a new and more useful mythology. The myth of the self-sufficient collection is dead, and Pat Battin, Dick De Gennaro and others call for a new atmosphere of effective cooperative activity and resource sharing on the national level. What is needed goes beyond *cooperative* collection development; what we need is *collaborative* collection development. Cooperation is indeed the environment for the needed programs, but it is only an environmental quality, not the goal itself. The goal is *collaboration*—working, laboring, together in new communities of enterprise which leap the walls of our local libraries—or even our large campus library complexes. Collaborative collection development requires communities of librarians who know their patrons and their programs well. It requires librarians who are active rather than static, less clerical and more professional than in the past. It requires librarians who are change agents rather than reagents—the agents of proactive change rather than the effects of it. It requires librarians who will manage library collections that are more program and client centered and less collection centered than in the past. Collection development librarians in the collaborative model examine, for example, the changing culture and structure of research and study on a campus, and modify collecting practices to conform to their findings, rather than being content only to preserve and enlarge the libraries historical collection strengths.[13]

COLLABORATION AND COOPERATION IN COLLECTION DEVELOPMENT

Collaborative collection development among research libraries must have as its goal the optimization of research library resources for scholars in the collaborating institutions. It also may serve to assure there is adequate collection coverage of subjects or areas of mutual interest and concern.

It was important in devising the Conspectus and its uses that the focus in collaborative efforts was on the common wealth rather than on what each library "could get out of it." Two ways of representing a healthy collaborative collection development or resource sharing program may be useful to keep in mind. The first is to look at the research collections of all collaborators as extensions of one's own. One should be less bound or constrained by local efforts, and become more aware of the potential of shared, collective resources. The second was coined by David Stam of the New York Public Library in an attempt to epitomize the RLG collection development and shared resources programs: "Think nationally, act locally." The idea is to keep the future in mind while working in the present, to think of the whole while working on the parts.

Another useful concept in the development of the national Conspectus effort was outlined in a paper by Ross Atkinson of the University of Iowa Libraries. Atkinson used the terms "synergism" and "complementarity" (in a position paper for the RLG Collection Management and Development Committee) to apply to the various models of attempted collaborative programs. By "synergistic" Atkinson meant programs which are managed or controlled to achieve a predetermined outcome or set of outcomes—usually cost savings. Synergism bears implications of managerial direction—even tinges of sanctions or coercion. "Complementarity," on the other hand, implied facilitative, consensual programs. It refers to the creation of facilitative and supportive tools that may be used by collaborators who may wish to use them to help them achieve self-determined goals—local or collective. Finally, Atkinson argued that a middle ground between synergism and complementarity is optimal—one which he called "complementary synergism." In this framework, collaborating institutions agree on a collaborative or distributed set of activities, goals or objectives which each then works locally to support or attain. This set of ideas and ideals was helpful in developing the Conspectus and NCIP programs.

The issue before us is the quality of the research environment and the books and the other materials available to it. All research libraries that find themselves confronted by significant interlibrary borrowing realize that no library or congeries of campus libraries is an island. Indeed, academic libraries, like their parent institutions, are united in kind and interest with others like them. If our concern is with the provision of extraordinary research resources to our faculties, there is every reason to support collaboration in ways which increase the pool of research materials available to all scholars, while preserving our autonomy, individuality, and our capacity to provide first to our own scholarly community. This sort of complementary approach to collaboration is a goal of the Association of American Universities.

"Redundancy in area-related collections, coupled with rising costs and increased in the volume of materials to be acquired and stored, make it urgent that plans be developed for complementarity and shared resources among universities."

The Lambert report goes on to endorse an RLG founding principle:

> RLG is founded on the recognition that neither significant increases in library purchasing power nor reductions in demand for library services are likely in the foreseeable future, that the volume of information on which scholarship depends will continue to grow, and that in the decades ahead, individual collections, regardless of their size and history, will be forced to move increasingly away from the concept of comprehensive acquisition policies.[14]

THE RLG CONSPECTUS

Essentially the Research Libraries Group/North American Collections Inventory Project is a "complementary" program, designed as a tool to help overcome some of the problems faced by former attempts to carry out collaborative collection development efforts.[15] It was created to deal with concerns expressed at meetings of the chief collection development officers of nine major U.S. research libraries, and was realized by the Collection Management and Development Program of the Research Libraries Group late in 1979. The Conspectus is meant to provide a comparable map of research library collections by LC class (there is a Dewey conversion table) according to nearly 5,000 subdivisions which represent an expansion of the collection development subdivisions recommended in the ALA RTSD *Guidelines for Collection Development.*[16] The Guideline breakdown was intended for all types of libraries, while the RLG/NACIP amplification is intended to distinguish specific emphases or "disemphases" within the specialized collections of libraries. I will not duplicate here the details of the

Gwinn-Mosher article on the Conspectus in the March 1983 issue of *College and Research Libraries*.

The Conspectus is an overview or summary, arranged by subject of existing collecting strengths and future collecting intensities of RLG and participating Association of Research Libraries and Canadian Association of Research Libraries institutions.[17] The Conspectus has also provided a base for communication and cooperation about collections among the libraries of Alaska, and for a projected cooperative program among academic libraries of the Pacific Northwest under the auspices of the Library and Information Resources for the Northwest program of the Fred Meyer Charitable Trust—efforts which will be described later in today's program.

The Conspectus was created to respond to the discovery of a number of collection development officers of large research libraries that we were all too ignorant of the detailed realities of our collections. It was hard, if not impossible, to collaborate in developing collections, or in any distribution of effort, if we had to deal chiefly with myth or legend. Some sort of comparable, empirical collection descriptions were needed to provide a base for action—whether synergistic or complementary—or both. The uses of the Conspectus identified by the RLG Collection Management and Development Committee were:

1. The need to identify collection strengths nationally.
2. Mutual reliance and interdependence in providing research materials.
3. Establishment of a tool to identify collecting levels at other institutions, to allow for changes, and to assess their significance.
4. Capacity to control better the physical growth of library collections and operating costs, and to distribute both collecting responsibilities and savings that might result.
5. Development of a mechanism to locate needed research material more adequately.
6. Rationalization and standardization of format and terminology of local collection development policies to enable libraries to achieve the above goals.
7. Development of a mechanism whereby an institution may store or dispose of locally unneeded materials with the knowledge and assurance that materials will be available elsewhere.

8. Establishment of a means for relating collection policy to preservation policy, both institutionally and cooperatively.
9. Development of a mechanism for relating collection policy and responsibility to cataloging priorities and for establishing centers of cataloging.[18]

As you can see, we hoped that the Conspectus would provide a basis for collaboration in cataloging and preservation, as well as collection development.

USES OF THE RLG CONSPECTUS

To date the Conspectus, which now covers all LC subjects but A (general), U and V (military and naval science), has been completed by about 25 of the 30 RLG libraries, and the Library of Congress. Indiana academic libraries testing the NCIP methodology have also completed certain segments. Special area or format conspectuses have also been devised for government documents, maps, East Asian Studies, Latin American Studies and South Asian Studies, and a number of libraries who are not regular RLG members have submitted data for these area or format segments, as well as for some regular LC segments such as art, music, medicine and law. We have found that the Conspectus has provided the basis for a good deal of complementary effort among our libraries, and some basis for both selected reductions and increases in collection strengths. The Conpectus effort has provided each participating library that did not already have one a copy of its own collection development policy for the first time. Conspectus data has also been used to analyze the adequacy of collections to determine if we feel collections and collecting efforts match the research and curricular programs of our institutions, and to attempt to identify, and provide at least minimal coverage of, esoteric areas and languages or topics felt to be "endangered species," to use the term coined by the Library of Congress representative. Local conspectus efforts have also been used, with success, for accreditation self-study.

RLG libraries have also used the Conspectus to negotiate about collection strengths with both new and older faculty, to negotiate collecting responsibilities and distribution of effort among campus libraries, and—increasingly—to examine interlibrary borrowing strategies.

But the most valuable part of the whole project for many of us—and our bibliographers—has proved to be the process itself. Often for the first time, collection development librarians were urged, and provided with time, to analyze their collections systematically. The favorable response to this effort has been overwhelming, and accounts for a good part of the growing enthusiasm in many parts of the country about undertaking the work, considerable though it is. Even while the project is under way, librarians find they are able to communicate more knowledgeably about their collections, make selection and management decisions more soundly, and generally take better control of the collections under their stewardship.

THE NCIP PROJECT

David Farrell, of Indiana University, will describe the Indiana Test Project and phases I and II of the North American Collections Inventory Project in some detail later on. I will restrict my remarks here to a short description of the project and its origins.

The RLG Conspectus was not created as a tool for a single consortium, but to help link research libraries of North America in ways that would facilitate knowledge of patterns of library resources. The approach of the collective inventors was to describe the combined research resources (and by this we mean lower-use, non-curricular materials) of all major U.S. research libraries as part of the largest scholarly research resource collection the world has ever known. It was to make comparable knowledge of these resources and their patterns of distribution more widely known and understood that the Conspectus was created. RLG provided the vehicle for creating, housing, experimenting with, and using this new device, and represents one of a number of consortia that are likely to use the information it contains.

The North American Collections Inventory Project, based at ARL and funded by the Council on Library Resources and other agencies, builds on the foundation provided by RLG, and seeks to put into effect a plan developed by the ARL Task Force on Collection Development and an Advisory Committee consisting of ARL, RLG and ARL staff representatives. This project seeks to create an on-line inventory of North American (Canadian as well as U.S.) research libraries' collection patterns, arranged by subject divisions guided by the Library of Congress classification schedules and the subject taxonomy of academic disciplines.

Libraries undertaking the project first analyze their existing collections by the assignment of standard codes to describe the functional support level of the collections, and the language patterns in which materials are collected. The same pattern is then analyzed and described for current collecting efforts. In addition, space is provided for detailed notes covering distinguishing specialties or emphases of each individual library's collections.

NCIP is the cornerstone of a national collaborative effort, and of other regional consortial efforts as well. The Office of Management Studies of ARL is staffing the project, and have developed with the help of the Indiana Project librarians and bibliographers from RLG member libraries, an excellent training program and manual to support the project.

The benefits of the NCIP program resemble, and amplify, those envisioned by the RLG and ARL test library participants. The Conspectus offers the following collaborative tools:

1. A map of North American research collection strengths through a standard tool for collection description and assessment.
2. A mechanism to locate significant research collections more expeditiously. By mapping existing patterns of collection strength, the inventory will serve as a powerful collection development and public service referral device.
3. The capacity to relate local collecting policies to collection levels at other institutions and to serve as the basis for collaborative and cooperative collection development, both nationally and regionally.
4. The capacity to relate collection development strengths to cataloging, retrospective conversion, and preservation needs, and to serve as a basis for cooperative cataloging and preservation efforts.[19]

The potential benefits of completing the NCIP Conspectus effort are not only collective or collaborative. There are major local benefits as well, which include:

1. Enhancement of the library's collection management program. The process of analyzing collections will facilitate the preparation of collection development policies, identify long-

and short-range collection needs, and establish priorities for the allocation of collection funds;
2. Establishment of a systematic program of collection assessment;
3. Development of broader staff expertise in collection management, especially collection assessment;
4. Establishment of a process to involve faculty in collection development and to serve them more effectively by expediting access to materials located elsewhere;
5. Development of a tool for communicating with university administrators. The assessments provide a means to demonstrate where collections are lacking, how the library's collections compare with those in other institutions, and where additional funds are needed; and
6. Enhancement of the library's role in the institutional planning process of providing information on collection strengths vis-à-vis academic programs.

Item #5 above is an important caveat. Collaborative collection development and the NCIP program do not necessarily imply budget cutting, but were devised to permit clearer delineation of the relationship between an institution's collection development and management efforts and it's academic programs. NCIP is also intended to allow a more knowledgeable and rational allocation or distribution of effort and resources. As Richard De Gennaro pointed out in a *Library Journal* article,

> we must husband [our] existing resources and increase them in the future. It would be a tragedy if those who fund our libraries were to misunderstand the purpose of resource sharing and use it as a rationale for further reducing library appropriations. Resource sharing will permit us to do more with less by pooling our resources, but only if we keep the pool replenished.[20]

It is our hope that NCIP will serve as a dynamic source of factual and comparable information about the nature, scope and patterns of the collections and collecting efforts of North America's principal research libraries, and that on this foundation of information, new collaborative programs will be constructed at the national, state and regional levels. We hope that the NCIP effort will provide a basis to assist collection development librarians in negotiating collaborative, distributed and cooperative programs for maintaining and sharing the richness of our nation's—and North America's—extraordinary library resources—in good times as well as bad.

NOTES

1. Bryant, Douglas W., "Strengthening the Strong: The Cooperative Future of Research Libraries," *Harvard Library Bulletin*, 24 (1976), 5. Mr. Bryant's reminders of inadequacy were rising Harvard interlibrary loan rates, and increasing faculty purchase requests.

2. Battin, P., "Research Libraries in the Network Environment: The Case for Cooperation," *Journal of Academic Librarianship*, 6 (1980), 68.

3. Cooper, W.S., Thompson, D.D., and Weeks, K.R., The duplication of monograph holdings in the University of California Library System. *Library Quarterly*, 45, (1975), 253-274.

4. Evans, G.T., Gifford, R., and Franz, D.R. *Collection Development Analysis Using OCLC Archival Tapes: Final Report.* U.S. Government of Health, Education and Welfare, Office of Education, Office of Libraries and Learning Resources, Washington, D.C., 1975 (ERIC Document ED 152 299).

5. Moore, B., Miller, I.J., and Tolliver, D.L., "Title overlap: A study of duplication in the University of Wisconsin System libraries," *College & Research Libraries*, 43 (1982), 14-22.

6. Arms, W.Y., "Duplication in Union Catalogs," *Journal of Documentation*, 29 (1973), 373-79.

7. McGrath, W.E., and Simon, D.J., *"LNR: Numerical Register of Books in Louisiana Libraries,"* Louisiana State Library, Baton Rouge, Louisiana, 1972 (ERIC Documents ED 070 470 and ED 070 471).

8. Potter, W.G., Studies of collection overlap: A literature review. *Library Research 4*, (1982), 3-21.

9. Scrimgeour, A.D., Hurd, A., Deering, R.F., and Thompson, D.D., *Collection Analysis Project. Final Report. Ad Hoc Committee for the Preservation of Theological Library Materials.* American Theological Library Association, 1981.

10. Mosher, P.H., "Quality and Library Collections: New Directions in Research and Practice in Collection Evaluation." *Advances in Librarianship*, 13 (1984), 226-27.13.

11. Battin, "Research Libraries. . . ," 70.

12. "Toward Cooperative Collection Development in the Illinois Library and Information Network." A Report submitted by the Cooperative Collection Development Subcommittee of the Research and Reference Center Directors. Illinois State Library, January, 1977.

13. On librarians as change agents, see: Tom G. Watson, "The Librarian as Change Agent," *Advances in Library Administration and Organization*, 2 (1983), 85-97.

14. Lambert, R., *Beyond Growth: the Next Stage of Language and Area Studies*, a Report by the Association of American Universities, Washington D.C., 1984, p. XX.

15. On problems of coordinated collection development programs and some chief models attempted in the U.S., see Paul H. Mosher and Marcia Pankake, "A guide to coordinated and cooperative collection development," *Library Resources and Technical Services*, 27 (1983), 422-25. These guidelines also contain suggestions for planning cooperative collection development programs.

16. *Guidelines for Collection Development.* David R. Perkins, ed., American Library Association, Chicago, 1979, 42-54.

17. Gwinn, N.E., and Mosher, P.H., "Coordinating Collection Development: The RLG Conspectus", *College & Research Libraries*, 44 (1983), 128-140.

18. Gwinn-Mosher, pp.130-131.

19. Adapted from Jutta Reed-Scott, *Manual for the North American Inventory of Research Library Collections*. Association of Research Libraries, Office of Management Studies, Washington, D.C., January, 1985 Edition, p. 9.

20. De Gennaro, R., "Resource sharing in a network environment," *Library Journal*, 105 (1980), 355.

The North American Collections Inventory Project (NCIP): 1984 Phase II Results in Indiana

David Farrell

Indiana University

ARL's Office of Management Studies brought the North American Collections Inventory Project (NCIP) to Indiana in 1984 as a pilot project funded by the Council on Library Resources and the Lilly Endowment and organized with the cooperation of the Research Libraries Group (RLG). The purpose of the project was to test and to develop a training program and a methodology, using the RLG Conspectus as a structure, for coordinating collection management among ARL institutions. It was the first major test of the RLG Conspectus in an environment where the corporate incentives of RLG do not operate.[1]

In my remarks this morning I will, first, address the points in the "Common Framework" suggested by the conference organizers; our model doesn't quite fit, but I can stretch it a bit. Second, I want to define "coordinated cooperative collection development." I feel certain we have nearly as many definitions of these commonly-used words as we have participants in this program. Third, I will describe four organizations or programs present in Indiana before the implementation of NCIP which contribute to the local cooperative environment and which are important to our success. Fourth, I will describe the progress of the Indiana project and its results.

THE COMMON FRAMEWORK

As a point of reference, you ought to know that the "Indiana model" is not an elaborate coordinated collection management system. It is a modest model, a developing but working model, that is being built on a subject-by-subject analysis of collections and collecting practices in three ARL institutions. Simultaneously we are analyzing our collections and the research and instructional programs they support. We are looking at complementary collections in our sister institutions to see if a coordinated approach to developing the collections and sharing information about how we manage them might help us to meet our local obligations more effectively and efficiently. At this stage we are not planning for a central staff supported by a "high tech" network. The people primarily involved in making our model work are the subject specialists in each institution.

Let me fill in the "common framework" as far as I'm able.

Goals: Our goals are to complete the Conspectus, using the common methodology and standard tools developed by RLG and ARL, to see if parts of the three university collections might be improved through a coordinated approach to their management. We hope to develop specific cooperative agreements and to use them in local resource planning and allocating.

Time in Operation: We have been addressing this task cooperatively since January 1984.

Governance: The chief collection development officers are guiding the project.

Financing: There is no budget, although each institution had a small grant during 1984 to cover the costs of travel, telecommunications, and student assistance. The high costs of Conspectus development have been absorbed in our routine work.

Make-up: Three voluntary ARL members: IU, the University of Notre Dame, and Purdue University.

Indiana University is a public institution with 1,400 FTE faculty, 32,700 students and 99 PhD programs. The library has 4 million volumes and 27,000 serial titles. Special collections include African, Slavic, Asian, European and American languages and literatures, history, music, and area studies. The humanities collections of the Lilly Library comprise 4 million manuscripts and 400,000 rare books. Collection development staff include an Associate Dean for Collection Management with 11.5 full time bibliographers and 25 other librarians with collection development responsibilities.

The University of Notre Dame is a private Catholic university with 768 FTE faculty, 9,200 students, and 26 PhD programs. The library collection has 1.5 million volumes and 11,000 serial titles; special collections include theology, church history, American

Catholic studies, Dante, and medieval studies. Collection development staff include an Assistant Director of Libraries for Collection Development, three full-time bibliographers and fifteen additional staff with some collection development responsibilities.

Purdue University is a public landgrant university with special strengths in science, technology and agriculture. It has 1,981 FTE faculty, 32,500 students and 53 PhD programs. The library has 1.5 million volumes and 18,000 serial titles. Collection strengths include physical sciences, agriculture, engineering, technology, veterinary medicine and computer science. Collection development is the responsibility of an Assistant Director for Research Library Services and 25 librarians who have specific collection development responsibilities.

Bibliographic Access: All are OCLC members.
Delivery System: Telefax, UPS.

General comments—the pro's and con's of our experience—will be addressed later in my remarks.

DEFINITIONS

Today and tomorrow we will hear a lot about "coordinated cooperative collection development." What does this mean? It depends on who's talking, what he's describing, and the context. Is there a common understanding of the meaning of "cooperative?" Does it refer only to materials, or does it refer to the cooperative use of knowledge and personnel? Does cooperation involve "core" collections as well as unique research collections? Are signed agreements and high technology necessary?

In their helpful "Guide to Coordinated and Cooperative Collection Development Among Libraries" Mosher and Pankake define "coordinated or cooperative collection development" as synonymous terms meaning "sharing in the development or management of collections by two or more libraries making an agreement for this purpose."[2] Mosher and Pankake take the concept further in their definition of "distributed" collection management. They note that "cooperative and coordinated collection development is normally achieved by the distribution of collection development responsibilities among libraries of a consortium . . . in a way that will provide greater coverage than is possible for any single library."[3] This is a crucial point; we cooperate because we believe it improves access for all to research materials.

As I thought about our work in Indiana it seemed useful to consider the terms "cooperative" and "coordinated" separately, one defining the pre-existing environment and the other defining the objective toward which NCIP leads us. I think that coordinated collection management is, by definition, distributed collection management.

ELEMENTS OF THE COOPERATIVE ENVIRONMENT IN INDIANA

In Indiana, cooperative systems have been a part of the environment a long time, but their impact on collection development has been largely passive if not negligible. For example, InCOLSA, the statewide bibliographic network, supports shared technical processing and bibliographic access as do similar networks everywhere. While InCOLSA provides an important link between the state's research libraries, it offers little direct benefit for collection management. This is a critical problem because collections (by which I mean both locally held materials as well as the capability to access remote collections) are the core of the scholarly enterprise. The utilities can do much more to make the machine-readable bibliographic databases work for us if they are willing and if we demand it. The Conspectus brings a new collection-centered focus to research library cooperation, and, if we are successful, the NCIP effort will redefine the meaning and use of the utilities as well as other organizations, systems, and networks.

Before discussing the progress of NCIP, I will describe briefly four organizations in Indiana's pre-existing cooperative environment that are critical for our success as we move into a coordinated environment.

The four organizations are the Indiana Four State Cooperative, the Committee on Institutional Cooperation, the OCLC/Research Libraries Advisory Committee, and the Midwest Cooperative Conservation Program.

The *Indiana Four State Cooperative* includes Indiana University, Purdue University, Ball State University and Indiana State University. These are the four state-supported universities that are signatories to an agreement made in 1969. By the terms of their agreement, each provides expedited reference and interlibrary lending services to the other three members. The current budget of $75,000 per year supports staff, equipment, telephone, postage and photocopying costs. The smaller institutions pay the largest shares because they require the most service. System traffic for IU's portion in 1984 totalled 1,314 books and 26,112 photocopy pages sent to the other three partners.

The top level library administrators of the four institutions (joined by their counterparts from the Indiana State Library and the University of Notre Dame) meet annually to discuss mutual concerns. Two recent results partly due to these meetings were the decision to participate in NCIP and the decision by IU, Notre Dame and Purdue this year to install telefacsimile equipment to expedite the transfer of materials and information between the campuses.

A second organization significant for Indiana's future in coordinated collection development is the *Committee on Institutional Cooperation* (CIC). CIC links the Big 10 institutions (Indiana, Illinois, Iowa, Michigan, Michigan State, Northwestern, Ohio State, Purdue, Wisconsin and Minnesota) and the University of Chicago. According to recent statistics, these eleven institutions award 10% of all master's degrees and 20% of all PhD degrees in the U.S. each year. Their libraries hold more than 40 million volumes and subscribe to more than 450,000 serials. The CIC sponsors cooperative programs supporting research, instruction, and faculty and curricular development. The library deans and directors meet occasionally and the chief collection development officers have been meeting twice a year at ALA since 1983. As a result of these initiatives, the Sloan Foundation has funded a collection management conference for 55 CIC science librarians and chief collection development officers this September at the University of Chicago. In preparation for our meeting, each institution is completing parts of the science conspectus divisions to allow institution-by-institution comparison of subject strengths. The librarians are also conducting a comprehensive survey of science collection management issues and practices. Two background documents produced from these efforts will provide common ground for conference discussions, and, I hope, for the development of an agenda for cooperation which may include closer coordination and cooperative collection development agreements. In the future we hope to extend the CIC conference series to include our humanities, social science, and area studies librarians.

OCLC's *Research Libraries Advisory Committee* is a third organization supporting the cooperative environment. RLAC was organized in 1980 by OCLC's research library directors to raise—some said to prod—OCLC's consciousness to the needs of large research libraries. RLAC has an important role in the national cooperative environment if it can bring OCLC's database, computers, and personnel to work for research library collection management. The RLAC Task Force on Cooperative Collection Development has proposed several ways for OCLC to assist its research library members. For instance, RLAC urges its members to complete the Conspectus through participation in NCIP and RLAC would like to see if the Conspectus Online can be mounted in OCLC. Pointing to the new collection analysis services offered by AMIGOS, RLAC proposes that OCLC produce similar products for gap and overlap studies, verification studies, and shelflist counts.[4] OCLC has responded with the Collection Analysis Project. This is a test using a sample of 1,000 OCLC records to assess the feasibility of analysing holdings and bibliographical data on archival tapes and in the Online Union Catalog to provide individual libraries and consortia with collection management information.

The fourth cooperative organization I will mention is the *Midwest Cooperative Conservation Program.* This was established at Southern Illinois University with NEH funding to provide information, training, and repair services to midwestern research libraries. Although the first two-year grant expires this year and MCCP's future is not clear, the program has had an important impact by calling preservation issues to the attention of regional research libraries. CIC members are now discussing the need for a regional preservation program and facility.

COORDINATING COLLECTION MANAGEMENT IN INDIANA: PHASE II RESULTS

I will now describe how NCIP is helping Indiana develop a coordinated collection management program in a structured and effective fashion.

NCIP was conceived in three phases. In Phase I (1983) Conspectus training materials and a training program were developed by ARL's Office of Management Studies and ARL signed an agreement with RLG for cooperative development of the Conspectus.

This is important, for by the terms of the agreement RLG opened the national database, the Conspectus Online, to non-RLG libraries and an ARL representative was appointed to RLG's conspectus task force. RLG and ARL have agreed to work together to develop and revise the Conspectus (and its associated verification studies and supplemental guidelines) so that it will be a truly cooperative instrument and a national standard for research libraries.

In Phase II (1984), the training program and materials developed in 1983 were tested in Indiana. We did this by simultaneously completing conspectus subject divisions and by adding our data to the Conspectus Online. In Phase III (1985), the project is being implemented in some 20 ARL member libraries. Four groups presently are working cooperatively in Canada, California, the Southeast and the Pacific Northwest.

NCIP developed from a project organized by ARL's Collection Development Task Force. In 1981 ARL charged the Task Force to plan a standard approach to cooperative collection development to ensure that specialized research collections in ARL libraries would be maintained as national resources. The Task Force also desired to support local libraries' collection management programs by encouraging the drafting of collection development policies, identifying long- and short-term collection needs, establishing priorities for fund allocation, developing staff expertise in collection evaluation, and involving teaching faculty in the collection development process. The Task Force recommended the RLG Conspectus (after an initial test in five libraries) as a vehicle because it appeared to be the best instrument developed to date for inventorying research collections and assessing their strengths. The Conspectus lacked a technical manual and a training program for bibliographers, so a major objective of NCIP was to develop these resources.

Based on the LC classification scheme, the Conspectus imposes a standard format and terminology which allows collection development librarians to discuss and compare collections with colleagues across distances, working in different environments, with common understanding. While the LC class schedule is not a perfect outline of scholarly knowledge, it is, taken as a whole, better than any other and it is the general scheme most familiar to research librarians. It is flexible and expandable. Mounted in an interactive data base, the Conspectus Online makes long distance communication easy, and can be searched a multitude of ways by combining terms, and is easily corrected and updated.

The goals of the Indiana phase of NCIP included the following:

1. To review and test the Conspectus format and training materials, including the bibliographer's manual;
2. To collect data on the time and cost of completing the Conspectus and in implementing the training program; and
3. To establish a schedule and plan for the three libraries to complete the Indiana Conspectus cooperatively.

Three task forces (one in each library) guided the local efforts while a committee of collection development librarians and OMS staff coordinated the statewide effort. A state-wide advisory committee representing public, special, governmental, college and university libraries and InCOLSA, the state network, provided general oversight and conducted a survey of research collections in the state's non-ARL libraries.

Our initial cooperative task was to select the first five conspectus subject divisions to complete. We chose subject divisions that represent collections we consider to be strong, or collections that we think might be significantly enhanced if we combined our resources. We also considered the subject expertise and availability of staff who would be completing the divisions, and we selected certain divisions because they have verification studies.

For example, each of our institutions has a strong chemistry collection, but the collections have different focuses; we want to see if the combined collection is significantly stronger than three distributed collections. IU's language and literature collections are unusually strong; Notre Dame and Purdue want to know if our strengths complement their weaknesses. Purdue has special strength in engineering, while IU is developing a new program; we want to know if Purdue's expertise and materials can support us in the expensive endeavor of developing an engineering collection. IU's religious studies program has proposed a doctoral program; we want to know if Notre Dame's strengths in religion can be utilized.

The organization of training and review of the progress at each institution was directed by local task forces. The progress at each institution varied according to local circumstances. At IU, for example, a task force member served as liaison to each group working on a conspectus division. As liaison for the languages and literature division I worked with about 10 subject specialists representing American and foreign, ancient and modern languages and literatures, linguistics, children's literature, journalism, film studies, and rare books. The group put about 250 hours into the project, not including about 100 hours spent to complete a verification study for English literature. In other areas, six bibliographers worked a total of 70 hours on the psychology division; three bibliographers put 64 hours into the art and architecture division; four bibliographers worked 25 hours on the technology division; and three bibliographers completed the physical geography and earth sciences division in 24 hours.

When the assessment of a division was completed at all three institutions, we compiled the values on a set of master worksheets and distributed it to our bibliographers for analysis. We asked them, first, to consider whether their collections were sufficient to support the local instructional and research programs. Second, we asked them to consider how the values for their collections compared with those of the other two institutions; were there significant lacunae and redundancies? Third, we wanted to know if collections at one institution might support programs at another institution.

Initial analysis suggests that we need to examine more closely our collections in chemistry, Latin American studies, religious studies, and environmental and chemical engineering. Engineering values as recorded in the technology division of the conspectus were surprising low and of special concern to IU as it develops a new program. Further analysis of Latin American Studies appears justified because IU has strong retrospective collections (including unique book and manuscript materials in the Lilly Library), but funding for the program is relatively low. At Notre Dame, on the other hand, a private institute has a special interest in Latin America but their collection is relatively new with little retrospective strength.

In their analysis bibliographers are looking at growth and change in faculty FTE and research interests, student enrollments, interlibrary borrowing, shelflist measurements, and verification studies. Our chemistry librarians are checking a list of 1,000 frequently cited journals and will compare the incidence of gaps and overlaps. We are completing a study of interlibrary borrowing transactions to determine by Conspectus category those items the three institutions could not procure within the state last year. Preliminary analysis of these data suggest that there is a higher number of transactions for strong collections in some divisions than for weak collections, including a fair amount of out-of-state borrowing for collections that are strong at all institutions. Analysis of specific items and users, and data for more years, will give us information about collection use and overlap among the three institutions.

Photograph by: Maurice C. Libbey and Gene W. Scholes, Eastern Illinois University.

NCIP PHASE II RESULTS

What are the pro's and con's of the NCIP process and the Conspectus methodology? I will consider the Conspectus itself first. It is something like the Jarvik-7 artificial heart; it's designed to regulate the lifeblood of research—scholarly knowledge—but it's in a developmental stage and if you use it you will have to tolerate some undesirable side effects. Its parts are not always consistent or logical. It's not a complete or full summary of knowledge. The Conspectus task force is correcting the flaws, but it takes time and the Conspectus will continue to try the patience of experienced bibliographers. The NCIP manual and training program go a long way toward addressing these difficulties.

Time is another factor to consider in evaluating NCIP. It is a costly process in terms of staff time. Libraries may wish to address this problem by doing the Conspectus piecemeal, although I recommend that the entire Conspectus be completed eventually.

Looking at the benefits of NCIP for Indiana I would include the following:

Our collection development librarians were introduced to new ideas and methodologies for collection planning and assessment, and we explored these issues together with Notre Dame and Purdue in a structured, cooperative way.

We gained experience and knowledge of national collection management issues and activities and we came into contact (in some cases for the first time) with colleagues in the state and region who are addressing the same issues. Conspectus work helped us develop relationships with sister institutions in the CIC including IU's primary interlibrary lending partners, Illinois and Michigan.

The chief collection development officers at IU, Notre Dame and Purdue established regular contact. Calls and meetings now occur nearly monthly; budgetary and collection data, serials, accessions, deaccessions, and desiderata lists, library newsletters, etc., are routinely exchanged. Our subject specialists, too, have increasing interaction.

Seven conspectus divisions were completed and our values were put into the Conspectus Online (the first non-RLG libraries to be included in the national database). Several verification studies were applied; overlap reports have been produced and will be used in further analysis of our collections. On the local level, our Conspectus training has prepared us to draft our collection development policy.

It will be LC class-based and use the Conspectus format and much of the standard terminology.[5]

One question I'm asked is "Has NCIP changed anybody's behavior? Does anyone do things differently as a result?" I think my remarks here indicate that our behavior is changing; we are cooperating more and our cooperation is based on a new collection-centered approach. There is potential for this approach to have greater influence on existing organizations, network and utilities; to redefine them, in part, for the purpose of better collection management. The question now is "Will the change last?" I don't know. Coordination is very difficult to bring off; it is difficult to make it work efficiently and effectively. I assume coordinated collection development will pay increasingly larger dividends, but I'm aware that not all librarians think so; certainly librarians are the critical factor in making changes work. Many are not interested in the new approaches; many do not wish to change old behaviors. And they may be right; if closer cooperation and coordination produce only negligible gains then they are not necesary; it may well be more costly to cooperate than to buy outright what a library needs. I don't think we know enough yet to make that judgment.

The cooperative environment has never been more supportive of coordination than it is today, and I believe we must seize the opportunity it offers for experimentation and progress. Building on and improving RLG's important work toward standardizing research collection assessment, NCIP is an important part of this promising venture.

NOTES

1. The goals and significance of the project are described in the *Manual for the North American Inventory of Research Collections* Prepared by Jutta Reed-Scott. Washington, D.C., Association of Research Libraries Office of Management Studies (January 1985 Edition).

2. See "A Guide to Coordinated and Cooperative Collection Development Among Libraries" Prepared by Paul Mosher and Marcia Pankake. ALA/RTSD/RS Collection Management and Development Committee (Fifth Revised Draft: December 1982), p. 6.

3. *Ibid*, p. 7.

4. See "The Research Libraries Advisory Committee to OCLC: An Informal History, 1980-1984" by David S. Zubatsky in *Research Libraries in OCLC: A Quarterly* 15(Autumn 1984):8-13.

5. The best example I've seen of this kind of policy is *The Brown University Collection Development Policy* (Providence, R.I., April, 1984).

A System Level Coordinated Cooperative Collection Development Model for Illinois

Karen Krueger

ABSTRACT. Coordinated cooperative collection development (CCCD) has too long been solely the province of large and usually research-oriented libraries. Illinois has been moving toward CCCD at a statewide network level since 1975. With State Library support, a data collection methodology was developed by King Research, and a how-to-do-it CCCD manual describing a statewide model was written by Karen Krueger. This paper describes the background leading to the development of this model as well as the model itself. Unlike many other approaches to CCCD, this model incorporates client-centered assessments of collections, is aimed at non-research libraries, and is based on data that are used in making *local* collection development decisions as well as cooperative collection development decisions.

Efforts toward cooperative collection development often differ in terms of their underlying models—the assumptions they use and the structure of their approach. The model I'll be describing is one which was developed with funding from the Illinois State Library and published by them in 1983.[1] This model is currently being used in some areas of Illinois but is not, at the present time, an example of coordinated cooperative collection development *in action* at the statewide level. I'll talk more about that later. First, I would like to give some brief background on the development of this model.

Illinois has long been interested in cooperative collection development. In 1975, the Illinois Research and Reference Center Directors, working with the State Library, appointed a subcommittee to study this topic. They issued a report[2] in 1977 which was debated (some might say, "hotly debated") across the state. Some of the questions that the subcommittee felt were important to answer were:

- —What resources currently exist in ILLINET and where are they? (ILLINET is the Illinois Library and Information Network)
- —In what areas are we repeatedly unable to fill requests for information?
- —Who will collect "junk" and esoteric materials?
- —How does interlibrary loan relate to CCCD?
- —What are appropriate levels of responsibility for local libraries, systems, and R & R Centers?
- —What are possible methods of CCCD?
- —How do we deal with getting enough popular material for everybody?
- —What is the impact of CCCD on individual institution's budgets?

This subcommittee, by asking these questions and by making the recommendtions they did, took an important step forward. They made CCCD practical and tied it to a tangible measure: the needs of users as identified by resource sharing activity in the state network.

Since many of the subcommittee's conclusions and recommendations are the foundation of the CCCD model I will be discussing today, I would like to mention a few of them.

1. The report concluded that the best approach for libraries is to provide items which are most frequently in demand by their primary clientele and to provide *access* to other resources and information which cannot be provided on site. (For Illinois libraries, this access is provided through participation in ILLINET.)
2. The subcommittee recommended that resource development at the local level be designed to respond to what users need to meet their *recurring* educational, recreational, and intellectual needs. The result, they believed, would be high use collections geared to primary clientele, which would ease the establishment of a cooperative collection development program to meet the needs of those seeking less frequently used materials.
3. The report clearly stated that the system level is where responsibility for cooperative collection development begins although the obligation for meeting these responsibilities may be shared with member libraries.

4. Last, the subcommittee recommended that each system involve all participants in design of such levels of responsibility.

Two key concepts upon which the report was based are "user oriented collection development" and "access to information." In regard to access, it is worth noting that this report recommended a plan be developed for the establishment of a statewide library delivery service that would minimize delivery times between any two points in ILLINET. This delivery service has been a reality since 1980.

A few years after this report was issued, the Illinois Valley Library System (IVLS) was given an LSCA grant to further explore the topic of Cooperative Collection Development. They contracted with King Research, Inc. (KRI) to develop a methodology for CCCD. This project was conducted from 1980-1981. The final report[3] was issued in February 1982 by Douglas Zweizig, the Project Consultant for KRI. The methodology that was developed in concert with an IVLS Advisory Committee incorporated a client-centered approach, taking into account use of and demand for materials, as well as assessments of holdings and acquisitions.

Upon completion of this project, the Illinois State Library felt a need for a tool which would help libraries actually begin to do CCCD. The King Research report described the data collection methods used, what worked and what didn't, and reported on experiences with four test libraries. It was not intended to be the kind of document that practicing librarians could pick up and use as a guide to implementing CCCD activities in their libraries.

Because I had been project officer for the KRI project while I was Assistant Director at IVLS, the State Library approached me about writing a how-to-do-it manual which would incorporate the KRI data collection procedures and expand on them to provide libraries with a practical step-by-step tool they could use. So, with LSCA funds and five months to complete the work, I wrote a three volume manual which is a detailed description of how a library and a system might go about coordinated cooperative collection development.

A difficult but important decision was made by the State Library in funding the development of this manual. Because minimal progress had been made in implementing CCCD activities in Illinois since the 1977 report, the State Library wanted something started fairly quickly. They did not want to wait two or three years before libraries began working toward CCCD agreements. This meant, however, that the manual would be published as an *untested* model. Although the data collection procedures were tested in the King Research project, none of the additional procedures included in the how-to-do-it manual were tested. The process itself was entirely new. Instructions for interpreting and using data, writing local collection development plans, facilitating library discussions on CCCD, etc. were all untried. Also, as a result of the KRI test, a number of changes were needed. One major change was in subject breakdowns. The KRI procedures used 23 subjects and the test libraries wanted data broken down in much more detail, into about 100 subject areas. This meant changes in sample sizes and extensive changes in the LC/Dewey conversion tables.

This brings me to the subject of the current status of this model in Illinois. Presently, the Illinois State Library is promoting use of this model, but not insisting that it be used by every system. Several systems are following this model, but I know of at least one other that uses an approach they developed themselves, prior to the existence of this CCCD manual. In addition, Illinois has a great many academic libraries linked together with the LCS automated system through the University of Illinois, and they are working toward CCCD using their own approach. Whether the work of the LCS libraries will be compatible with the model I'm describing today is yet to be determined. In recent developments, the state has awarded an LSCA grant to Terry Weech at the University of Illinois to evaluate CCCD efforts in the state and make recommendations for a coordinated effort. This evaluation will be completed by June 30, 1985.

That seems like a very long introduction for a model which will only take me twenty minutes to describe. The manual is called *Coordinated Cooperative Collection Development for Illinois Libraries*, and the first three volumes are available through the Illinois State Library, free of charge. The first volume is a brief overview of the subject. It explains cooperative collection development in general terms, describes benefits, assesses methods used to date, and proposes a new approach for ILLINET. It describes the approach that is the basis of the manual and provides a general overview that is intended to give library directors, staff, and governing authorities an understanding of this process and enough information to make a decision about their willingness and ability to participate.

Volume II is a how-to-manual *for local libraries* which describes step-by-step the procedures to be used in collecting data on holdings, use, and acquisitions, and in interpreting and using these data for local collection development decisions. It includes specific instructions, worksheets, forms, and numerous examples. Volume III is a how-to-manual *for systems* which describes step-by-step the procedures to be used in collecting and using data on interlibrary loan, along with data from local libraries, to develop a coordinated cooperative collection development plan for the system. It includes specific instructions, worksheets, forms, examples, conversion tables, and information on data analysis.

The premise behind this model, and I can't stress this enough, is that CCCD has too long been solely the province of large, and usually research-oriented libraries. I believe that all libraries can be involved in CCCD and the benefits from such involvement will occur both at the individual library level and at the network level. The strength of a network is directly related to the strength of its members. Weak members will weaken a network. To reiterate a recommendation in the 1977 Illinois report, local libraries (school, public, special, and academic) must do their best to meet the primary needs of their clientele, and then, and only then, rely on the network. I don't believe libraries can effectively participte in CCCD until they have analyzed their own collections and have clearly established their own collection development policies. The building blocks of a CCCD plan, whether it be at the system or state level, must be effective local collections.

Another premise at work in this model is that libraries agreeing to undertake certain activities as part of a CCCD plan should do so in their own self-interest. There are few libraries today that can justify buying and housing materials that are not used by their primary clientele—even if the argument is that neighboring libraries are doing the same as part of a CCCD agreement. It is in everyone's interest that some libraries are able and willing to do so, and fortunately many large public, academic, and other research-oriented libraries are doing just that. But of the approximately 3800 libraries in Illinois, I would venture to guess that at least 80% are not in that position. If they are to agree to CCCD activities which affect their collection development decisions, they will have to do so because the materials they purchase will be of interest to their own clientele. Evaluating their collections is the first step in this process, and a CCCD model which is intended for this audience must be based on this assessment at the local level.

Related to this is the premise that CCCD should not be imposed

54   COORDINATING COOPERATIVE COLLECTION DEVELOPMENT

Photograph by: Maurice C. Libbey and Gene W. Scholes, Eastern Illinois University.

from the top down, but rather begin with local libraries of all types and progress to the reference and resource libraries of the state. Cooperative collection development must allow libraries to formulate local collection development policies which best serve their clientele, and then to use these policies as the foundation for system CCCD plans and eventually for a state CCCD plan. Unless libraries make informed collection development decisions at the local level, they will not be able to effectively enter into agreements with other libraries and with the system. Although this process is based on local collection development policies which many libraries may already have, it is also based on detailed data about library collections, use, and acquisitions, which very few libraries have.

A fourth premise in this model is that CCCD decisions should be tied to something tangible in terms of objectives. A problem with CCCD is that the results are difficult to measure. If the objective is to ensure that at least one copy of every title available is being acquired by some library somewhere, the measurement becomes easy. But in user-oriented collection development strategies, this is not the desired end result. At least some degree of measurement and continuing evaluation can be achieved by using the interlibrary loan fill rates in a network to identify areas that are in need of improved collection building.

The definition I have used in the Illinois manual for cooperative collection development is as follows: "the acquisition and maintenance of collections of materials by local libraries which meet the needs of the people they are intended to serve, enhanced by agreements between these libraries to cooperatively acquire and maintain materials which are not available at the local level and which are needed by their collective clientele." The emphasis in this definition is on responding to identified needs for material, not on collecting materials for the purpose of covering all fields of knowledge. *Coordinated* cooperative collection development refers to a more centralized approach which takes into account the overall objectives of the participating libraries as a group and monitors the effectiveness of cooperative agreements on these objectives.

The model I developed, like any CCCD model, is based on assessments of library collections. Using definitions from a report on collection analysis produced by the Association of Research Libraries, I make a distinction between collection-centered assessment and client-centered assessment.[4] Collection-centered assessment "treats a collection as a resource irrespective of actual demand and use. It focuses on the intellectual breadth and depth of the collection and responds to the concept that a research collection's value is intrinsically related to the unknown needs of future scholars." Client-centered assessment "focuses on the actual utility of the collection to its current users." Collection-centered methods will be most effective for libraries with large collections which have decided that they serve a dual mission—both to provide materials to meet the current needs of their users and to build collections (in at least one or more subject fields) of an in-depth nature which will serve as a resource for future users and/or for clientele other than their own. The data collection methodology developed by King Research fits into the client-centered assessment definition. This method of assessment is fundamental to the model I am discussing today.

In this model there are four levels of CCCD activity, as follows:

At the *local level*, a collection development plan would be developed by every ILLINET library, which would:

—be based on assessments of their collections (for most libraries this would be a client-centered assessment)
—identify areas of special emphasis
—specify future acquisitions plans.

System level activities would result in a coordinated cooperative collection development plan which would:

—identify high and low interlibrary loan performance areas within the system based on the ability of participating library and system collections to fill requests
—specify CCCD strategies to be used for improving in those areas needing improvement.

At the *intersystem level*, libraries with similar interests, regardless of system boundaries, such as libraries with special collections in a narrow field, would develop CCCD agreements.

At the *state-wide level*, a coordinated cooperative collection development plan for ILLINET would be written which would:

—identify areas of high performance and low performance in the network as a whole based on the interlibrary loan fill rates within ILLINET
—identify in-depth subject collections in the state
—specify CCCD strategies to be used for improving low performance areas

The major focus of this model, at least at this stage in its development, is on analyzing collections and reaching CCCD agreements by libraries in subjects that are not highly specialized. Volumes 4 and 5 which deal, respectively, with intersystem and statewide CCCD activities, remain unwritten. It is at this level that libraries with in-depth subject collections may wish to combine a client-centered and collection-centered approach to collection assessments, or to solely use the latter.

Crucial to any CCCD effort is the existence of comparable data, upon which to base CCCD decisions. This means a common list of subject categories must be used. It also meant that a conversion table had to be developed so that libraries using Dewey and LC classification systems could analyze their data so that they were comparable. In the manual, I have included a conversion table for a very broad level of analysis which includes only 20 subjects, and for a second, more detailed level of analysis, which includes 119 subjects. The majority of libraries will want to analyze their collections at the second level, and the systems will analyze interlibrary loan data at this level. There is a third level in the manual which includes 507 subjects and is the same as the LC National shelflist subjects (published in *ALA Guidelines for Collection Development*)[5] except expanded in certain subjects. It includes, however, LC classification ranges but not Dewey.

So far I have talked a lot about data collection without describing the data that will be collected. There are five categories of data: holdings, use, acquisitions, interlibrary loan, and publishing output. Each of these, except publishing output, is broken down into a minimum of 119 subjects. Publishing output, at least as compiled by R.R. Bowker in 1983 when this Illinois manual was published, is only available in broad subject breakdowns. I would like to now further describe these data collection activities.

1. *Determining number of holdings, median age, and availability of titles in each subject area*. An example of the results, at the lowest level of subject analysis, would be as follows: Library X finds that 2.9% of its non-fiction monographs are in medicine (or approximately 3,436 titles), that the median age of holdings in medicine is 1966, and that 69% of the medical holdings in the library are available at any given time.
2. *Determining subject distribution and age of items circulated and used in-house*. In doing so, Library X discovers that 7.8%

of circulation and in-house use are in medicine, and that the median age of medical items used is 1977.
3. *Determining subject distribution of previous year's acquisitions.* For example, Library X finds that 3.7% of the previous year's acquisitions are in the field of medicine.
4. *Determining subject distribution of the previous year's interlibrary loan and back-up reference activity.* For Library X, the result is that 6.9% of their interlibrary loan requests are in medicine.
5. *Determining subject distribution of publishing output.* As an example, Library X finds that during the previous year, the percent of U.S. non-fiction title output in medicine was 9.1%.

With this information, a library makes collection development decisions and writes a collection development plan. The library sends information to the system on the number of their holdings in each subject, number of titles acquired annually in each subject, and an indication of the areas which they will be emphasizing in collection building in the near future and in which they have a particular interest in CCCD.

Data collection at the system level relates to performance in interlibrary loan. The system collects data on interlibrary loan for the system as a whole, including requests that are handled directly by libraries as well as those handled by the system. These data include the subject distribution of requests, fill rate and non-fill rate by subject, and median age of requests by subject. For example: System X finds that 7.1% of the total interlibrary loan and back-up reference requests generated within the system are in medicine. Of those 36% are filled within the system, 44% are filled elsewhere in ILLINET, 8% are filled outside ILLINET, and 12% are unfilled. It also finds that the median age of titles requested in medicine in the previous year was 1976.

At this point, CCCD really begins. This model proposes that subject Groups be formed. I use GROUP as an acronym standing for Greater Resources Of Use to Patrons. These GROUPs would be made up of the libraries that expressed an interest in that particular subject from a collection development point of view. They would be responsible, on an on-going basis, for *cooperative* activities taking place in their assigned subject, and as I mention in the manual, these activities could cover more than CCCD. Continuing education activities, for instance, related to collection development in the

GROUP subject areas, might be appropriate. For practical purposes, I recommend the 20 broad subject categories be used as the basis for forming subject GROUPs. Within the GROUPs, more specific subjects will be discussed.

The subject GROUPs would have the following information available to them as they begin their discussions:

—The number of holdings of each system library in that subject.
—The number of titles acquired annually by system libraries in that subject.
—A summary of the libraries which expressed interest in CCCD for *specific* subject areas within that field.
—A summary of the system-wide interlibrary loan performance in that subject.

As a result of discussions by the subject GROUPs, CCCD decisions are made. These could include cooperative purchasing agreements, last copy centers, central switching point for discarded materials, on-demand purchasing by some libraries in response to titles requested through interlibrary loan, agreements to purchase heavily in a certain subject and having other libraries suggest titles in that subject, and checking one another's files (when feasible) to avoid unnecessary duplication.

This has been a fairly brief description of the CCCD model I have developed. I am going to spend the last few minutes talking about particular topics the symposium planners wanted each speaker to cover. These are governance, financing, coordination, participation, bibliographic access, delivery, resource sharing, needed changes, and benefits and drawbacks. I will address each topic very briefly.

Governance: Although there should be written agreements, there is no need for separate governance. The structure is based on the 18 library systems in Illinois, and on overall coordination by the Illinois State Library.

Financing: This model was designed in a way that makes special funding unnecessary. At the local level, most libraries have little if any funds to "give to CCCD" in the traditional sense. I tried to develop a process that allows them to build collections based on need and expected use, so their contribution to CCCD is in their own best interest. What is different is that it is a planned, "advertised" CCCD program based on some basic data, so that other libraries can make decisions in the same context.

Coordination: This is the job of the systems and of the Illinois State Library. While small groups of libraries around the state may initiate and implement cooperative collection development activities, in order for them to have an impact on ILLINET as a whole, systems must take the lead in expanding upon and coordinating these activities. Coordination for intersystem and statewide CCCD efforts is the responsibility of the State Library. I recommend that each system have a CCCD coordinator, which may only need to be a part-time position depending on the number and size of libraries involved, and certainly the state library needs to have someone on the staff with this responsibility. I also think there should be a Coordinating GROUP which would serve as an advisory group, working with the System consultant to oversee the CCCD process, establishing timetables, writing the system plan, and recommending collection development decisions related to the system. I believe the system should take responsibility for training library staff in data collection methods, arranging for computer analysis of the data, collecting the data on interlibrary loan, meeting with the various subject GROUPs, facilitating discussions, being responsible for further analysis of data if needed, etc. A side note: IBM PC software for analyzing the data is available through the Illinois State Library.

Participation: I wrote these manuals with the intent that all 3800 libraries in ILLINET could be involved if they chose. However, it is unrealistic to expect some small or poorly funded libraries to be able to participate. For instance, of the 595 public libraries in Illinois in 1983, when the manual was published, over half spent less than $4,000 on library materials each year; over 40% were open less than 25 hours a week; and 63% did not even have one professional librarian on the staff.[6] Certainly, in each type of library, there will be some which are too small or are too occupied with trying to improve their services in basic ways, to get involved in this. On the other hand, my experience in conducting workshops around Illinois in 1984 which were attended by staff from many small libraries showed that most of these staff really wanted to find out more about their own collections and were acutely aware of their limitations and dependence on the network. They were therefore eager to do whatever they could to ensure that they did their best at the local level and in doing so could contribute to the overall strength of the network. I think that any library that analyzes its collection according to this model and, based on that analysis, makes collection development decisions which better serve their primary clientele, is participating in this CCCD process at the most basic level. For some, this will be the only level at which they can participate, yet resource sharing in the network will be improved as a result.

At the other end of the spectrum, I expect special libraries and large academic and public libraries to be most interested in intersystem CCCD. A special or academic library which collects heavily in chemical engineering, for example, will find few, if any, libraries in its own system with the same interest. CCCD at the intersystem level is the only way for them. But, almost every library, no matter how specialized, has some subject areas that may be peripheral, or that are not a primary interest, yet they have clientele which demand such materials. Certainly, college students use the public library for a great many materials, from literary criticism to art history. Not every college can acquire what they want in all areas, and it seems likely that system-level cooperation in collection development in some subjects can benefit their clients a great deal.

Bibliographic Access: CCCD is not very effective without easy bibliographic access among libraries. Fortunately, almost all Illinois library systems now have shared automated circulation systems which include many of their member libraries. Illinois also has a large OCLC network, although small libraries are not often a part of this. Because of the diversity of automation activities in the state, I made no specific recommendations on expansion and enhancement of bibliographic access as part of this model. I assume the current trend for development of on-line bibliographic data bases will continue and even be accelerated if meaningful CCCD agreements are reached around the state.

Delivery: All library systems, with perhaps one exception, provide two to five direct delivery stops to member libraries each week. Daily statewide delivery service (ILDS) is in place and would be very capable of meeting the demands placed on it from system, intersystem, and statewide CCCD plans. The volume of items transported by ILDS in 1983 was 6,018,621.[7]

Resource sharing: Illinois has a lot of interlibrary loan and reciprocal borrowing activity, and CCCD would increase this level of activity. I like to envision, as part of any CCCD plan, that each participating library would have cards in its card catalog or entries in its online catalog indicating that in a particular subject the library is only able to collect moderately but that Libraries X, Y, and Z have more in-depth collections which are available through interlibrary loan, reciprocal borrowing, or in-house use.

Needed changes:

—I would expand the section of the manual on analysis of data, as it is the most difficult aspect of this process.
—I would incorporate fill rates and turnover rates by subject as an optional data collection activity. Turnover rates are easy figures to collect and interpret, and fill rates would be a better indicator of unmet needs. Of course, determining fill rates by subject is difficult and time consuming and for many libraries, not a possibility.
—I would try to make the whole process less time consuming—but if I knew how to do that and still accomplish my goals, I would have done it to begin with. There may not be a way to simplify.
—The model is untested. I would really have preferred to have delayed publication until some testing was done.
—I would involve more people in the development of the subject breakdowns and Dewey/LC conversion tables. I intended that libraries with specialized collections would develop their very detailed subject lists as an expansion of the second and third levels in the manuals. It may be that the better route would have been to develop the very specific lists first and then combine them to get the broader list of 100 that most libraries would use. I am not totally convinced of this, however. The limitations of trying to mesh Dewey and LC classification schemes might have prevented this from working. By not writing volumes 4 and 5 for intersystem and statewide CCCD, I did not go beyond the third level subject breakdowns, and I know many libraries in the state feel they must have more detail than the 507 subjects at the third level allow. The topic of subject categories and conversion schemes is one of the most crucial to CCCD, especially when dealing in a multitype environment.

Drawbacks and benefits: The major drawbacks in this model are that it is:

—Time consuming
—Difficult to evaluate degree of success, even if measuring inter-

library loan performance, due to the number of variables involved.
—Difficult to interpret collection assessment data.

The major benefits of this model are that it:

—Allows libraries to prioritize areas of purchase and to have a more planned approach to collection development at the local level.
—Provides libraries with an opportunity to become more familiar with their own collections as well as other collections in their system or in the state.
—Increases the library's ability to provide on-site access to materials most in demand.
—Allows for participation by all types and sizes of libraries.
—Relies heavily on data, not subjective assessments.
—Is designed so that the effort a library puts forth will be worthwhile at the local level, even if that library does not participate in CCCD activities.

Obviously, I believe the benefits of this model far outweigh the drawbacks, and I am hopeful that as libraries and systems in Illinois have more experience with it, needed changes can be made and a truly statewide CCCD program will result.

REFERENCES

1. Karen Krueger, *Coordinated Cooperative Collection Development for Illinois Libraries*, Springfield, IL.: Illinois State Library, 1983.
2. *Toward Cooperative Collection Development in the Illinois Library and Information Network.* Springfield, IL.: Illinois State Library, 1977.
3. Douglas L. Zweizig, *Test of Data Collection Approaches to Coordinated/Cooperative Collection Development.* Rockville, MD.: King Research, Inc., 1982.
4. *Guidelines for Collection Development.* Chicago: American Library Association, 1979.
5. *Collection Analysis in Research Libraries: An Interim Report on a Self-study Process.* Washington, D.C.: Association of Research Libraries, 1978, p.9.
6. *Analyses of the 1982-83 Illinois Public Library Statistics.* Prepared for the Illinois State Library. Urbana-Champaign, IL.: Library Research Center, University of Illinois, 1983.
7. *ILDS Annual Report, 1983.* (Inter-Systems Library Delivery Services, unpublished report to the Illinois State Library.)

Cooperative Collection Development Among Research Libraries: The Colorado Experience

Joel Rutstein

Assistant Director for Collection Services
The Libraries, Colorado State University

Johannah Sherrer

Director of Public Services, Michener Library
University of Northern Colorado

ABSTRACT. Cooperative collection development among research libraries in Colorado began in 1978 when a formal structure for cooperative purchasing was developed. Since that time the philosophical framework for that structure has become more sophisticated and complex. This paper outlines the development and growth of cooperative collection activities among research libraries in Colorado with a special emphasis on the development of uniform policy statements.

PART I
DEVELOPMENT OF COLA AS A COOPERATIVE ACQUISITIONS GROUP

An article in the Chronicle of Higher Education in the fall of 1984 might be an appropriate starting point for this paper. The article described the difficulty faced by the State of Colorado in funding its institutions of higher learning. Simply put, there are too many colleges and universities doing too much of the same thing for the number of potential students and resources available. This dilemma has been understood for several years, at least since the period of the mid-1970s, when the combined impact of recession and inflation diminished the sources of revenue necessary to maintain and vitalize the higher education structure.

As creatures of their institutions, libraries have been equally affected. Until 1981, academic libraries in Colorado were funded as separate line items in the state's budget, apart from the general allocations for each college or university. As resources became scarcer, librarians complained not only about the lack of funding, but its method of distribution as well. In the mid-1970s, two state agencies, the legislature's Joint Budget Committee and the executive branch's Commission on Higher Education, requested librarians to develop an equitable method for library funding, staffing, and cooperation.

With an incentive to cooperate, many associations were formed, one of the most important being the Colorado Alliance of Research Libraries. CARL's aim was not just to speak as one voice for academic libraries in the state, but also to formulate cooperative activities among its seven members, the largest libraries in Colorado.* These activities included the development of a network base linking members through a compatible online circulation system, as well as an automated public access catalog.

Begun separately, the Colorado Organization for Library Acquisitions was formed to seek ways of cooperatively purchasing expensive publications needed in the state. In 1978, this group was incorporated as part of CARL, and became known as the Committee on Library Acquisitions (COLA). CARL's interests were thus expanded into the realm of cooperative collection development—not dissimilar to other consortia which were linked by a common network.

The original goals of COLA consisted of 1) the joint acquisitions of unusual or expensive library materials not available in any Colorado library; 2) improving standards of library services through the interlibrary loan of jointly acquired material; and 3) exchanging information concerning acquisitions, services and procedures. Goal number one was further modified to include only lower use material. Guidelines were also established for items that should not be considered for cooperative purchases, as follows:

1. Items which are already owned or about to be purchased by any member libraries.
2. Any heavily used indexing journals (such as citation indexes or current contents), abstracting journals, or published catalogs.

---

*Auraria, University of Colorado, Boulder, Colorado School of Mines, Denver Public, Colorado State University, University of Denver, and University of Northern Colorado.

3. A title or a multi-volume set which is priced $1,000 or less.
4. Little-used materials which fall within the collection scope of CRL and particularly those materials which can be obtained through the "demand purchase program" of CRL (e.g., foreign dissertations, U.S. state documents, newspapers in microform, and archival materials in microform).
5. Rare books and collectors' items.

In actual practice, the guidelines had to be refined. Item no. 3 was reduced from $1,000 to $300. Item no. 4 was almost impossible to monitor, since only 4 members of CARL (later reduced to 2) belonged to CRL. The feeling was also expressed that CRL's acquisitions did not reflect the specific requirements of Colorado. COLA believed its main objective was to purchase materials supporting the collective research needs of the State, while CRL serves the individual research needs of an institution, or even more specifically, an individual patron.

Funding for cooperative purchases was drawn from the CARL membership, each library agreeing to pool a percentage of its acquisitions budget, derived from an assessment of 1% or less of the allocation. The following procedures were developed regarding CARL purchases: 1) anything purchased with COLA funds must be available for loan; 2) the heading "CARL" will be placed above the call numbers on cards and materials for identifying items purchased with CARL funds; 3) the "host" or home library will send extra catalog cards to the other participating COLA libraries; and 4) the materials purchased will be housed in the library which expects the most use.

PART II
MOVEMENT TOWARDS
A BROADER COOPERATIVE BASE

COLA remained exclusively a cooperative acquisitions committee for the first years of its existence. By the beginning of the 1980s, the structure of the Committee began to change, and, with it, a questioning of its objectives. At first comprised exclusively of acquisition librarians, the composition shifted more to collection development librarians, reflecting national trends. The Committee's chair, it should be pointed out, has been and continues to be the library director of the University of Colorado.

Selecting materials for cooperative purchases had been done in a relatively ad hoc manner. Items could be brought forward without preliminary screening by the Committee, giving the impression that expensive purchases were aiding only select faculty, not program requirements. Decisions for selection were based on a simple weighting scale of one to five. The top candidates received the highest scores; the home institution was chosen according to program emphasis. Some committee members felt this method was arbitrary, and more "scientific" measures should be adopted. Some of the questions and issues raised included the following:

1. A methodology for evaluating use. How do we appraise the utilization of our cooperative purchases? What other means besides card catalog entries can be implemented to ensure publicity for these materials?
2. If printed guides to purchased sets are available, should they be furnished to all members?
3. Should CARL evaluate member holdings strengths and weaknesses to improve cooperative acquisitions program? Another purpose would be to determine collecting priorities for CARL and devise a rationale as to who should get what.
4. A review of selection methods may be necessary. Items now brought forward as purchase candidates are chosen in a whimsical manner, and may have no bearing on the information needs of Colorado's research libraries.

Concurrently with the work being done by COLA, Colorado's academic libraries commenced drafting a statewide master plan to meet the challenges of the 1980s. CARL, as a consortium of the largest libraries in the state, determined that in this spirit COLA should re-examine the direction of cooperative acquisitions and examine new approaches to cooperative collection development. New goals were identified and subsequently approved for COLA in 1982. They were:

1. To carry on a program of cooperative acquisitions.
2. To exchange infomation regarding acquisitions and procedures.
3. To prepare up-to-date Union lists of serials.
4. To consider pre-order coordination as part of the CARL online system.
5. To coordinate resource sharing.

6. To develop uniform collection policy statements.
7. To cooperate with other collection development activities on a statewide basis.

COLA determined that as a first step, library holdings should be assessed, through the medium of collection policy statements. Stricter guidelines were also developed for the cooperative acquisitions program, to wit:

1. Copies of requests, blurbs, and PR descriptions will be sent to each COLA member by the requesting member. From this, a complete listing will be generated for all requests.
2. Prior to a COLA meeting, each member will check requests against individual institutional holdings.
3. Prior to a meeting, each member will determine the level of interest for each request at the home institution in terms of collecting intensity indicators.
4. Those requests satisfying the collection intensity indicators will be further documented by a collection conspectus from each library insofar as it is feasible.

It should be pointed out that, although COLA was prepared to expand its responsibilities from a somewhat narrow focus into the state's leading cooperative collection development agency, all the work has been and continues to be carried on by committee members themselves. Though an incorporated entity, CARL's central staff was tiny (basically an executive director and a secretary), and most of its interest centered on the systems projects. The success of COLA depended almost exclusively on the committee members' enthusiasm and commitment—a difficult task since job descriptions did not include cooperative collection development tasks. Some relief was provided by the State Library, whose resource consultant in collection development also served on COLA, and aided in the development of collection policy statements.

PART III
THE FOCUS ON POLICY STATEMENTS

In the early 1980s, the focus shifted away from the cooperative purchase program and towards the notion of developing uniform, standardized collection policy statements. COLA members agreed that a stronger base was necessary to support the cooperative purchase program. But there were also several other factors influencing this decision:

1. Collection development had become an important trend in librarianship. It grew into a philosophy of management reaching beyond the boundaries of basic selection and de-selection of material resources. This included:
   a) evaluation and assessment,
   b) policy statements which describe both the collections and the level of collecting,
   c) appropriate staff to carry out collection development activities,
   d) the allocation of funds to build and maintain these collections, and
   e) preservation policies to ensure the availability of resources.

2. The growth of networking spawned various consortia utilizing bibliographical data bases for shared cataloging. Collection development as a cooperative venture incorporated the idea of shared resources. CARL could easily be categorized as a consortium with a collection development function (COLA).

3. The Research Libraries Group was developing a coordinated collection development tool, the Conspectus, which could easily be modified for regional applications.

4. ALA's Resource and Technical Services Division issued their *Guide for the Formulation of Collection Development Policy Statements* for utilization by both individual libraries and consortia. Also under their auspices, regional collection management institutes were organized to aid in the better understanding and application of policy statements.

In the spring of 1981, a survey was developed to determine the status of collection development in Colorado's academic and research libraries. The survey revealed that the vast majority of these libraries did not have detailed collection development statements or even written guidelines.

The survey revealed that collection development, as an element of library management, was in its infancy in Colorado's academic and research libraries. In isolated cases, it had been formally incorporated into daily library activities through the creation of a full-time position in collection development, or through the existence of written collection development policy statements. In general, however, academic libraries in Colorado were just beginning to construct a formal framework for collection management. Colorado's academic and research libraries were presented with the opportunity to develop definitions that described individual library collections in a uniform manner. The CARL library directors collectively agreed that uniformity in definitions and methodology would allow a more rational approach to collection comparison between institutions, enable more effective cooperative purchasing, and provide a mechanism that justifies collection development on a state wide basis.

With the approval of the CARL Board of Directors, COLA began the testing which would lead towards a series of collection policy statements as the driving force for cooperation in the sphere of collection management and development. A subcommittee was appointed consisting of the co-authors of this paper and Geri Schmidt, the State Library Resource Consultant in collection development. The subcommittee chose bibliographers from selected CARL libraries who represented the unrelated subject areas of literature, music, and mathematics.

A model policy statement with broad guidelines was developed in order to determine how bibliographers would apply the policy statement for their discipline. At this point, the subcommittee was unsure how the final format should appear. Many questions required answers before the statements could be equitably applied to institutions with different infrastructures and different missions. Should CARL adopt the RLG Conspectus without changes? Are program narratives necessary? Should each library determine its own disciplines to describe? Are the collecting intensity levels from either RLG or ALA adequate, or are modifications necessary? How detailed should the conspectus classifications be?

PART IV
THE WORKSHOPS

The completion of the trial statements revealed very individualistic styles and approaches among the involved bibliographers, ranging from lengthy essays to short, clipped responses. No concensus was apparent, and the subcommittee decided that the format needed tightening. Most important, the subcommittee decided that a program of education was in order, so that bibliographers could come together and learn why these statements were important, and what would be expected from them. It became clear that the next step was to introduce the formats to the bibliographers of the CARL libraries and, approximately 100 bibliographers were identified.

With CARL's approval, COLA decided that the best approach would be the workshop method, which would bring the bibliographers together for training in the use and application of the CARL collection policy statements. Only after such workshops could the real work begin.

In order to ensure the possibility of a uniform presentation, it was determined to introduce the project to the bibliographers in a daylong workshop. In this way, it could be assured that the details of the project would be presented in a consistent manner.

Workshops were held on March 9th and March 22nd in 1983. Prior to the workshop, each bibliographer received a packet which contained an outline of the workshop objectives and photocopied articles used in the development of the formats. Each bibliographer was requested to read the material prior to the workshop.

Throughout each session, the presentors were peppered with questions as well as suggestions for improving the formats. Most of the suggestions dealt with ways to further clarify the narrative descriptions and nearly all of these were incorporated into the final draft.

The explanation of the conspectus, however, elicited a great deal of concern from the bibliographers. Many felt uncomfortable evaluating a segment of LC class range in terms other than their own institution's program support.

At this point, the difficulties of engaging in a cooperative written collection policy statement when six of the seven institutions had not yet documented their own collections in writing was CLEARLY brought home.

Reactions from the bibliographers were ones of skepticism. They expressed doubts both as to the feasibility and to the practical value of what was termed an "exercise." When queried, however, consensus emerged that written statements should exist and that advantages could indeed result from a common approach.

As a result of the workshop feedback and the valuable input from the bibliographers, the policy statement formatting was finalized.

PART V
ANATOMY OF A COLLECTION POLICY STATEMENT—
MASTER LIST OF DISCIPLINES

A master list of disciplines was compiled to document broad subject areas as represented in the participating research libraries. The disciplines decided upon were intentionally broad. Opportunity to define a specific body of knowledge in narrower terms is provided in the each of the Library of Congress class breakdowns, located in the conspectus portion of each policy statement.

Since the A.L.A. Guidelines recommend use of the *National Shelflist Count* as the minimum refinement of the Library of Congress Classification scheme, an effort was made to utilize this breakdown in such a manner. However, local funding and collection patterns suggested that in some subject areas the *NSC* was itemized too specifically; while in others it was perhaps too broad. Added to this dilemma were the obvious institutional differences and variances within the group attempting to devise a standard breakdown for cooperative use.

The disciplines designated for analysis with their corresponding L.C. breakdowns were the result of a time consuming but valuable consultative process. COLA's subcommittee put a trial list together and distributed it to the bibliographers in the participating schools.

Almost one hundred recommendations were made concerning the draft structure. Most of these recommendations were incorporated into the final list. More than once, the subcommittee found it necessary to remind itself that the process being defined must meet the objectives of the group rather than the needs of an individual institution. Various questions arose:

1. Was the *National Shelflist Count* an appropriate minimum vehicle for structuring an interinstitutional class based analysis?
2. Could a broadly based policy format be developed that would accommodate individual institutional expression?
3. Would a broadly based policy format permit individual institutions the opportunity to incorporate modifications for internal use? Should it?

The process of identifying compatible, shared, disciplines for the seven institutions was no easy task. Almost immediately communication difficulties arose with terminology.

CARL's group of "like" institutions soon discovered subtle but distinct variations not only in institutional terminology for academic programs but significant variances in curricular support for similar degree programs.

Clearly the only way to proceed was to accept the recommendation in ALA's Guidelines for Collection Development and use classification schemes to identify or target individual subject areas.

Six of the seven libraries used the Library of Congress Classification Scheme. For the seventh library, Denver Public, a Dewey crossover guide was created.

Eventually thirty one disciplines were identified. The disciplines and their corresponding L.C. breakouts are presented on the screen.

NARRATIVE DESCRIPTIONS

In the CARL policy statements, a narrative description accompanies each discipline. It is in these individual descriptions that both institutional and specific programmatic objectives are delineated.

The format of the narrative description breaks down into seven major sections. Sections one and two simply identify the DISCIPLINE, the BIBLIOGRAPHER, and the institution.

Section three, PROGRAMMATIC INFORMATION, identifies the academic departments for which the subject is collected. It defines the subject boundaries for the discipline including the curricular emphasis, branch libraries, if they exist, and their relationship to the main library and special subject limitations. This section also provides information on the program or user needs that impact collection building in the discipline. Degree programs serviced should be listed as well as the existence of any special institutes or laboratories which affect collecting decisions. Institutional users should be identified in addition to any outside or corporate borrowers. If regional or local interests impact on collection maintenance they should be noted here as well. Interdisciplinary information also merits special attention. Questions that should be considered are: Do other programs identified in other disciplines have a relationship to this discipline? Are there areas or special studies programs that influence collection decisions? Are there other bibliographers involved in managing this subject area?

Section four requests information regarding possible SUBJECT MODIFIERS of the discipline. Are there geographical, language or chronological emphases or limitations in the collecting activities of this discipline?

Section five is titled COLLECTION DESCRIPTION. It provides for a general description of how the discipline is collected in terms of bibliographical support, primary or secondary materials, and retrospective collecting activities. Also included in this section are provisions for identifying methods of acquisitions of materials. This

Photograph by: Maurice C. Libbey and Gene W. Scholes, Eastern Illinois University.

is the place to mention approval plans, contracts with foreign vendors, or blanket order plans.

This section also requires a description of the format of materials when format determines if an item is selected or excluded. Information supplied could include references to government publications, newspapers, dissertations, micro-form collections, cassette recordings, symposiums, annual reports or proceedings.

Section six, COOPERATIVE AGREEMENTS, permits a description of any formal collecting agreements with other institutions. In addition, if the holdings of other libraries or membership in a research or resource sharing operation influence collecting priorities, it should be mentioned here as well.

The final section, SPECIAL CONSIDERATIONS, provides for the documenting of any legal requirements in the institution concerning archival or special collections, exchange or gift programs or external funding enhancements that may impact the collection management of the discipline.

CONSPECTUS REPORTING FORM

The conspectus reporting form was designed to reflect the level of collecting intensity for each L.C. class breakout assigned to the individual disciplines. The subject fields are identified both parenthetically and by the L.C. class equivalent. Thus, the subject field identified as "conservation of natural resources" is also identified by its L.C. classification of S900-972.

The existing collection strength and the current level of collecting intensity are analyzed for each subject field. In addition, the section labeled "scope notes" provides an opportunity for the bibliographer to include additional comments or to indicate the desirable level of collecting. In those instances where a bibliographer would like to further refine or break down the L.C. class listed, he/she may do so by simply indenting those lines directly under the assigned subject field. However, the assignment of intensity levels to each *prescribed* L.C. breakout is requested in addition to any further refinement by the bibliographer.

INTENSITY CODES

Intensity codes are defined as the descriptive values assigned to a specific L.C. class range. They are used to identify both the existing strength of a subject field and the extent of current collecting activity in the field.

Definitions of collecting levels are not to be applied relative to a given library or program. Collecting levels are to be assigned in an objective manner based on the publishing output in each subject field.

It is, therefore, quite likely that a large number of libraries will not hold comprehensive collections in any area nor would their curriculum or programs require that they should. Academic libraries that do not support doctoral programs or those types of libraries that are not oriented toward special research may not have any collections that would fall within research levels as defined by the collecting levels. The definitions are intended to interpret the depth and scope of a limited area of knowledge, not the appropriateness of the collection to the degrees or programs offered by the institution.

The Colorado Collecting Codes consist of six levels and are a modification of the *RLG INTENSITY LEVELS*. The levels range from 0-6 with 0 being out of scope and 6 representing exhaustive collections. The levels are to be applied to each class range from the modified *National Shelflist Count*. The application of these definitions to specific class breakdowns has been the most difficult task to interpret to the subject librarians involved.

Most of the bibliographers instinctively think in terms of program and institutional support. There is an irresistible impulse to think of the narrowly defined conspectus breakouts only in terms of institutional needs. Therefore, if it is necessary for an institution to purchase only minimum support for Anglo-Saxon literature to more than adequately satisfy program needs at the Ph.D. level, the instinct of the bibliographer is to assign that area a level 4 which is advanced research. In fact, the area of knowledge known as Anglo-Saxon literature should be evaluated independently of program needs.

The main purpose of the CARL conspectus is to serve as a mechanism for identifying collection strengths in research libraries on a statewide level. The appropriateness of collecting intensities will always remain local decisions based on program or user needs, priorities and funding patterns.

CONCLUSION: A LOOK TO THE FUTURE

The target date for completion of the first draft of all 31 disciplines was March 1, 1985. A comparative examination of each discipline is now in process. A reporting form titled the Colorado Comparative Matrix has been developed for this purpose.

The Colorado Comparative Matrix (CCM) is a device used to compare discipline strengths and weaknesses by institutional collecting patterns. With this matrix, it is possible to compare the current level of collection activity as well as the existing strength of each discipline.

For the most part, the bibliographers have done an excellent job in consistently applying the definitions. Although refinements in selective analyses may prove necessary, the initial drafts look very promising.

The next step will be to conduct validation studies on selected disciplines. The process for these procedures is still in the formulation stage. Every attempt, however, will be made to draw on previous activities in this area.

COLA is also in the process of drawing up draft formats for government document collections, maps, and newspapers. Various sub-committees are at work and tentative completion dates are scheduled for summer.

Central to the entire project's success is the ability to incorporate online access and data retrieval mechanisms into co-operative collection management strategies.

Online access to CARL policy statements is an integral and, therefore, essential element in the success of cooperative collection development activities. The long range goal of CARL's collection development endeavors is to make all of the policy statements and accompanying studies available to libraries throughout the state. Online accessibility appears to be the only realistic means of attaining this goal. It is anticipated that the conspectuses and the comparative matrixes by discipline will be accessible at all data points and combinations thereof; most specifically desired is the ability to search and retrieve data with Boolean search strategies.

On another level, an online maintenance system permitting in-house adjustments to all sections of the statement, including the narratives, is essential to maintaining a current, efficient, and reliable online database. Collection policies are meant to be dynamic. An online maintenance system is a critical factor in the success of co-operative collection development.

The process of formalizing collection development policies has provided each institution the opportunity to thoroughly acquaint itself with its own collection. Bibliographers now find themselves accountable for all phases of collection management, not simply selection processes. Institutions whose subject librarians have worked independently and in isolation from other bibliographers now find themselves in communication with their counterparts at other schools and even with their colleagues at their home library.

The major premise of CARL is that the libraries collectively represent one research collection for the benefit of the State of Colorado.

The CARL libraries collectively participate in a single Online Public Access Catalog available at each institution and which is fully integrated with circulation activities.

This focus on a single research collection supported by the six libraries* clearly mandates a continued emphasis on cooperate collection development. Library cooperation in Colorado is a goal achieved. Its reality can be witnessed not only in the online endeavors of its research facilities but in the conceptual framework which governs its future.

The Colorado experience in cooperative collection development has been a profitable one and one that continues to stimulate, probe and challenge her participants.

---

*In June of 1984, Colorado State University withdrew from CARL reducing the number of participants to six.

Indiana, Colorado, and Illinois— Comments on Three Approaches to Coordinated Cooperative Collection Development (CCCD)

Terry L. Weech

Associate Professor
Graduate School of Library and Information Science
University of Illinois
Champaign-Urbana, Illinois

The three papers present three different approaches with, of course, certain common concerns. For purposes of discussion I will review each paper separately and then comment on them as a group.

COMMENTS ON DAVID FARRELL'S PAPER

David Farrell, in describing the development and testing of procedures for applying the RLG (Research Libraries Group) Conspectus in research libraries outside RLG, raises some provocative issues. For example, Farrell suggests that one result of applying the Conspectus to collection evaluation might be the change in the meaning and use of "utilities" (presumably OCLC, RLG, etc.). One assumes he sees this change as a result of using the Conspectus online as a source for assisting in collection purchase decision or interlibrary loan routing. If this is the case, it seems to me that we are returning to the concept of "subject collection lists." I am not convinced that we really gain that much from classified descriptions of subject holdings, no matter how specific these subject classifications might be. It also seems to me that we should be demanding more of our electronic tools than developing a successor to Ash's *Subject Collections*. At least, the assumed benefits of the use of the RLG

© 1986 by The Haworth Press, Inc. All rights reserved.

Conspectus online deserves more discussion that it sometimes seems to get in the literature.

Farrell indicates verification studies have been undertaken, but does not share the results of these studies. From the information we have on the methodology of verification studies, it appears that standardized lists of materials are most often used as criterion for "verifying" the judgment of the subject bibliographers. One wonders if there might not be a better method of verification, or at least consideration given to the development of additional verification methods.

Farrell asks the question as to whether the Conspectus process will change the behavior of collection development specialists, but we might also be concerned with the question as to whether the behavior of users will change. The lack of concern with user evaluation in the process seems to this author to be a real lack in the Conspectus methodology.

It is refreshing to see someone admit it is likely to be more costly to go about collection building through CCCD and the use of the RLG Conspectus, but one wonders how the funding agencies of libraries would view such a statement. The whole question of cost-benefit and cost-effectiveness of collection evaluation procedures, such as the Conspectus, has yet to be explored.

The promotion of the RLG Conspectus as a standard evaluation procedure for research collection evaluations is interesting in light of the extent of modification of the Conspectus which seems to be taking place by various groups. Of course, the modifications by the Indiana project can be justified since part of the testing of the application of the Conspectus methodology would presumably be the testing of alternative approaches. But the freedom with which others seem to be modifying the methodology could become a real problem for the successful realization of a single standard for evaluation of research collections. It might be helpful if the testing of the methodology included measures of willingness on the part of libraries to accept a standard methodology.

One cannot help but wonder if the comparison of the RLG Conspectus to the Jarvik-7 artificial heart, although topical, is also a possible indication of the future of the Conspectus' use. The artificial heart is always likely to remain an emergency device, used only after all other efforts fail. I would hope we could anticipate a less mechanistic and more natural solution to CCCD. If not, I do not see much hope for standardization, for like the Jarvik-7 artificial heart, the RLG Conspectus will continue to be tinkered with and will always be subject to "improved" versions.

COMMENTS ON KAREN KRUEGER'S PAPER

The most striking aspect of Karen Krueger's paper is the potential scope of the CCCD model she describes. Her model has its origins, as she notes, in a 1977 report, which predates the RLG Conspectus by at least two years. The methodology on which her model is based was tested about the time data were being gathered to support the RLG Conspectus concept. The three volume manual that Krueger developed was published approximately a year before the ARL's Office of Management Studies brought the North American Collections Inventory Project (NCIP) and the pilot testing of the RLG Conspectus to Indiana. Thus of the three papers, Krueger presents the most independent model of CCCD, since most of it was developed simultaneously, but separate from, the RLG Conspectus process.

It is thus not easy to compare this model directly with the others discussed in this group of papers. As Krueger indicates, her manual only carries CCCD through the system level as defined by the 18 Illinois Library Systems, although her model permits intersystem and state/national levels of CCCD to be developed should volumes four and five of her manual ever be written. But it is significant that Krueger is approaching CCCD from the local level (from the "bottom up"). This is quite obviously a different perspective of CCCD than that found in the other papers. Phrases such as "client centered evaluation" and "meeting user demands" make much more sense from the "bottom up" perspective, while they seem much less relevant from the "top down" (the state and national perspective). I personally do not think the "client centered" approach is any less relevant to the state or national level of CCCD, but I can understand why it is not as much in evidence in the thinking of those with the "top down" perspective. It is likely that the distinction between the two perspectives is a matter of degree. It is unlikely that a model from the state or national perspective could sustain itself long if it did not take evaluation by users into consideration and in Krueger's model collection centered evaluation is certainly evident once one goes beyond the local level of CCCD. The important difference in the two perspectives lies in the starting point. The initial orientation of a model will undoubtedly influence the degree of emphasis given client centered evaluation as opposed to collection centered evaluation as the model progresses up the levels of the CCCD hierarchy. This may explain some of the apparent lack of communication which seems to be present among proponents of "top down" models and "bottom up" models.

Krueger's responses to the specific concerns of the symposium planners regarding questions of governance, financing, coordination, participation, bibliographic access, delivery, and resource sharing, are forthright and concise. Her response to the question of governance is presumably in the context of CCCD at the local and system level. I wonder if she would feel that there was no need for separate governance if she were considering the question from the intersystem or state/national level? It seems to me that some form of "coordinating" governance separate from the units being coordinated would be necessary for the intersystem and state level. Her view that no special funding would be necessary at the local level seems rather optimistic to me, but I assume she would find special funding necessary at levels above the local level, although she does not comment on this in her paper.

Within her model, capped as it is by the 18 Illinois Library Systems, Krueger's comments on "coordination" and "participation" are predictable and appropriate. But if the model were to be expanded to intersystem, state, or national levels, considerable adjustments would be necessary in the pattern of coordination and participation. How would the concept of "Subject Groups" fit into intersystem or state level CCCD? What is the optimum size or geographic area of a "Subject Group?" These and other questions would have to be answered.

Bibliographic access, as many have pointed out, is essential for effective CCCD, but Illinois is in a difficult, although probably not unique, situation of having at least five separate, non-compatible, bibliographic access networks. Although work is going on to make some of these compatible, the diversity of protocols for the variety of bibliographic access networks is a barrier. OCLC is probably the most comprehensive bibliographic network, but those networks tied to online circulation systems are undoubtedly the most effective for gaining physical as well as bibliographic access. Fortunately, delivery and resource sharing in Illinois are well established and the Krueger model takes good advantage of these strengths.

In addition to the limitations of the model pointed out by Krueger, such as the complexity of the manual and data analyses and the time it takes to work through the process, the lack of modeling for the intersystem and state/national level would appear to be one of the greatest shortcomings of the model. But rather than rejecting the model because of its local orientation, perhaps we should consider how the model could be expanded to include the upper levels of CCCD.

COMMENTS ON JOEL RUTSTEIN'S PAPER

Joel Rutstein presents an interesting review of developments in Colorado. Although he discusses some of the motivating factors for the libraries cooperating, one cannot help but wonder if there are not more political factors motivating Colorado cooperation than the author is sharing. His paper also raises many issues which deserve more exploration.

The probable financial motivation noted by Rutstein for cooperation in Colorado deserves further comment. The statement that CCCD grew out of a call for " . . . an equitable method for library funding, staffing, and cooperation," suggests that some Colorado libraries were getting a larger share of the state's budget for library development. It would be interesting to explore the impact of CCCD on the budgets of state supported libraries in Colorado. Does CCCD result in more equitable distribution of funds? Or does it result in more access to more materials without fund redistribution?

Rutstein reports that CARL (Colorado Alliance of Research Libraries) was founded with one private academic library (University of Denver) and a public library (Denver Public), yet financial support came from each participating institution assessing their own acquisition budgets. Assessing one's internal budget for cooperative activities is unusual, especially in a private/public mix of cooperation. To accomplish this, as appears to be the case in Colorado, is indeed a positive sign for CCCD and deserves more study.

Rutstein indicates that in the course of developing a cooperative plan in Colorado, three elements called for were: 1. a method of evaluation of use; 2. an evaluation of holdings of cooperating libraries; and 3. an identification of needs. There is little indication that much has been done in the areas of evaluating use or identifying needs (1 and 3) except through the subjective perceptions of the subject bibliographers in the cooperating institutions. Why these client centered evaluations were not pursued deserves further examination. Colorado selected three subject areas (music, literature, and mathematics) for applying the collection centered evaluation methodology and held workshops for staff from the participating libraries. It might be helpful to have more background on why these three subject areas were chosen and some data on the effectiveness of the workshops a year or two after the fact.

In the course of delivering the paper, Rutstein noted that one of the original Colorado libraries participating in CARL had withdrawn because it had chosen to pursue a different online catalog. The issue of the importance of access to resources online and its role in successful CCCD has been brought home by many of the presenters at this conference, and I think it is important to explore this issue further as we evaluate models for CCCD.

Certainly Colorado provides an interesting and potentially generalizable model of multitype research library CCCD at the state level using the RLG Conspectus concept. Some of the problems and achievements are undoubtedly due to the specific characteristics of libraries in Colorado. Rutstein provides a clear and forthright description which should be helpful to others developing similar models.

OVERVIEW OF ALL THREE PAPERS

When reviewing the three papers as a group, I arrived at the following schematic outline:

General Description

IN—Research library emphasis—Collection centered evaluation—National/multi-national orientation.

IL—Multi-type library cooperation emphasis—Client (user) centered evaluation—Local/regional orientation.

CO—Research library emphasis—Blend of collection and user centered evaluation with current emphasis on collection centered—State orientation.

Motivation

IN—External motivation to develop and test a method for constructing an inventory of research collections in North America.

IL—Internal motivation—Analyzing and meeting unmet needs at local, regional and state level in all types of libraries.

CO—External with internal support—Distribution of state funds and resources for research collections more equally among research libraries in the state.

Means

IN—Organization of academic libraries in the state.

IL—Multi-type library systems in the state.

CO—Organization of research libraries in the state.

Perceived Benefits

IN—More complete national research library resources [at less cost?].

IL—More client needs satisfied.

CO—A single research collection in the state supported by six cooperating libraries.

Unique Elements

IN—Top down orientation—National perspective.

IL—All types and levels of libraries included—Client centered—Subject interest groups—Decentralized governance.

CO—Self-assessment from member acquisition budgets.

Common Elements

IN/IL—Process of evaluation is time consuming.

IN/CO—Research libraries focus—Collection centered evaluation—Use of modified RLG Conspectus intensity levels.—On-line access to results.

IL/CO—Developed own subject categories for analysis of collections based on DDC/LC.

IN/IL/CO—Workshops and/or manuals on collection evaluation process.

All in all, these three rich and varied papers provide a basis for much thought and consideration. The questions of financial support, governance, types of library involved, and similar issues need further investigation. But most significant to the concerns of this symposium, in my opinion, is the need to reconcile the variety of orientations and assumptions contained in each model of the models presented. It seems to me that the client centered (bottom up) approach deserves as much consideration for planning purposes as the collection centered (top down) approach. In fact, it is my guess that when a successful and lasting CCCD model is developed, it will contain the best of both approaches.

Photograph by: Maurice C. Libbey and Gene W. Scholes, Eastern Illinois University.

Discussion #1

Discussion Leader, Terry L. Weech

I would, thus, invite you to address your questions to one or more of the speakers (or comments, they don't have to be questions) for purposes of discussion. I would also ask you to come to the microphone. They're not there to intimidate you; they're there to make everyone else more aware of what your concerns are and it might help if you were to state who you are and your affiliation just for the sake of orientation to the rest of the audience. Do we have a volunteer?

* * *

Doris Brown, De Paul University. Could we have some discussion of faculty involvement in these various projects, and faculty reaction as your projects are on-going?

* * *

I think that's a very interesting question. Let me just speak about it from the point of view of the NACIP progress in Indiana. We made many attempts to involve the faculty and have involved the faculty in our work. I think we did not involve them to the level that we had initially hoped to involve them, but they were involved. They were invited to discussions about the project and the Conspectus and what we were doing with it initially, and they were informed of our progress as we went along.

One of the steps that our bibliographers were asked to do was to review their Conspectus work, the values they had assigned, for two purposes. One was to check their perceptions with those of the faculty. The other was to let the faculty know that we were going through this process of assessing our collections and assigning priorities, and that they would have implications for the future.

In every case I can think of, in fact, that happened. The bibliographer working on a section of the Conspectus discussed it with relevant faculty members to get their feedback and to inform them of what was going on. We did not get a universal expression of interest in the Conspectus, and I can't say I was surprised or disappointed in it. I think it is the librarian's task to do the Conspectus work and to initiate the interaction with the faculty.

A couple of comments that we've had from the faculty are: one thing is, some faculty—and I'm not speaking for all of them by any means—some of them were very impressed with this work and excited by it. Others were critical of the Conspectus divisions and the Conspectus analysis of scholarly knowledge, just as some librarians are. Teaching faculty felt this did not reflect the world of scholarly knowledge as they knew it and, in fact, they had some specific examples to counter with to say, "This is really the way knowledge is organized from our point of view." They would discuss indexes and systems of organizing knowledge of their used and reviewed journals.

One other group I want to mention is administrators. I must say we've universally had enthusiastic responses from university administrators, both when we described the process we're going through and the results. They asked us to use this information in budget requests and reports to them, and they feed it right back to us, when they give us money. They tell us, "We're giving you this money because we're impressed with the effort you're making and we want to encourage it."

They're doing similar things in the programs at Indiana University. The different programs are supposed to be assessing their strengths and weaknesses, the academic and research programs, and comparing them with similar programs at peer institutions. Our effort has dovetailed very nicely with that.

* * *

The faculty contact, that I am aware of, was done on the local level with the bibliographers and the faculty in the various disciplines that they were representing. I can only speak for individual instances that I am aware of. Some of our bibliographers at CSU [Colorado State University] were very much involved with faculty, depending upon the amount of contact that was normally on-going between faculty and the subject librarians. This, of course, would always vary depending on the bibliographers and depending upon how the institutions arranged their coterie of bibliographers.

David also mentioned that administrators, and I might add that since this was coming from the top in the beginning, at least, were involved in various associations such as the Association of Public College and University Presidents which is interested in this, and also interested in the formatting or reform of creating formulas for allocating monies to the various institutions. This was reported up through their Library Formula Finance Committee in terms of what was going on in CARL. There was no other way around in that particular area.

* * *

I'm Scott Bennett from Northwestern University. I have a question for Joel. Every speaker this morning, starting with Mr. Wallhaus, emphasized the importance of libraries intending to cooperate with one another being able to read one another's catalogs. This [to be done] through a common cataloging system. It, therefore, struck me as really quite remarkable that Joel reported that Colorado State had to withdraw from CARL as a result of making a decision about an on-line catalog.

I wonder, Joel, if you would speak to the question of the precariousness of cooperative collection management in that context, and speak further about the ability to champion collection concerns in making decisions about on-line catalogs.

* * *

Thank you, Scott. I presume, of course, you're relating to the whole situation of when you have networks, cooperative collection development is an offshoot of the development of those networks and the shared cataloging process. That is true of this. The consortium did, at first, get very much actively involved in developing on-line circulation systems which is still developmental, although it is available to all of the CARL institutions except, of course, Colorado State University. We, by the way, have NOTIS.

The public access catalog, also, is available and Johannah might speak to that because that's available at the University of Northern Colorado plus the other institutions. You might notice, also, that the development of COLA was almost (in the beginning) independent of the shared cataloging processes. We sort of came into it through the back door when it started out as a cooperative purchase program and then was integrated into the CARL system. In that sense, there's never been any direct contact with what was going on in the on-line systems activity and the work of the committee members of COLA, which is exacerbated by the fact that there were no staff people involved in the essential projects to work with the committee in developing the cooperative collection development node. In that respect, that is correct: We did not have a direct relationship and that probably makes us somewhat different than other networks around the country.

* * *

The Executive Board of CARL has verbalized, and also written, that they have now a dual commitment—not only to their on-line system, but to the utilization of the on-line systems in collection development activities.

As Joel mentioned, the staff itself is quite small, but one of the very first things they noticed was that on the CARL system we have over 1.5 million records. So far, there's only about 25 percent duplication. Naturally, that prompts a lot of questions. Either we're doing something wrong, or we're doing something right. We can't decide. At the moment, we're gathering the statistical information on all the MARC records that are currently in the CARL data base. I think the cooperative collection development aspects are taking on a prominence they didn't have even three months ago.

* * *

I have a general question. I'm Bill Jones at the University of Illinois at Chicago. In terms of the kinds of systems, and proposals, and ideals that have advanced today, it seems to me that there should be some opportunity for mathematical modeling and simulation of the various kinds of programs that have been developed. I was just wondering whether any of the speakers have been involved in any kind of mathematical modeling and simulations that might, in fact, give them some predictability in terms of how one might expect to share one's resources and where one might expect queuing problems to occur. What would be some of the problems that Mr. Wallhaus spoke about in terms of delay, access, and dispersal of collections? Just in a general way, I would appreciate a response.

* * *

Let me just mention that Research Libraries Group has a study underway which is sponsored by CONOCO, which will involve a significant modeling exercise. The object of the modeling has less to do with the delivery of documents and more to do with the cost of alternative arrangements for managing our collections. If all goes well, the study will be completed by the end of the year.

* * *

I'm Phyllis Rearden from Eastern Illinois University. For those of us who are not primarily collection development managers, what are "verification studies?"

* * *

A verification study (these definitions are given in the ARL manual that is developed for the NACIP Project which is available from ARL) is a collection evaluation instrument. It's a way of measuring the strength of a collection. What's peculiar about it is that it's conspectus-based; it's related specifically, directly to a subject line of a conspectus or a group of lines of a conspectus. Typically, a bibliographer or subject specialist will look at some lines, or a line of the conspectus and construct, perhaps, a tailored list (a bibliographic list, citation studies, or a few hundred items up to over a thousand items) which is then checked. Every institution can check that list against their holdings and then get a fix, relatively, on how their collection matches up with others who have rated their collection, perhaps, at the same value (one, two, three, four, five) and see how they compare according to this list.

From verification studies some very interesting reports can be generated: overlap studies or gap studies. The results of the lists can be manipulated by a machine and you can get a report, say at Indiana University, showing which of those titles we held uniquely in the state, which ones Notre Dame held uniquely, which ones Purdue held uniquely, and if we were to combine our resources with Purdue what that means in terms of the total percentage of the sample that's been checked.

It's a way to evaluate your collection. A way to verify your values against the values that somebody else assigned to a certain line or collection of lines, and a way to build on that and decide where your best opportunities for cooperation [are] or where you should be putting your money for further development of your collection. [It shows] which is the best avenue to take.

* * *

RLG has developed several verification studies, and they've proven quite useful. They're used as an opposite, I would say, to doing shelf-list assessments which can skew the results. I think the approach of verification studies is a very good one, by drawing upon the bibliographers and central staff within the network, and picking a wide range of material to focus upon these strengths and weaknesses of the collection. As David pointed out, it's a very good method to analyze the levels of collecting that have been selected by the institutions. They have been very useful within the RLG network.

The only problem with it is it is very time-consuming to do. A lot of times you're starting from scratch since again, as David pointed out, you're using specific lines to measure and if you consider the number of lines that are in the LC breakdowns and the conspectuses, it could take forever.

* * *

I just wanted to add that when King Research was working with us on this, that was identified as one of the options or one of the things that has been used in cooperative collection development. Because we were trying to emphasize a multi-type environment, where we were looking at school districts, and public libraries, and a variety of libraries, it was impossible for us to come up with a standard list. Again, of course, we tended to reject that a little bit more just from the basis of the client centered approach, but partly because of the multi-type environment as well as the client centered, we did not do that.

* * *

I'm surprised—maybe I'm overly naive here—but I was first of all surprised at Karen's statement of "no special funding needed" for her particular model. Local resources could provide that support, and although it wasn't contradicted by the other speakers it seemed to me that there was an implication (at least in the case of David's presentation) that it actually might be more costly, as we've read in other sources, too, to go that route. You're getting a different type of benefit rather than cost savings, you're getting more of a cost-effectiveness approach. I'm wondering if anyone has any comment or response to that at this point, or whether you'd rather reserve it to talk about, or explore further, later in the conference.

* * *

I guess it's later in the conference.

* * *

Cooperative Acquisitions Within a System: The University of California Shared Purchase Program

Marion L. Buzzard

Head, Collection Development and Acquisitions
Main Library
University of California

ABSTRACT. The Shared Purchase Program, now in its ninth year, was implemented mainly to prevent unnecessary duplication of expensive, low-use materials among the nine campuses of the University of California. Stanford University also has been a full participant for the past six years. Although shareability of materials is an important consideration, the Program permits the acquisition of manuscripts and archival collections. Funding is provided by taking a percentage of the total University library materials budget each year before campus allocations are made. The Program is considered a success by its participants, in spite of problems of methodology and access that remain to be resolved.

The University of California's Shared Purchase Program has been in effect since 1976 and represents an attempt to acquire library materials cooperatively within a nine-campus system. To date close to four million dollars have been dedicated to this Program, which was implemented in the face of virtually universal opposition on the part of librarians at all ranks. Almost a decade later, it has won acceptance from the same people, or their successors, although the need for some modification and improvement is recognized by all.

PROGRAM GOALS AND BACKGROUND

The stated goal or purpose of the Program, to begin with, was the acquisition of materials which, because of their high cost or anticipated low frequency of use, should be shared among the campuses without unnecessary duplication. Several years later a further goal was added, namely, "to reduce competition for, and to promote sharing of, manuscript and subject area collections among the various campuses of the University of California."[1]

The concept of shared acquisitions was one of several proposals for intercampus cooperation made by the University in response to a study on its management and operations by the State Department of Finance Audits Division in 1971 and 1972. The unfavorable economic climate of the late sixties had caused the auditors to focus on the large sums that the State of California was spending for higher education, which at that time was provided to all residents at a nominal fee. As luck would have it, the auditors decided to begin with the libraries of the University of California's nine campuses.

The two-part study was intended to cover both collections and library operations, but concentrated almost entirely on the collections. Its basic finding was that these libraries were developing nine separate collections numbering a total of 10.6 million volumes in 1970, with an increase to 17.5 million expected by 1978. The study concluded that it was doubtful this increase could be financed and that other alternatives should be sought. As an example of the proliferation of unnecessary duplication of materials, the auditors mentioned several times in their report the purchase of eight separate copies of *The Irish University Press Series of British Parliamentary Papers*, at a collective cost of over $350,000. The one campus which had purchased the publication in microform was given credit for having saved the University over $40,000.

The study's overall conclusion was that "substantial opportunities exist for increased interdependence, cooperation, and coordination."[2] A number of recommendations, ranging from viable to highly questionable, were included, as was the suggestion that budgetary restraints be used to insure compliance. The issuance of the study caused dismay and some anger among University officials and librarians, but it led eventually to the appointment of an Executive Director of Universitywide Library Planning and to the creation of a master plan for developing the libraries. By the time the final version of this document was published in 1977, several of its proposals, such as the Shared Purchase Program, were already in place.[3]

GOVERNANCE

The Program is administered by the Assistant Vice President for Library Plans and Policies (formerly the Executive Director), who must approve the recommended acquisitions. This approval has become largely a pro forma exercise, although in the early years some reservations were expressed regarding the division of materials among the campuses. The chief responsibility for operating the Program lies with the systemwide Collection Development Committee, a group made up of the collection development officers of each campus and several others who serve as liaison with interested bodies. General oversight of the Program is provided by the Library Council, which is the present body of the Committee and whose membership consists of the nine University Librarians, the Assistant Vice President for Library Plans and Policies, and others.

FUNDING

Funding for shared purchase acquisitions is provided out of the University's library materials budget, which is a line item in the library operating funds allocated by the State. A percentage is skimmed off the top of the library materials allocation before the latter is divided among the campuses according to a formula (now somewhat modified) which was set forth in the Master Plan. In order to give the libraries time to work out effective procedures, the funding began at 1 percent of the total book budget the first year. It was slated to rise by one percentage point each year until a maximum of 5 percent was reached.

Both the collection development officers and the University Librarians fought the annual increase, arguing that the Program tended to encourage the purchase of items of lower priority than might have been purchased by the individual campuses from their own local budgets and that there was a point of diminishing returns in the expenditure of shared purchase funds. But they were overruled by Systemwide Administration, who saw the Program as a highly visible good faith effort on the part of the University to promote intercampus cooperation. Three years later, with the funding at 3 percent of the total library materials budget and approaching half a million dollars, the University gave in to pleas that the line be held at that level, where it remains today.

EXPANSION OF THE PROGRAM

Two interesting developments took place in 1978. In the first, the University of California libraries all became members of the Center for Research Libraries, fulfilling another recommendation of the Master Plan. At the time this step was taken, only two of the campuses were members. The cost of membership was substantial, but it was anticipated that use of the Center by the University libraries would grow as its resources and services were publicized to faculty and students.

The University's participation was expected to encourage CRL's development as a national periodicals lending center, so that reliance on it might hopefully extend beyond nonduplication of materials to the point where the campus libraries would dispense altogether with certain titles and depend on the Center to supply them whenever requested by users. To date the latter has happened seldom, if ever. Since the University libraries cannot require the Center to buy specific titles and since the results of their votes are uncertain, they prefer to rely on having one or more copies of most serials and microform sets within the system. Indeed, by the time queries on titles for possible acquisition by the Center are received, many of them have already been acquired by at least one UC library, which will usually return the form indicating that the title in question is already held by that particular library and that it may be borrowed. Nevertheless, membership in the Center for Research Libraries is viewed positively by most UC librarians, particularly those involved in interlibrary lending activities, in spite of the high cost of transaction per item. The University libraries are currently also providing additional shared purchase funds to the Center by participating in its Latin American Microfilming Project.

A further expansion of the Shared Purchase Program in 1978 involved the inclusion of a private university. Late in 1976, UC Berkeley and Stanford University had received foundation grants to promote a cooperative program between the libraries of these two institutions. Among other goals, the program was intended to facilitate a coordinated acquisitions policy for books and other materials. In 1978, when the libraries were already well on their way to producing coordinated collection development policies, Stanford requested that it be allowed to participate in the University of California's Shared Purchase Program. The UC Library Council agreed to this request, and Stanford's collection development officer attended the meetings of the Collection Development Committee as an observer for the first year. In 1979 Stanford requested full participation as a voting member and stated its willingness to commit to the Program a percentage of its budget each year for materials to be proposed and housed by Stanford, but selected by the Collection Development Committee. Approval of this request was given, although several of the University Librarians expressed reservations about Stanford's having a voice in the use of University of California funds, and some wondered if this might open the door to similar requests by other institutions.

OPERATION OF THE PROGRAM

At present the Program operates in the following manner. Recommended titles or collections, which must meet specific criteria and other requirements, originate with librarians on each campus at the beginning of the academic year. Each proposal is submitted on a special form that requests the following information: bibliographic description, justification for the purchase, cost, access, suggested location, whether one or two copies or sets are recommended, and whether it is held by the Center for Research Libraries. The completed forms are reviewed and signed by the campus collection development officer, and copies are then sent to each of the other campuses for comment and assignment of priorities. This information is forwarded by the collection development officers to the Chair of the Collection Development Committee, who tabulates and summarizes the responses on a second form, after which an overall priority rating is assigned to each item, based on those assigned by the campuses. The Chair also compiles a master list of the recommended acquisitions, and sends copies of the summary forms and the lists to each member of the Committee.

A four-priority system is used in the rating of shared purchase recommendations. Priority 1 indicates that the material is considered essential; Priority 2 is assigned for materials considered important, but of lesser significance; Priority 3 means that materials are of sufficient value to the overall University program to be acquired, although they may not support the programs of the campus assigning the priority; Priority 4 means "do not purchase." The latter is assigned to recommendations that are already held by one or more participating libraries, or that fail to meet the criteria for shared purchase. It may also be assigned for other reasons deemed to be appropriate. Finally, there is a Priority X which is used in conjunction with a numerical rating to indicate a question or problem relating to the material which may require discussion and review by the Committee.

The Collection Development Committee usually meets twice to review and vote on the materials recommended for shared purchase each year, with the collection development officers being the only members allowed to vote. The process described above follows a schedule that is geared to both the academic and the fiscal years. It begins early in the academic year, so that faculty input may be solicited, and it concludes before the end of the fiscal year, to allow sufficient time for the transfer and encumbering of funds.

In addition to deciding whether or not to acquire a particular item, voting is used to determine where the materials will be located and unless they are unique, whether one systemwide or two regional copies or sets will be acquired. (California is usually thought of as having two major regions, the northern and the southern; there are four UC campuses in the north, plus Stanford, and five in the south.)

TYPES OF MATERIALS ACQUIRED

The guidelines under which the Program operates allow for the acquisition of materials without regard to form or format. Eligible materials include, but are not limited to, computer based services, newspapers and other serials, archival and manuscript collections, and large microform collections. Certain types of materials, such as facsimiles, library catalogs, and collections of dissertations are discouraged unless special conditions are met. The guidelines require that all materials selected meet the following criteria:

1. Materials must be specifically related to the programs of more than one campus;

2. Items selected must be currently unavailable for shared use in the system either on a Universitywide or a regional basis, although funds may be used to assume payment of ongoing publications;
3. Adequate bibliographic and physical access must be available or provided to permit effective sharing of resources;
4. The selection of materials requiring on-site use normally should not exceed 15 percent of the annual shared purchase funds;
5. Materials costing less than $1,500 will not be considered, except for subscriptions to serial titles;
6. If funding is used to acquire a portion of a title or collection already held by a campus, the entire body of material will be available for sharing.

BIBLIOGRAPHIC ACCESS

The very important matter of access is dealt with in some detail in the guidelines, but nevertheless, it remains a problematic area for a number of reasons. Bibliographic access in particular has proven itself to be a complex and difficult issue to resolve. The Program guidelines state that indexes or registers of the contents of collections will, where available, be acquired with shared purchase funds by all campuses requesting them. It is further required that any participating library that creates such a register for a previously unindexed shared acquisition must distribute copies of the register to all interested campuses.

The guidelines recognize that it is generally not practical to incorporate catalog cards for the contents of large microform and other collections acquired with shared purchase funds in the catalog of libraries other than the one that holds the material. The registers and indexes are expected to provide at least partial access to materials on other campuses. There is also now available, thanks to the efforts of several campuses and of one librarian in particular, a list of all microform sets held by the University of California libraries through 1983.[4] The list is not limited to sets acquired with shared purchase funds. Unfortunately Stanford's holdings are not included in this bibliography.

Bibliographic access to materials acquired through the Shared Purchase Program is limited by the fact that the campuses do not all use the same bibliographic utility; some use OCLC and others are affiliated with RLIN, although several libraries now have access to both. An important source of bibliographic information is the University of California's new online catalog, MELVYL, which includes records of holdings of all of the campuses. Its database, however, is still far from complete, although it reflects current acquisitions.

There has been no agreement on whether or not it is important to tag shared purchase materials in the MELVYL database. Tagging or coding might be important only for items housed at locations that normally do not lend, or for titles only partially acquired with shared purchase funds. Also, for microform or other collections that are not analyzed, bibliographic access through MELVYL is very limited indeed. However, the OCLC Major Microform Project is capable of solving this problem over a period of time, and acquisition of OCLC tapes of bibliographic records for sets held by UC libraries has been endorsed by the Collection Development Committee. As a final caveat, since Stanford's holdings are not included in the MELVYL database, those campuses not having access to RLIN may find it difficult to identify materials owned by Stanford.

At present reliance for information about shared purchase titles rests almost entirely on a list that is cumulated manually each year and sent to Collection Development Committee members for distribution in their libraries. Since it is put together by a non-librarian attached to Systemwide Administration, the citations often do not conform to AACR2 rules. The list is supplemented in part by a photocopy of catalog cards for these materials prepared by one of the campuses and shared with other Committee members.

DELIVERY

The Program provides for physical access to materials acquired with Shared Purchase funds by requiring that users of the University of California and Stanford libraries be permitted to borrow the materials by direct or interlibrary loan of the original, or a photocopy or microform reproduction of the original. It allows also for use by remote consultation through reference assistance, in the case of certain catalogs and indexes, and for on-site use of archives and manuscripts, or other special materials, provided the Committee members agree that this constitutes adequate access. A related consideration recognized by the guidelines is the importance of efficient delivery systems and transmission of information, and this has at times affected the choice of location for specific items.

LOCATION AND OWNERSHIP

The choice of location may be dictated by a number of factors, including academic programs, strength of collections, projected use, and reasonable consideration of equity in the distribution of materials among the campuses. The latter criterion was added to insure that the smaller campuses with fewer programs and usually weaker collections would be able to capture some of the shared purchase materials, either in areas where a particular library might have a special strength, or where materials under consideration would support the programs of all campuses. The accessibility of materials may be a factor where use is required on site, or the likelihood of more effective use in conjunction with other scholarly resources at a particular library may be considered.

The larger campuses, especially UCLA and Berkeley, have received a very large portion of shared purchase materials, in part because of the strength of their programs and collections, and partly because they are regarded by the other campuses as major regional and systemwide resources. In addition, daily jitney buses from the northern campuses to Berkeley, and from the southern campuses to UCLA facilitate on-site use and borrowing of materials. Although dissatisfaction has been expressed from time to time with the uneven distribution of the funds compared with the allocation formula for the rest of the library materials budget, the majority of the collection development officers and the University Librarians have supported the criteria for selection of location that is used and have accepted the division of materials that results from the discussion and voting of the Collection Development Committee.

Materials acquired with shared purchase funding are included in the holdings of the campus designated to acquire and lend them. Special marking is not considered necessary unless it is required to insure availability of the material to other campuses. There have been a few problems in borrowing some titles acquired on shared purchase, as indicated earlier, but the identification and awareness of the availability of shared purchase materials by librarians and users may be a more significant problem.

Photograph by: Maurice C. Libbey and Gene W. Scholes, Eastern Illinois University.

STRENGTHS AND WEAKNESSES

Interviews with collection development officers, University Librarians, and other University officials clearly substantiate their generally positive and, in a few cases, enthusiastic view of the Shared Purchase Program. This has replaced an initially negative attitude on the part of most of those involved in the Program from its inception, who felt it had been imposed on the University for political reasons and might be detrimental to campus academic programs.

Certain benefits were cited frequently by the librarians, particularly the fact that the Program has prevented the unnecessary duplication of a lot of expensive low-use materials, with a consequent enhancement of the University's collections at lower cost. The political benefits were recognized by most, since the University has been successful each year in its requests for an increase in the library materials budget. Some of the University officials believe that the Program has been instrumental in obtaining funding from the State Legislature to support other segments of the Master Plan by convincing the legislators (and the Department of Finance) that the UC libraries are making progress in coordinating their collection development activities. The benefit mentioned most often was the sense of genuine cooperation that has evolved among the collection development officers and bibliographers, as well as their greater knowledge of the interests and collections of the other campuses.

Other strengths of the Program include the acquisition of valuable archival and manuscript collections by the University of California, for which funding might not have been available, particularly in the case of the smaller campuses. Special projects, such as the provision of funds for the microfilming of rare or deteriorating materials, were cited as a way in which the Program has increased available resources. This has been supplemented by the acquisition of commercially available microform collections.

There is general agreement that it has promoted the idea of sharing resources within the system and has also legitimized the concept of one University rather than nine separate campuses, with the result that the groundwork has been laid for at least limited cooperative collection development. In addition, the voluntary participation of a private university of the stature of Stanford is seen as underscoring the credibility of the Program, as well as increasing available resources.

A weakness of the Program identified by everyone queried is the extremely cumbersome and labor-intensive nature of its procedures, which require a great deal of consultation and communication both within and among the campuses, accompanied by much photocopying and paper shuffling. The Chair of the Collection Development Committee, who is selected on a rotating basis between the north and the south for a two-year term of office, bears the brunt of the burden. The time-consuming task of assembling, analyzing, and summarizing the data received from all participants that is the responsibility of the Chair has been carried out to date with only minimal clerical support provided by that individual's library.

It is unfortunate that no significant administrative or staff support is being provided for a program in which already millions of dollars have been invested. The University Librarians have accepted the more or less hidden overhead costs of the Shared Purchase Program to their libraries, including the time of the collection development officers and others, plus photocopying and travel. They are understandably reluctant to go further, since library operating funds have not shown the increases of the library materials budget and must be used to support local automation costs. The University, for its part, has taken the position that any administrative costs for the Program not paid for by the campuses would have to come from shared purchase funds, and this the collection development officers have been reluctant to agree to.

Consequently nothing has been done to solve this continuing problem. Suggestions have been made that some of the logistical and paperwork problems be resolved through the use of electronic mail, conference calling, and the use of a machine-readable scoring method for tallying the votes. It is doubtful, however, that the collection development officers would be willing to give up their face-to-face meetings, which have resulted in a valuable ongoing dialogue and exchange of information and ideas.

Another problem mentioned by many of those involved in the Program is the weakness of bibliographic and, in some cases, physical access for the material that is acquired. The implementation of the University of California's online catalog has been a big step forward, but as noted earlier, it does not include Stanford's holdings, nor is it of much help where large unanalyzed collections are concerned. At the very minimum, an accurate, up-to-date computer-produced master list should be made available for wide distribution. The list should also indicate what registers or indexes, or other access tools, are available for each of the items listed. This would require a relatively small amount of administrative support.

There is a belief, particularly on the part of the smaller campuses, that a lack of equity exists in the distribution of shared purchase materials. At present a major portion of the Program's annual budget goes to support continuations costs, including both serials and large collections published over a period of time, with most of this material going to the larger campuses. Although at present no collection development officer or University Librarian espouses a strict division of funds according to a formula, it has been suggested that the distribution be looked at periodically and that some adjustment be made wherever major inequities exist.

Other weaknesses seen in the Program include the criteria for selection, which are regarded by some as too subjective or inconsistently applied. Also mentioned is the questionable value and lack of shareability of some of the acquisitions.

The newer members of the Collection Development Committee who were not involved in fleshing out the Program are somewhat impatient with the rather hidebound and time-consuming process, as well as the fact that the focus has been on the acquisitions of traditional materials. There is a feeling that the Program should seek new ideas and that cooperative collection development should not be limited to this one effort.

NEW DEVELOPMENTS

Although the guidelines of the Shared Purchase Program are broad and flexible with regard to the types of materials that may be acquired, there has perhaps been a lack of imagination in applying them or in following through on some of the suggestions that have been made.

An idea that surfaced early in the Program involves the use of shared purchase funds to support unique copies of serials, so that at least one copy of each title will be held somewhere in the system. The University of California campuses with medical schools had applied this concept by identifying all medical titles held by only one of the medical libraries; they then successfully requested shared purchase funding to support these subscriptions on a continuing basis.

Recently an attempt was made to expand the concept to include non-medical serials as well. After much discussion, a list was prepared of serial titles held by three or fewer UC libraries, and a pilot project was approved. Its intent was to protect existing serial resources in California, to effect savings through cancellations of unnecessary duplicate copies, and to increase the net number of titles in the system. There were, however, some serious flaws in the proposed methodology and also a lack of consensus on the criteria for selection. As a result, the Collection Development Committee concluded that the amount of effort required to undertake such a project would be worth while only in a period of budgetary retrenchment, and voted to table it.

Another direction in which the Program is moving, with a greater probability of success, is toward the funding of computer based services. Although permitted in the guidelines, support for bibliographic and nonbibliographic online databases with shared purchase funds has not yet occurred. This year a request has been submitted for a subscription to the American and French Research on the Treasury of the French Language (ARTFL), a user-friendly online textual database that is designed to be accessed by individual researchers without intermediaries, on any standard computer terminal with a modem. Its acquisition has been endorsed enthusiastically by all Program participants. The subscription would be paid for out of shared purchase funds, with the individual campuses picking up the additional online and communications fees.

In another instance, a grant proposal has been prepared by the University of California health sciences libraries requesting funding from the National Library of Medicine to mount a current (three-year) file of MEDLINE on the MELVYL catalog, to permit free online searching by UC library users. A further request has been made to the Collection Development Committee for funds to purchase the MEDLINE database, beginning with the second year of the grant. Even though only one physical tape is needed for loading into MELVYL, the five campuses with medical schools would each be charged individually for the database, so the continuing cost would be high. There are a number of other issues, in addition to cost, that require discussion and resolution before an informed decision can be made on this request.

As a final note, last year with the encouragement of the University Librarians, the Collection Development Committee asked to participate in the Association of Research Libraries' North American Collections Inventory Project. Since UC Berkeley, UC Davis, and Stanford have already completed the analysis of their collections as part of the Research Libraries Group conspectus project, only seven of the campuses are currently involved. Although not really connected with the Shared Purchase Program, this multi-campus effort was undoubtedly made possible by the success of the Program and the spirit of cooperation that it has helped to build.

REFERENCES

1. "Guidelines for University of California Library Acquisitions with Shared Purchase Funds." Rev. ed. University of California, Library Council, Collection Development Committee, 1984. Photocopy.
2. California. Department of Finance. Audits Division. *The Library System of the University of California.* Management and Operations of the University of California, vol. 1. Sacramento, Calif., 1972.
3. University of California. Office of the Executive Director of Universitywide Library Planning. *The University of California Libraries: A Plan for Development, 1978-1988.* Berkeley, Calif., 1977.
4. Eichhorn, Sara. *Guide to Research Collections on Microform in the University of California Libraries.* Irvine, Calif.: University of California, Irvine, 1983.

The New York State Experience with Coordinated Collection Development: Funding the Stimulus

Joan Neumann

Executive Director
New York Metropolitan Reference
and Research Library Agency

ABSTRACT. The nations' first state aid for college and university libraries contributing to resource sharing has been the stimulus for coordinated collection development planning in New York State. The planning effort is carried out within each of the nine regions of the state by regional committees involving 177 academic libraries. The program fits within a framework of other state-supported library programs and, as a result, builds on well-established regional multi-type library resource sharing systems which provide coordination, bibliographic access, and delivery. Both existing systems and the collection development effort have been strengthened by the other.

In 1981 New York State became the first state in the nation to financially recognize the contributions college and university libraries make to statewide resource sharing. As a result of this state aid, 177 academic libraries and an increasing number of other libraries are now participating in coordinated collection development in the nine regions of the state.

New York State has more institutions of higher education (community colleges, four year liberal arts colleges, universities and professional schools) than any other state except California and has the second largest student enrollment in the country. Academic library holdings total more than 54 million volumes out of 172 million volumes held statewide. In the 1960's, in early recognition of the need to facilitate resource sharing for reference and research, the State established nine reference and research library resources systems with academic, public, and special libraries as members. Although hampered by years of insufficient funding, the 3R's provided the support structure for the more recent coordinated collection development effort.

GOALS

The State's Coordinated Collection Development Program is intended to augment collection strength and encourage regional resource sharing. The impetus for the program came from the 1978 Governor's Conference on Libraries which recommended that independent college and university libraries which share their resources with other libraries should receive state financial aid in recognition of their public service. The Regents' 1980 legislative program, building on this recommendation, proposed grants based on the size of collections, ranging from a minimum of $4,300 to a maximum of $75,000. Once the bill was introduced into the legislative and the public arena, public and independent sector interest was raised and legislative leaders indicated willingness to consider a bill which would aid libraries in both the independent and public sectors.

Aid for both sectors became part of the Regents comprehensive library legislation proposals in 1981. Costs and well-established resource sharing were used to justify the proposals. As the *Fact Book on the Board of Regents 1981 Legislative Program for Libraries*[1] pointed out,

> Skyrocketing prices of books, serials, and other library materials have prevented the continued growth and development of college and university libraries which have been noted for the quality of their resources. Over the past six years, the average prices of books and periodicals have risen 87 percent, substantially higher than the overall general inflation rate.
>
> Colleges and universities contribute to regional interlibrary loan and resource sharing activities.
>
> Strengthening these libraries will ensure continued access to resources within the regions of the State, thus enabling users of all types of libraries to have access to quality resources.

The legislation enacted late in 1981 provides that any academic library participating in the regional resource sharing program of a Reference and Research Library Resources System is eligible for a grant.

What had begun as a movement for aid to independently funded research libraries had ended in establishment of aid to all academic libraries who share and who will plan together for collection development. While grant funds are to be expended for materials within the subject-area commitments of each library, no distinction in openness of access is made between state-funded and locally-funded materials. Established regional resource sharing was accepted as a given in the program. Coordinated collection development is simply the most cost-effective way to stretch finite public funds within the sharing environment of the 3R's systems.

These systems devote a high percentage of their funding to facilitation of interlibrary loan, providing delivery service and bibliographic centers for location and routing of requests. The systems also have variously used or experimented with direct access referral passes, cooperative acquisitions programs, order awareness files, HFA IIA projects, gifts and exchange lists, cooperative retention agreements, and other methods of formal and informal resource sharing.

The coordinated collection development program in New York State overlays a regional structure of support services that provides for its administration and facilitation with minimal additional cost. At the same time the program strengthens the resource planning and sharing for which the regional systems had come into being.

TIME IN OPERATION

The legislation was signed by Governor Hugh Carey on June 30, 1981, and by September draft regulations were being reviewed by groups of librarians around the state. Regulations were adopted by the Regents in November 1981. Applications for the initial (1982) grants were due December 15, 1981. About fifteen months was allowed for the preparation of the regional coordinated collection development plans. Regulations called for submission of a "plan to prepare a plan" in December 1981, in mid-1982 a report was to show substantial progress in planning, and a final plan was due early in 1983. Applications from 1983 on were based on the regional plan.

GOVERNANCE

Long-established regional boundaries determined who would plan together. State law and regulations determined the outline and the approval process for the plan. Law and regulations set the state aid formula, the application process, and the maintenance of effort requirement.

The coordinated collection development plans, however, are the products of committees in each of the regions. In May 1982, the State attempted to provide these planners with "some shared experience in plan development in order to assure common understanding of the parameters, format, and potential of a coordinated collection development plan."[2] Several systems, including METRO, asked preexisting committees to take responsibility for collection development planning; most formed committees for this purpose. In some regions, planning meetings include a representative of each participating library—which was not difficult when the number of academic libraries planning together was ten to fifteen.

The METRO region, with 62 libraries in the plan, has had a more complicated planning process. Our Resources Development Committee, which has focused much of its energy on collection development planning, is now reworking a list of subject descriptors in preparation for a meeting of all participating libraries in May. They expect to have a revised plan completed for approval in September. The revised plan must be approved by every participating library and by the Board of Trustees before submission to the State Library.

Again, this planning effort is in the context of a multitype library system that is governed by Trustees elected by the members, almost half of whom participate in the collection development plan. Staff support for the planning effort is high. The database is being manipulated on one of our IBM PCs. By the time the revised plan is approved this fall, we will have made thousands of pages of photocopies to keep all involved fully informed.

FINANCING

The legislation that passed in 1981 established base funding of $4,000 for each chartered institution, plus a formula of 46 cents per full-time equivalent student. The full-time equivalent student is also a formula: each full-time undergraduate is weighted as 1; part-time undergrads as .33; full-time first professional students, 1.5; part-time first professional students, 1; full-time grad students, 1.5; and part-time grad students, 1.

In the first full year, aid ranged from $4,067 for the College of Human Services to $19,616 for New York University.

To continue to receive aid, the library materials expenditures per full-time equivalent student must be maintained by the parent institution. Actually, 95% of the average expenditures for the last two years for library materials must be maintained, either as total expenditures or expenditures per FTE student.

In 1984 omnibus library legislation raised the aid formula to 60 cents per full-time equivalent students.

The balance in the aid formula does not reflect the thinking of the original recommendations that would have favored large research libraries. The aid driven by the relatively large base has the most impact on small, relatively poorly-funded libraries. For these libraries, the aid helps them to better meet their own curriculum demands so that they may not need to turn to the region for basic materials.

COORDINATING

Building on a pre-existing system takes minimal funding, but it does require some funding. Because no funding was provided to the 3R's specifically for administration of this program, or for another new program in the same legislation, the 3R's were hard pressed during the first years to coordinate the planning and administer grant applications; Library Development had similar problems with program aid outgrowing the ability of staff to effectively administer the new programs.

Use of pre-existing systems for coordinating collection development had advantages besides low cost. The cooperating libraries were experienced in working together, and the program was developed as an integral part of systemized sharing.

In addition, although the funding was limited to academic libraries, because the 3R's systems are multitype library systems, many of the planning committees include representatives of public and special libraries. Now that school library systems have become part of the mix—with their own mandated coordinated collection development programs—they, too, will have a part in planning the resource development that is intended to benefit users of every type of library. It is hoped that, building on the 1982-83 experience of six Education Consolidation and Improvement Act Chapter 2 competitive grant projects, school library system cooperative effort will not only be among high school libraries but also will encourage articulation of collections and resource sharing among high school and college libraries.

MAKE UP: PARTICIPANTS

I said earlier that every academic library participating in resource sharing through the reference and research library resources systems was eligible to participate in the program. If a distinction is made between participating in coordinated collection development planning, and receiving aid, all members of 3R's systems can participate in planning, and the trend is for more and more of them to do so.

To receive aid, however, each academic library must a) be a member of their 3R's system, b) participate in regional interlibrary loan, c) document the fact that their parent institution is continuing to fund the library as well as it had in the past. In addition, the parent academic institution must be eligible for state aid called Bundy aid. We have a few academic libraries in METRO that are not eligible for aid, such as Union Theological Seminary and St. John's University, although Yeshiva University and St. Joseph's College, sounding equally religious, do receive aid. Apparently details of governance make the difference. With these few exceptions, all academic libraries in the state, both publicly and independently funded, receive state aid through the program.

MAKE UP: THE COORDINATED COLLECTION DEVELOPMENT PLAN

The State required the systems to describe the resources within the region (identifying the participating institutions, their subject strengths and their resource sharing programs), describe the needs, and set out a plan to meet the needs (regional goals and objectives, obstacles, monitoring and maintenance of the plan and related information). Each region's plan developed independently of the others and, probably, differently. The ALA *Guidelines for Collection De-velopment*[3] was used across the state for definition of subject strengths, but "A. *Comprehensive level*: aim exhaustiveness", "B. *Research level*: major published source materials", "C. *Study level:* a collection which supports undergraduate or graduate work", (C1. Advanced study level, C2. initial study level), and "D. *Basic level:* highly selective collection which serves to introduce and define the subject" are hardly rigorous definitions, and application undoubtedly varied. (More on this later.) Each reflects its region, whether it deals with 150 subject areas in a dozen libraries or 300 subject areas in 62 libraries, as METRO's does.

In the METRO region, because so many libraries are involved, the planning committee worked with the participating libraries by mail. The first input from participants was taken from their first grant applications in which they listed subject strengths and collection areas they were building up that were not yet at A, B, or C strength. At the end of this first pass we had a list of subjects being collected in depth in each library described in each library's own terms.

This method of planning collection development was based on the assumption that what libraries were actually doing in collection development in their institution's self-interest, they would be willing to continue to do in the region's interest. It was expected that institutional needs would change over time. It was hoped that as the plan became a part of the regional sharing environment, institutions would compare their own collection development with that of their neighbors and make adjustments, again, primarily in their own enlightened self-interest. No monitoring or enforcement had been built into the State's program. Enlightened self-interest was, therefore, both the only motivation for following the regional plan and the most appropriate one in a cooperative system.

Once METRO had compiled this list of subjects being collected in depth, we had an ungainly and uneven list of descriptors. Staff reviewed the subjects and collection levels indicated and attempted to impose structure and uniformity by translating some descriptors into common terms. These revised listings were submitted to the originating library for approval or further clarification. The returns from this second pass were incorporated in the plan submitted to the State not because we were satisfied, but because, in the State's timetable, time had run out. Terms still reflected one library's insistence on "liberal arts" and another's special collection in "health advocacy." Perfection was going to have to wait for the second edition.

The format for the plan was dictated by state forms with one exception, the charting of regional subject strengths and subject areas in which collection depth was going to be developed. METRO admittedly used the opportunity to make something of a political statement by dramatizing the fact that four or five times as many libraries, with far greater collections, were cooperating in our region without proportionate funding to facilitate resource sharing. Our chart, 62 libraries across and 300 subjects down, was four by eight feet when unfolded. In 1984, legislation began to redress this inequity by adding formula funding, based on population and square mileage, to the 3R's systems' base funding, and the second edition's chart will be in an easier-to-use 8½" by 11" format.

BIBLIOGRAPHIC ACCESS

There is no requirement that participating libraries provide machine-readable records for access to their entire collections, their subject responsibility, or even the materials purchased with grant funds. Most academic libraries, however, are members of a bibliographic utility: OCLC, RLIN, or UTLAS, and their records can be accessed on-line by other members of their respective databases. In most of New York State, these records are being entered into OCLC. In metropolitan New York, all of the above utilities are being used. Until linkage becomes possible, no single electronic source will provide holdings information for the whole regional collection pool. METRO's bibliographic clearinghouse is intended to bridge the gap. System funds, augmented by grant funds from the new Regional Bibliographic Data Bases and Interlibrary Resource Sharing Programs, will make it possible to have all bibliographic databases on-line at the Clearinghouse. Through this service, OCLC users can locate materials in RLG libraries, UTLAS users can tap OCLC . . . and unautomated libraries can have access to them all.

The possibilities of a multiplier effect enhancing programs is real within the systems. Funding for Regional Bibliographic Data Bases and Interlibrary Resource Sharing Programs is a result of 1984 library legislation. The region's five year plan for this program includes improving linkage through the Clearinghouse and

Photograph by: Maurice C. Libbey and Gene W. Scholes, Eastern Illinois University.

retrospective conversion of members' records. One of the priorities for selection of records for conversion will be making subject strengths identified through the coordinated collection development plan more accessible. Serial records are being made machine-readable through the LSCA-funded regional union list of serials projects across the state.

DELIVERY SYSTEM

The 3R's systems also provide document delivery between member libraries. METRO's regional delivery, provided through contract with two of the public library systems, has 3.5 FTE drivers and vehicles on the road. Stopping at each academic library two or three times a week, material moves rapidly across the region's six counties. The delivery system provides support for any sharing arrangement between members.

RESOURCE-SHARING EXISTANT

New York State has multi-tiered subgroups of sharers. Some sharing is utility-based. OCLC members share among themselves with or without benefit of the ILL subsystem. The Research Library Group shares similarly.

The 64 members of the State University of New York (SUNY) form an affinity group, as do the 20 units of the City University (CUNY) system. In the private sector there are also special relationships such as the Research Library Association of South Manhattan that includes N.Y.U., The New School of Social Research, Parsons School of Design, and Cooper Union libraries.

Geographic proximity also has fostered special arrangements, especially where it is assumed that users go and use neighboring libraries. Among these groups are the Academic Libraries of Brooklyn consortium, a Queens group and the Westchester libraries.

Regional state-supported systems encourage resource sharing not only by facilitating location and delivery, but through regional interlibrary loan agreements. Through negotiation, the system works to increase access; through its interlibrary loan procedures, it seeks to equalize the burden of requests. Requests that have not been located in the region are transmitted by the 3R's to the New York State Library Interlibrary Loan (NYSILL) system which provides further search at the State Library and in nine referral libraries.

Planning for coordinated collection development on the regional level should add value in each of the exchange groupings in which members participate—particularly if consideration has been given to these sharing relationships during the planning. I know that CUNY's coordinated collection development plan is being compared with METRO's for consistency. More attempts to synchronize collection planning on the various affinity levels are likely to follow as commitment to the plan grows.

WHAT WOULD YOU DO DIFFERENTLY?

METRO has had a coordinated collection development plan now for close to two years and is preparing a revision. The State has revised regulations once to increase flexibility in meeting the maintenance of effort requirement, and the legislature passed new legislation increasing the funding in 1984. All actors are likely to continue to tinker with the aid package and the plan itself, fine tuning and adjusting.

But none will turn back the clock and start all over with the benefit of experience. For your benefit, I asked a number of people what would have been better if done differently, what side effects were good or bad, and how they would like the program to evolve.

Even before plans were submitted, Joseph Shubert, the State Librarian, remarked that "Whatever success may come of the coordinated collection development planning effort in New York State, it seems to me, will be based upon four important conditions: the resource sharing experience of the reference and research library systems; new tools for describing and measuring collections; a new technology for resource sharing; and strong incentives for resource sharing."[4]

The first-named factor contributing to success is in place: the program has built on the experience and support services of the 3R's with good results. Side effects identified by my respondents were all good. Generally cited were: good will in the region, good feeling toward the 3R's systems, and leverage in achieving greater cooperation from some less willing libraries. In the METRO region, the coordinated collection development grants for academic libraries brought in new members. In the other regions where there are only a dozen or so academic libraries and regional state aid had not been spread as thin as in METRO, all academic libraries, I am told, had joined the 3R's. But in the metropolitan region, the grant incentive persuaded 7 academic libraries to join the system. As a result, these libraries have been drawn into the full range of resource sharing activities in the region, strengthening the library service they are able to offer their own users, and strengthening the library service of the rest of the region.

No funds were allocated for coordination and administration of the program on either the regional or state level. With the expectation that there would be considerable work involved, even if building on existing structures, legislation should have provided administrative support for the program in the region and in Library Development.

Suggestion that funds for the participating libraries be disbursed through the regions came from the 3R's directors who emphasized increased speed in members' receipt of aid, and added that regional handling would increase leverage in strengthening resource sharing. There was some thought that if funding passed through the region, it might be easier to encourage joint activity such as cooperative purchase of expensive materials.

Mr. Shubert's second factor in success, "new tools for describing and measuring collections," needs considerable work. Patricia Young, Head of Circulation at Brooklyn College, and Chair of METRO's Resources Development Committee which is responsible for the region's coordinated collection development plan, believes that the planning process would have been much easier if the regions had been given a set of terms with which to work. The State Library was not unaware of the need.

Mr. Shubert had declared, "In the case of collection development planning, a common vocabulary and set of descriptors is paramount."[5] Although planners had been refered to the ALA *Guidelines* for common descriptors of collection depth, Ms. Young points to the disparate collections with the same labels as evidence that collection levels were too vaguely defined, and left too much to subjectivity and local pride. Collection levels remain subjectively described with neither quantitative nor qualitative measurement. Funding for measurement of collections might have yielded more uniform collection depth descriptions. Ms. Young referred to RLG's Benchmark evaluations of serials collections in the sciences as a rigorous model. For this revision of METRO's plan no more measurement will be done, but libraries will be asked to compare their collections with others in the region collecting in the same subject areas to assess relative strength of collection.

Ms. Young feels strongly that a standard list of collection subject areas would have made the planning process easier and would not have been a costly addition to the project. The Resources Development Committee is currently developing a more rational list for use in the revised plan. The Committee is comparing their developing list against LC classification and may identify collection areas in which the region is weak. If their product is likely to be as useful for others as the Committee believes a similar list would have been for them, METRO will make the plan available in the fall.

Mr. Shubert's third factor for success, "new technology for resource sharing," is also one that is receiving attention. In New York State, two related efforts have begun. The State is funding a major study for redesign of NYSILL, the statewide interlibrary loan system that still functions much as it did in the 60's. In addition, each region has prepared a five-year plan for use of $80,000 to $200,000 in state grants for development of regional databases and resource sharing.

"Strong incentives for resource sharing," is Mr. Shubert's fourth factor in success. Everyone would like state aid increased. Small libraries look for an increase in the base funding, and large libraries seek increases in the FTE student formula. Some 3R's directors point to falling enrollment as reason to increase the base. After the first year's experience, Joseph Shubert, reported that "The per capita, anticipated to be a useful measure of effort in a period of declining enrollment, has proved somewhat inflexible as colleges experienced substantial increases in part-time enrollment."[6]

For threatened academic libraries, a side effect of the maintenance of effort requirement has been that it is a tool to be used as needed to help libraries resist budget cuts from their administrations. If a reduction in the materials budget will result in additional loss of state aid of at least $4,000, administrators may be wary of making what might have been easy cuts in the library budget.

Dorothy Smith, Associate in Library Services and Section Head, Library Development Division, spoke for funding increases in the FTE student factor in recognition that the amount of aid has relatively little impact on the largest libraries who do share quite liberally (and who might be induced to be still more liberal with better funding). Already technology seems to have enabled much of the burden of interlibrary loan to be shifted from a few large suppliers and spread among all. More rigorous analysis of ILL exchange, facilitated by technology, would aid in recognition and reimbursement of libraries which may still remain significant net lenders. Overall, coordinated collection development aid amounts to only 2% of the academic libraries' acquisitions budgets, hardly enough to have major impact, but sufficient to be incentive.

Funding should increase not only for the current participants, but incentive aid should be extended to the public libraries, special libraries and school libraries. In time, coordinating collection development with libraries with which there is affinity will be as basic as having a collection policy. Incentive funding would stimulate action now.

It is too early, and the stimulus of funding is still too small, for impact on collection development to be measurable. Yet without the stimulus of funding, it is unlikely that coordinated collection development planning would have begun in New York State.

In considering the New York State pattern for Illinois, or any other location, it is most important to remember that coordinated collection development in New York is not a stand-alone program. Its relative success has been synergistic: both existing systems and the collection development effort have been strengthened by the other. It is for you to decide whether Illinois's movement toward multitype library systems could or should be similarly stimulated, and coordinated collection development similarly supported.

FOOTNOTES

1. New York State Library, *Fact Book on the Board of Regents 1981 Legislative Program for Libraries.* Albany, New York, 1981.
2. Shubert, Joseph. "The Coordinated Academic Libraries Collection Development Program," *Bookmark* Fall 1982. p. 4.
3. Perkins, David L. editor. *Guidelines for Collection Development.* Chicago, American Library Association, 1979.
4. Shubert, Joseph S. "Coordinated Collection Development for the Purpose of Resource Sharing." Speech, Spring, 1982, pp. 7-8.
5. *Ibid.* p. 8.
6. Shubert, "The Coordinator Academic Libraries Collection Development Program," p. 5.

Discussion Summary of the California and New York State Plans

Mary Alice Moulton

Associate Director, Government Relations
Illinois Board of Higher Education
Springfield, Illinois

We have just heard two very different approaches to the establishment of cooperative collection development among libraries. California started with a very specific goal for a specific group of similar libraries. New York, on the other hand, started with an inducement to develop a collection sharing plan within an established regional system of multi-type libraries. Given these very different starting points the two efforts have very much in common. Both states have experienced reasonable success in achieving their goals. Both states are still providing funds to support the activity. Both systems have grown by the addition of private institution libraries. Both report that inter-library relationships have improved as a result of their experience.

Since our goal today is to identify criteria for model cooperative collection development, I would like to highlight similarities and differences of these two programs and raise some questions for both the presenters and for audience participation which might help us determine the necessary criteria for cooperative collection activities.

My first observation is that both programs were initiated by a force outside of the libraries themselves. State statutes were adopted which mandated the activity and were accompanied by a source of funds to support the activity. Perhaps, because cooperative collection development requires dramatic change, conceptually and operationally, an external change agent is required to start the process. I would like to know whether others think this is the case. Also, it would be interesting to know, if either of the presenters think their states would have progressed with any form of cooperative collection development more rapidly without the state mandate.

Another observation is about the mandate. In California it leads to the production of an obvious product among a system of academic libraries, while in New York the mandate emphasizes the participation of multi-type libraries in the development of a coordinated collection plan. We can argue whether a plan is a product or not, but I have a couple of questions about the New York model which I understand is based upon self-interest decision making. Will a plan be sufficient to induce the New York libraries to make decisions together about acquisition, weeding, preservation and storage of materials? Or is cooperative decision making even necessary, if the New York concept of self-interest decision making is sufficiently improved by automated information sharing and common collection descriptors?

The singular goal in the California model is desirable, if the motive is to achieve an end quickly and efficiently. The questions I have about the California model are: How difficult will it be for the shared purchasing model to be expanded to include other collection development activities such as cooperative weeding, preservation and storage? Also, can the system be expanded to include other types of libraries outside of the current system? What would it take to expand the system?

As I read the papers, both states are now moving in the direction of improving information about the collections of participating libraries and both have made progress in developing an automated on-line catalog system. Common information about collections and access to that information are major criteria in my mind for any cooperative collection activity. New York is currently improving common descriptors for quantitative and qualitative measurement of library collection strengths. I would like to know more about the use of this data and what it is expected to do for cooperative collection activity. In addition, it seems that information about user needs is required for effective decision making in collection management and financing. I would like to know what type of user needs assessments are being conducted, and in what ways user needs assessment data would assist decision making in cooperative collection activities.

The final observations I have are related to the geographical proximity of the cooperating libraries and user access to the material. In

California some duplication is permitted to house documents in both the north end and the south end of the state. In New York the entire concept of cooperation is tied to a regional system. I also observe

Photograph by: Maurice C. Libbey and Gene W. Scholes, Eastern Illinois University.

that these two state experiences were initiated before common automated collection information systems were in place among the participating libraries. It seems to me that one of the major barriers to cooperative collection development is the user perception that access to documents is too slow. My question is this: how critical is the location of the document or the proximity of the libraries, if rapid and reliable information about documents is available, and if an efficient, reliable document delivery system is operational?

I will stop now for a response from the presenters, and after they have had a chance to respond to these questions or to ask each other questions we would welcome questions or comments from the audience.

Discussion #2

Discussion Leader, Mary Alice Moulton

At this point, I will stop to provide the presenters an opportunity to respond to the questions I have raised and to see if there are any questions that the audience would like to raise or comments that you would like to make regarding either what I have said, or the presenters.

* * *

I'll try to remember all of the questions. First of all, would we have done something like this if it had not been forced on us? I think, certainly, it would have taken much longer, but even if we had received the additional funding for the collections (which is somewhat doubtful), I think eventually we would have been brought to it because when you consider the cost of collections you have to worry also about the costs of storing them and processing them. I do remember, however, I was one of the early people when we were trying to implement the program, and the sentiment was very much opposed at that time to cooperative collection development.

As far as whether this would lead into weeding, preservation, and storage, I didn't try to address these related issues in my paper, but the master plan that I mentioned several times does cover these. It has made provisions for two regional storage centers that are somewhat euphemistically referred to as "regional library facilities." There's one in the North in the vicinity of Berkeley that has been open for several years now and that is almost reaching capacity at present. It serves the libraries of the North. There is a provision for other libraries (including private libraries) to use the storage facilities.

In the South, we expect to have a facility on the UCLA campus that will be open for business sometime in 1987. We are already weeding our collections and wondering how we're going to select these materials and trying to calm faculty fears. There's quite a bit of faculty sentiment about this, except, interestingly enough, at

Berkeley and UCLA where they have already been storing materials. Of course, the facilities are much closer to them than to the other campuses.

The delivery: If you're talking about delivery within the same region, whether it's the North or the South, the turnaround time is pretty good as long as it's on the shelf at the time the request is received. Between regions, it takes a little longer. One of the fears expressed with regard to the regional library facilities was that delivery would be very poor, but in the North they have actually had a 48 hour turnaround time. I think that's as good as we can expect. We rely on UPS for delivery between the regions. This is not as satisfactory, obviously.

* * *

As I said before, I don't believe that we would have become involved with coordinated collection development without something from outside. It's conceivable that other places could. Certainly, areas are all different. Generally speaking, I have felt that any group of libraries that sees itself as more equal—all medium sized academic libraries or all research libraries—peer groups will share most easily. I think the greater disparity in size and type, the more fear there is built in, ("If they know what I have, they're going to raid me," all of those kinds of things.) People are very cautious. They have enough fighting within their institution between the academic faculty and staff over where they're going to spend their acquisitions funds. It is not easy to get them to voluntarily give them away to other people for other people to make decisions.

On the other hand, it has happened in our region without anything outside. The CAP program, (the Cooperative Acquisitions Program) is a long established program. It has some people who firmly believe in this program and the importance of it. It has many other members who don't understand it at all. That's one of the things that happens in our kind of a system. There are some programs that people are devoted to that other people don't use and visa versa, but in terms of trying to draw in great and very disparate groups it is very helpful to have something from the outside—the carrot—to bring people along. I don't think it would have happened as soon—someday, maybe.

On some of the other things it's a little harder to answer. For instance, your question, Mary Alice, on whether a plan is sufficient to induce the New York libraries to make decisions together about acquisition, weeding, preservation, and storage of materials. Actually, most of these things have come up at one time or another. There have been strong advocates of storage of materials, for instance. Only, given the cost of space in New York City, we didn't know where we were ever going to get that kind of money.

Acquisitions: We did continue to do some things that didn't have outside funding and that isn't (at this stage) even part of the coordinated collection development planning. There are separate activities although the same committee, the Resources Development Committee, does oversee the whole activity.

Weeding: I think, this is the very natural one. It's the other side of acquisitions and should be built-in for the future. We just simply haven't arrived there, but I think it is one that follows naturally.

The plan, at this stage, is just beginning. It is not a finished product by any stretch of the imagination. People's reaction to it and what it means in their internal decision making . . . it's just beginning. It's too new to know the answers on whether it will work. I think it will. I see a tremendous change in the last three years, where I had the sense in 1982-83 that, "Yes, we'll do this plan in order to get the money." Now the plan itself is an important thing and, of course, the money stays important. I think it's an evolutionary change.

Your next question was, "Is the cooperative decision making even necessary if the New York concept of self-interest decision making is sufficiently improved by automated information and common to collection descriptors?" I think so. I think there has to be a methodology, at least procedures for things like last copy. You just can't assume when people see on their screen 'this is the last copy' that they are automatically going to know whether it's worth having, what should be done with it. I think it does need to be thought through, but we're not quite ready yet.

Some of the other questions I'm going to leave for Pat, such as the one about the common descriptors, because that is what she's been working on. The other major general questions such as the information about user needs: "Is it required for effective decision making and collection management and financing?" Yes, but I certainly hope the libraries locally are paying attention to their user needs because our thinking is based on their knowing what they need.

Hopefully, what they think they need is based on what their users need.

I don't think—certainly, within our region—it would be politic or even very "do-able" to reach down into some of the kinds of uses of materials within a library. On the other hand, we do believe that analysis of interlibrary loan statistics leads to knowledge of what kinds of things should be collected, what kinds of things should be made machine-readable for our retrospective conversion efforts, and that kind of thing. I guess I hadn't thought about it in terms of a user need study, but more in terms of another level. We really do count on the local level (the local library) to know what their users need and to make their decisions based on that. If we can't count on informed self-interest on that level, we're in trouble.

Our feeling is that the most used materials should be on campus. No matter what, moving stuff around is not terribly fast. We do the very best we can, but by the time you go through all the varying steps and count on some other library fishing things off the shelves and getting them into the system, it is not anywhere near like having it on the shelf. If libraries concentrate on having the most popular materials on the shelf or the things that most closely support their curriculum, then maybe other things can be a little slower. Hopefully, people who are doing research have a little longer time frame than undergraduates—certainly, more time frame than when we deal with high school assignments. The most used things should be at home already. Maybe one of these days, when we have everything machine readable, (I don't know how long it's going to take us to get 25,000,000 more things in), it will be different. We have an awful lot yet that we don't know where it is. That's one of the joys and one of problems of being in our area—we just have so much that getting it under control is quite a problem. If we work with what has highest need at any particular time, I think we're probably going to work it out.

I'm hoping for things like telefacsimile, but I don't think we're ready for that yet, to bridge some of that.

Everyone thinks of our region as being "small" and "compact." In fact, it's even been said, "Why do you need a delivery system at all?" In this case, the user can go to the book instead of the book to the user. I discovered, when I was attempting to put together an experimental delivery system, that it isn't quite as simple as that. I ran into trouble because New York City is all an island. I had this clever idea (I thought) of getting each of the public library systems to do the delivery for the other types of libraries within their geographic area. No problem, except that no one would cross the bridges. [They said,] "Do you know how long you get tied up in bridges?" No one was going to go into that.

Just moving people around isn't too easy either. I would like to think that we could make delivery transparent. You know, location isn't going to matter—it *does* matter. It takes a lot of convincing that it can be somewhere else. You have to make the choices of what has to be local and what has to be somewhere else pretty carefully.

* * *

I just wanted to speak very briefly about the idea of common information, because it's actually the goal of our revised report that's going to be submitted to the State in the fall. Most of these applications have been filled out by the academic libraries by themselves. I mean, they just sit down and say, "I'm very strong here, and I'm without this." Then they give themselves a rating and they send it in.

It's not until our committee, the Resources Development Committee, sat down with a list of all these subjects, the schools, and the level they gave and [we] said, "Wait a minute. I think we all better get together and talk." They're taking any subject they want (like Liberal Arts) and saying, "I have a C-1 in Liberal Arts." What does that mean? Or they say, "I collect in Japan." We have Japan as one of our terms; there's Japanese Literature, Japanese . . .

We need people to think more clearly about what they are telling the State so that we can share that information among ourselves. This is what will be the benefit of this final report. The terms will be more precise. The levels, hopefully, will reflect an interaction with other colleagues and also the LC class will give us even another sense of descriptions.

We would like to, in the final report, submit a list of historical strengths. For instance, back in the sixties they had a lot of money to collect in such and such; they don't now, but they still have a very big collection. We would like that to be added so we're having a better overall view of what, actually, we have in our region and what our subject strengths are.

That's what I mean. Common information is very essential and we're just getting to the point where we're about to share that information with each other with this process.

* * *

I have a question for Marion, please. I'm interested in why California stopped at 3 percent instead of going on to 5 percent, as was originally planned. Was it because, by some systematic analysis, you found that the 3 percent represented the upper limit of value in such a program; or did you find that the mandate simply could not be pushed any further against an ever stiffening resistance?

The other question I'd like to ask is, perhaps, the same question stated differently. That is, if the mandate for 3 percent were lifted now, would it stay where it is and if so, why; or would it float down and float down to where, do you suppose?

* * *

I think the answer to the first question is that there was nothing systematic at all about the decision. It was simply the system wide administration giving in to the feeling of the university librarians and the collection development officers that there was a limit beyond which the funds would not be, perhaps, as well spent through the program as by the individual campuses. You're talking about a lot of money: 3 percent of the University of California Library Materials Budget.

I asked that same question, "Where is the ideal percentage?" of the people I interviewed and almost all of them seemed to think that 3 percent felt about right. We could spend that usefully, but if we had more money it might be difficult.

One of the things we're concerned about is that our continuing commitments are taking an ever larger share of the available funds, so that the discretionary funds seem to be smaller each year. How we're going to deal with that, I'm not sure, but I don't think that most people would want to increase the percentage beyond where it now is.

There's nothing sacred about 3 percent, though.

* * *

Cooperative Collection Development Programs of the Triangle Research Libraries Network

Joe A. Hewitt

Associate University Librarian for Technical Services
University of North Carolina, Chapel Hill

ABSTRACT. The libraries of Duke University and the University of North Carolina at Chapel Hill have cooperated in the development of their collections for over fifty years. North Carolina State University in Raleigh became a party to the agreements in 1978 and the University of Virginia participates on a limited basis. The programs are intended to increase the range of research materials available to the libraries' users and are based on assignments of areas of collecting responsibility at the research level and the avoidance of all unnecessary duplication of library materials. The programs operate through frequent communications among the collection development staffs. This paper describes these programs and makes several general observations on the operation of cooperative collection development programs based on the experience of these libraries.

The University of North Carolina at Chapel Hill and Duke University, located nine miles away in Durham, have coordinated the development of their research level collections since 1933. As you might imagine, cooperative collection development agreements which have managed to survive for 50 years have a rich and complex history. Over the years these programs have been subject to ebbs and flows of emphasis, to periods of drought in terms of funding and the attention of administrators and collection development officers, and periods of stagnation with respect to program development. They have also enjoyed periods of rejuvenation and elevation to new levels of refinement, and I am happy to report that it is in such a period that we find ourselves today. Indeed, these long-standing collection development agreements have become the impetus and the foundation for the collaborative systems development projects of the Triangle Research Libraries Network, which I believe to be one of the preeminent examples of a local area research library network in the country.

In preparing for this presentation I went back to the source documents relating to these agreements and traced their development decade by decade from 1933 to the present. It seems to me that there are many lessons and insights embedded in these documents—far too many for me to touch on, even in a superficial way, within the limits of this program. But I would like to share a little of this general historical perspective before describing the current status of our collection development programs.

I assume that many of the participants of this symposium are from the state of Illinois. For that reason I should not fail to mention that the early documentation on this project consists largely of correspondence between Robert B. Downs, then Librarian at North Carolina, and Harvie Branscomb, the Librarian at Duke. Aside from the letters, the early documents consist of program statements apparently written collaboratively by these two eminent librarians. A very striking feature of these documents, now over 50 years old, is the fact that they seem totally modern. They deal with the same issues and express the same concerns that we attempt to deal with today in discussions of cooperative collection development—bibliographic control, document delivery, access to collections, faculty acceptance, analysis of collections, a need to confine cooperative programs to research collections rather than general and curriculum support materials, and emphasis on cooperative collection development as a means to expand access to materials rather than to limit the development of the local collections.

As an expression of these concerns, the very first grant for this project, received in 1934, was used to develop the support services required to operate effective programs of cooperative collection development. Bibliographic control was approached through what was called the "exchange of catalogs project," and document delivery was provided through a daily interlibrary delivery service. The delivery service, greatly expanded to include a number of libraries in Raleigh and the Research Triangle Park, has operated continuously since 1934. The exchange of catalog cards was continued until this method was supplanted by the use of OCLC in 1975.

It is interesting to note the technology used in 1934 to duplicate and exchange catalogs. The libraries adopted a photostatic technique called Dexigraph, developed by Remington Rand to compete with the real Photostat. (Photostat, by the way, like Xerox, is a trade name which has come to represent a process.) The Dexigraph was not only an extremely cumbersome process but one which resulted in a negative print image on heavy, treated stock that tended to warp grotesquely when used as a catalog card. You can imagine the problems these white-on-black cards presented when we microfilmed the catalog in 1970 and Dexigraph cards had frequently to be filed on the same frame as conventional cards.

The point of this diversion, as you have probably gathered, is to contrast the advances in technology since 1934 to the progress toward resolution of the policy and program issues related to cooperative collection development. In comparison to online bibliographic networks, online public access catalogs, and the whole range of computing and telecommunications technology that we can bring to bear on library problems today, the Dexigraph is a quaint and primitive technology indeed. Yet the issues raised by cooperative collection development are essentially the same today as they were in the early 1930s. This contrast seems to me to underscore a couple of points. The first is that there is still a great deal to be learned from early programs of cooperative collection development because they are not in fact as far removed from our current experience as we might assume. The second point is that we seem considerably less successful today in exploiting the capabilities of existing technology for purposes of program support than forward-looking librarians were 50 years ago. Perhaps the widespread attention now being given to cooperative collection development, as exemplified by this very symposium, will work in the direction of allowing us to capitalize on both the historical lessons of cooperative collection development programs and the extraordinary capabilities of current technology.

Let me note briefly several other impressions that emerge from the perusal of historical documents that may be instructive to today's program. The first is that cooperative collection development programs, for all their apparent fragility in their early stages, can become remarkably persistent once they are firmly ingrained in a library's budgetary process and operating procedures and, perhaps more importantly, its organizational mythology. If cooperative collection development agreements are soundly conceived in the beginning they can have a survival quality that transcends all sorts of institutional change and vicissitudes of funding. The single greatest threat to the survival of these programs appears to have been collection development staffs which were either actively opposed to or not strongly committed to the programs.

Another point is that visible pay-offs may be long term in the extreme, but they can be massive once they begin to appear. It took a number of years before the agreements between Duke and the University of North Carolina became major influences on the shape of the collections. But looking back over a period of decades, it is obvious that the coordination of collection development has vastly extended the range of research materials available to our users beyond what would have been available had collection development proceeded independently. Obviously, this point is clearly intended as a caution to those just beginning cooperative collection development programs who may be inclined to give up the effort if sizeable and immediate benefits do not materialize.

As a final general observation I would like to call attention to the vision and the noble social purpose contained in the program statements of early efforts at cooperative collection development. In their proposals to the General Education Board and the Rockefeller Foundation, Downs and Branscomb visualized the result of their collaborative efforts as a great research library center serving the entire Southeast, then an impoverished area in terms of library resources. There is another example much closer to home for those of you from Illinois. John Shipman, the University Bibliographer at North Carolina, and I are conducting a survey of existing programs of cooperative collection development in research libraries. The oldest, continuously operating program that we have so far identified dates from 1866 and is right here in Chicago. It involves seven theological libraries and has the stated purpose of ensuring that the Chicago metropolitan area remains a major national center for religious studies. I regret to say that it is in this sense that more recent initiatives in the direction of cooperative collection development seem lacking in comparison to their historical models. The rhetoric of an ambitious social mission has been largely replaced by the management rhetoric of cost containment, which, however unavoidable in the modern world, seems somewhat less effective in capturing our imaginations.

Let me now briefly describe the cooperative collection development programs of the Triangle Research Libraries Network. Although North Carolina State University, with significant collections in technological areas not held by Duke and UNC, became a party to these agreements in 1978, the collection development program is for the most part still based on long-standing arrangements between Duke University and the University of North Carolina at Chapel Hill. At the broadest level, of course, the programs are based on the disciplines and areas of study which are offered in one institution and not in the other. On this basis, for example, Duke took responsibility for Forestry and Engineering, and North Carolina took City and Regional Planning and Library Science. Duke collects Egyptology and North Carolina Linguistics. These programs, based on what we call the principle of "mutual exclusivity," represent the easy part, and their number is in any case not large when dealing with one or more comprehensive research universities. The real challenges of cooperative collection development arise in assigning areas of responsibility in subject areas of interest to both campuses.

One type of agreement is based on broad categories of materials, government documents being a principal example in our case. While both libraries have large collections of U.S. federal documents, in 1935 we reached an agreement regarding the collecting of state documents, the documents of foreign nations, and the documents of international organizations. These programs have undergone considerable refinement over the years as we have adjusted to factors such as the documents collections at the Center for Research Libraries and the growing difficulties of maintaining extensive acquisitions networks for state documents. The general direction of these adjustments has been for Duke to specialize in foreign documents and North Carolina to specialize in state documents, and there has been a restriction in the range of collecting state documents to those states and state agencies of special interest to both libraries. There is a similar agreement related to collecting microform backfiles of newspapers, with North Carolina collecting exhaustively in North Carolina, and comprehensively in the southeastern U.S., and Duke specializing in foreign newspapers.

Perhaps the real cornerstone of our agreements are those relating to area studies. The oldest such agreements date to 1940 when Carolina, Duke and Tulane received a grant from the Rockefeller Foundation for the coordinated purchase of Latin American materials. Although Tulane has ceased to be an active partner in the agreement, the assignment of responsibilities between Duke and North Carolina continues to the present time. Similar agreements exist for the Commonwealth Nations. Duke, for example, specializes in Canadian materials and North Carolina collects Australian materials. An extensive agreement was reached in 1965 on the collecting of African materials and the early 1960s also saw the development of agreements on Slavic, East European, and East Asian publications. Duke, for example, specializes in Polish publications and North Carolina in Czech; Carolina collects in Chinese and Duke in Japanese.

The principle of division by geographic parameters is very important to our programs. Latin America and Africa are divided country by country; essentially the entire Third World has been divided among the libraries. In our experience, programs based on clear, unambiguous country of origin divisions are much easier to operate than those based on subject divisions or historical periods, unless the latter programs fall under a mutual exclusivity arrangement.

The libraries also maintain a number of less formal understandings in a number of fields and subfields based on specialized strengths of the collections. These agreements frequently are based on historical periods of general interest such as the French revolution, and involve only retrospective purchases of materials actually published during the period, with both libraries purchasing modern editions and secondary works as they see fit. As another example of such an agreement, North Carolina specializes in Russian literature and history before 1917 while Duke specializes in Russian literature and history of the early Soviet Period.

As an example of program development in recent years, in 1980 we overhauled the African agreements and extended coverage to countries which were not assigned under earlier arrangements. In 1978 the University of Virginia became a party to our Slavic agreements, accepting responsibility for the south Slavic area. At the same time special interlibrary loan privileges were extended to University of Virginia faculty and graduate students for Slavic materials. Recent discussions have focused on the countries of Western Europe, traditionally a difficult area to bring under cooperative agreements because of the wide-spread overlap of interest in publications from these countries. We are making progress on this front, however, and our most recent agreement, signed in March 1984, assigns coverage for collecting French regional history.

Overlaying all of these agreements is a general understanding that there will be no unwarranted duplication of research materials regardless of whether or not they fall within the scope of specific agreements. Thus we have mechanisms for alerting each other of

Photograph by: Maurice C. Libbey and Gene W. Scholes, Eastern Illinois University.

expensive purchases. Justification forms for new subscriptions require information as to whether the other libraries subscribe or intend to subscribe, often the determining factor for publications of marginal interest or value. We make numerous ad hoc decisions, particularly with respect to microform sets, that one library will purchase and the other will not. Over the years we have also made a number of joint purchases, with each library contributing a share of the cost but housing the material in the collection where it most logically belongs, a practice which is apparently quite rare when it involves both public and private institutions. The *Landmarks of Science* is an example of microform set purchased in this way.

Supporting this activity is the practice of continuous consultation among the collection development staffs of the three libraries. Our Slavic bibliographer, for example, sends purchase requests for Polish materials to Duke. Duke sends requests by their faculty for Chinese materials to us. All three libraries purchase materials at the request of unaffiliated agencies in the Research Triangle Park, such as the National Humanities Center, and these requests are routed to the library where the material would best complement existing collections. Gift materials received at each institution are often redirected to match existing cooperative responsibilities. The entire collection development staffs of the three libraries meet as a group a minimum of once each quarter; over the past year there have been special monthly meetings of the bibliographers at Duke and North Carolina; we estimate that each bibliographer at North Carolina communicates by telephone with his or her counterpart at Duke at least once weekly.

If this program is broken down into its component parts, it is obvious that it consists of three principal elements. The first is the formal agreements which assign responsibility for defined areas of coverage at the research level. Collectively, this series of agreements provides an important general framework for coordinated collection development, but I feel that too much can be made of such arrangements as the primary instrumentality of cooperative development programs. The other two elements seem in our experience to be more critical.

The second element is active commitment to the general principle that all unwarranted duplication of research material should be avoided. This involves much more than mere affirmation; there must be a constant and assiduous promotion of an atmosphere in which this principle can operate. In Fiscal 1983/84 the three TRLN libraries spent well over $9,000,000 on library materials. Our collection development staffs are constantly encouraged to use these funds to develop a unified research library resource to the fullest extent possible within the context of three separate institutions. Another aspect of creating this atmosphere is the constant promotion of our programs among faculty and other constituents, so that they clearly perceive the benefits of cooperation.

The third element is the practice of continuous interaction of collection development administrators and selection officers both in formal and informal settings, which encourages an active mind-set to perceive opportunities for cooperation and collaboration in the course of their daily work. This may well be the real bottom line, the critical element that determines success or failure of cooperative collection development programs.

Let me close by making several observations on topics that seem to be of particular interest to the organizers of this conference. The first has to do with funding. Over the years we have received grant funding from the General Education Board, the Carnegie Corporation, the Rockefeller Foundation, and most recently from the Department of Education's Title II-C program for the support of coordinated purchase of library materials. This type of funding is particularly useful as seed money for initiating or expanding programs. When used for this purpose it is important that funds be available over a period of time, ideally perhaps three years, so that the patterns of cooperation in a given area can become firmly established. Special funding has also been used when we have discovered through program review that the libraries were slipping in their coverage of assigned areas and special funds were needed to shore up their collections through retrospective purchases. When special funding is acquired for either purpose, it tends also to restore emphasis on the cooperative programs generally. There is no doubt that periodic, well-timed infusions of extraordinary funds are important to programs of coordinated collection development.

On the other hand, in our experience, the long term maintenance of programs of cooperative collection development depends upon incorporating their support into the ongoing budget allocations of the participating libraries. At Carolina we allocate a small amount, some $40,000 a year, to be used exclusively for cooperative purchases. This encourages bibliographers to develop truly cooperative projects, such as joint purchases, but by far the largest part of the support for the programs come from budgets to regularly funded units. The East Asian bibliographer, for example, uses materials funds allocated to the East Asian Biblio Centre to purchase materials which fall within the scope of our assigned coverage.

Although TRLN is a small consortium of three libraries, it may still be suggestive in terms of a model for a statewide plan of cooperative collection development. The University of North Carolina at Chapel Hill and North Carolina State University are part of a 16 campus university system. Although neither library maintains formal collection development agreements with the other libraries in the university system, the students and faculty of the other institutions have access to our collections and the resources in the two formally designated Research Universities are considered a systemwide resource. Indeed, the collections of all three TRLN libraries are tacitly viewed as a general resource serving all libraries and users in the state. Thus, anything we do to expand the range of research materials available to our own users works also to the advantage of those who depend on our collections as a secondary resource.

It may well be the case that the most cost-effective approach to cooperative collection development on a statewide basis would be to concentrate on coordination of research collections in the largest libraries. I say this for several reasons. First, we have found that there must be a certain degree of parity if cooperative collection development is to work as a mutually beneficial enterprise. Our success with Duke is closely related to our relatively similar size and mission. Collectively, small and medium sized academic libraries contribute enormously to the materials available for resource sharing, but this collective strength is not by design. I can think of only a few cases in North Carolina where a smaller library can collect *systematically* at a level that would be useful to the research libraries, without seriously overbalancing the collections of the smaller library.

I have mentioned the great amount of interaction among bibliographers required to maintain cooperative collection programs on an ongoing basis. This interaction can be extremely costly in terms of staff time. We feel that while it is definitely worth the cost for TRLN, that may not be the case if we were to expand this level of communication to a much larger number of libraries in programs for which the payoffs are not as clear and certain.

We have also found that this interaction is facilitated when there is some degree of congruence between the organization and staffing of the collection development function in the cooperating libraries, and we would expect cooperative collection development to be less effective as these factors diverge. At North Carolina, for example, we have 14 full time staff positions in our Collection Development Department. We have in fact encountered some problems in integrating North Carolina State University into our programs due to the fact that they do not staff collection development on anything approaching this scale.

The idea that I am suggesting for your consideration is simply the possibility that in Illinois the greatest return on the effort invested in cooperative collection development may come by emphasizing these programs in your largest research libraries, while, of course, making these resources available to users throughout the state. Collection overlap studies have generally shown that there is less duplication among small and medium sized academic libraries than one might expect. An extensive computer analysis of the collections of the SUNY libraries showed this to be the case.[1] This study found that in ten institutions, the number of unique titles was above 50% in all but two disciplines. In libraries collecting below the comprehensive level in any given field, the selection process, for whatever reason, seems to result in a great diversity in collections beyond a certain core of high demand materials that almost everyone must acquire. (In the SUNY study, only 10% of the titles were found to be ubiquitous in the ten collections.) For this reason, the laissez-faire approach in a sizable group of small to medium sized libraries might be expected to result in a total research resource of considerable variety and richness without any particular attempt at coordination. This is not to say that the adoption of the practice of avoiding unwarranted duplication of especially expensive research materials might not work as a statewide goal. On the other hand, elaborate and finely drawn agreements assigning specialized areas of responsibility may very quickly reach a point of diminishing returns when applied below the level of the research libraries.

The TRLN model might also suggest, however, a series of local area consortia involving compatible libraries practicing cooperative collection development on a scale appropriate to their individual collection development goals. In the University of North Carolina system, for example, three libraries in the western part of the state—Appalachian State University, The University of North Carolina at Asheville, and Western Carolina University—have formed the Western North Carolina Library Network and are beginning to think about cooperative collection development. This pattern follows the recommendations of a 1982 King Research report to the State Library which proposed the concept of Zones of Cooperation, or ZOC's as we call them, as the basis for a statewide multitype library network plan.

Finally, let me say something about the relationship of local area collection development programs and the emerging national and regional programs such as NACIP and the program being initiated under the auspices of SOLINET. At TRLN we view such programs as complementing rather than conflicting with our own. We are tracking these developments closely and, so far, the evidence suggests that our long established programs of cooperative collection development at the local level prepare us well for participation in national and regional programs. The areas of specialized collection depth developed under our local programs are more likely to make a useful contribution to the goals of national and regional programs, than if our collections had been developed in a vacuum. The ongoing practice of collection analysis with which we support the TRLN collection development programs can be adjusted to reflect the methodologies of broader area programs. Above all, our experience has refined our sensitivities to both the promise and the limitations of cooperative collection development, and we are prepared to greet the era of expanded cooperation in a posture that is both hopeful and realistic.

NOTE

1. Evans, Glyn T., and A. Beilby. "A Library Management Information System in a Multi-Campus Environment." *In Clinic on Library Applications of Data Processing: 1982*. Graduate School of Library and Information Science, University of Illinois at Urbana-Champaign, pp. 164-196.

HILC at Thirty-Four: A View from Within

Billie Rae Bozone

College Librarian, Smith College

ABSTRACT. The evolution of the Hampshire Inter-Library Center from a repository for little-used serials to an umbrella for cooperative projects of HILC's members is examined. The paper reviews briefly what HILC used to be like, what happened, and what HILC is like in its thirty-fourth year.

The Hampshire Inter-library Center, Inc., affectionately known as HILC, is an example of a cooperative library effort that has evolved over time from a Center with a jointly-owned, jointly-selected, jointly-managed collection to an umbrella organization for cooperative library activities among the five higher education institutions in Hampshire County, Massachusetts. The institutions are: Amherst College, from 1821 to 1977 an undergraduate liberal arts college for men, presently coeducational; Mount Holyoke College, founded in 1857 and Smith College, founded in 1875, both undergraduate liberal arts colleges for women; the University of Massachusetts, founded in 1876 as an agricultural college under the Morrill Land Grant Act but presently a university supporting doctoral programs and research as well as undergraduate liberal arts programs; and, Hampshire College, an experimental college founded in 1965 by the other four institutions, and opened for classes in 1970.

A complete history of the Center does not exist nor is it appropriate to recite a complete history here, but a brief outline of the first thirty-four years of HILC is certainly in order.[1]

The Hampshire Inter-library Center, Inc., incorporated under the laws of the Commonwealth of Massachusetts in 1951, was established for the purpose of maintaining a center to provide centralized

© 1986 by The Haworth Press, Inc. All rights reserved.

services for nonprofit educational, charitable and scientific institutions by fostering cooperative circulation and exchange of books, periodicals, microfilm and other articles or documents. The founding members were the head librarians of Amherst, Mount Holyoke and Smith Colleges. Though the librarian of the University of Massachusetts was included in planning sessions the University did not participate as a full member until 1954. The Center was given space in the Mount Holyoke Library at no cost, thereby setting a precedent whereby the Center always expected free space. In 1957 no less a figure than Keyes Metcalf was brought to the Center to survey its background and make recommendations for the future.[2]

Recommendations made for HILC but not acted upon could well be the topic of another paper; however, the major direction of HILC was set for some years by Metcalf's report. His recommendation of an associate membership for the Forbes Library (Northampton's public library) became a reality in 1962. Libraries were not the only cooperative educational endeavors in the Pioneer Valley: in 1965 an umbrella organization, Five Colleges, Inc., made formal the many existing cooperative arrangements, and after years of planning, study, and fund-raising, the four institutions gave birth to a fifth in 1965: Hampshire College. Upon its opening in 1970, Hampshire became a member of HILC. Though membership has been proposed for libraries from Dartmouth to Trinity (going up and down the Connecticut River) and from Williams to Bowdoin (in a mountains or oceans vein) since 1970 there has been only one change in membership. The Western Regional Public Library System (WRPLS) of which the Forbes Library is a part, decided that the Regional budget could not afford to continue the Forbes' membership and since the early 1980's, WRPLS has maintained an "observer" rather than a member status. The present members of HILC are Amherst, Hampshire, Mount Holyoke and Smith Colleges and the University of Massachusetts/Amherst. The HILC libraries now own over three million volumes and serve a student population of over 33,000.

In its early years, HILC's primary goal was to encourage and facilitate cooperation between its members. At HILC's founding in 1951, the librarians envisioned cooperative use, cooperative acquisitions, cooperative cataloging and cooperative storage as their goals. HILC's founders—Flora Belle Luddington, Newton McKeon and Margaret Johnson—set about establishing selection procedures for a collection of serials which were of research value to the three members but were thought to be too expensive for any single member to afford. In 1954 when the University joined the endeavor, there was still great validity to this simple sharing of serials. In the 1960's, however, the University grew from an institution not much larger than its neighbors into a mammoth very different university supporting doctoral-level programs in many areas. HILC's major activities at this time were the running of the Center which now was located at the University, and the coordination of a delivery system which moved (and still moves) materials to and from each of the libraries twice daily on weekdays. The person who drives the car/truck/van from campus to campus is still known as the HILC Messenger—a title that evokes perfectly the era in which HILC began. Increasingly, however, there were concerns that had more to do with the individual libraries than with HILC. Though the daily delivery system and the interlibrary loan system in the valley were made available to all faculty, students and staff, the early 1970's brought pressure for borrowing in-person at all of the libraries.

The HILC Board and various five college student groups worked out an arrangement in 1973 whereby any student, faculty or staff member of each of the five institutions may use the main library of each institution for what is called "direct borrowing" and may return borrowed material to whichever library is most convenient. Since the cross registration of students had increasingly brought students to each of the campuses other than their own, and since funding from federal, state and local government had made available a transit authority for the provision of public transportation in the area, direct borrowing was the logical next step in library cooperation.

However, the 1970's also brought a budget squeeze to each of HILC's member libraries and for the first time since its inception, HILC began to be viewed as an expensive luxury rather than as a moderately priced necessity. The HILC Board could not agree on HILC's future direction. In the mid 1970's a new Five College Coordinator was brought on board and was given the "HILC problem" as something to cut his teeth on. The administrators of the five institutions, trying to stretch library dollars as far as possible, were certain that coordinating collection development could save money. Elimination of unnecessary duplication of monographs, cancellation of subscriptions to duplicated titles, the possibility of expanding HILC for the storage of little-used monographs, even the possibility (again) of making HILC a regional facility, were explored by the

Photograph by: Maurice C. Libbey and Gene W. Scholes, Eastern Illinois University.

librarians and a group of four consultants.[3] The basic conclusion drawn was that the conception of HILC and its emphasis on little-used serials was no longer valid in a time of retrenchment. The five institutions were having considerable difficulty supporting five libraries and since HILC's collections were selected from items that were judged likely to be little-used, no rational justification for maintaining such a sixth library could be found. A secondary conclusion drawn was that for four of our institutions, the commonality of our offerings made duplication a necessity, and that rather than consider cancellations to effect savings, intentional duplication should be considered to improve service to users. The five library directors appointed representatives from their libraries to a Collection Development Committee and charged that committee with devising procedures whereby the HILC collection could be dispersed among the five college libraries. The parts of the collection, now located in space in the Amherst College Library, were assigned to one of the five institutions without regard to original ownership, or were declared an unnecessary duplicate of material owned by one of the five and sold. The Collection Development Committee additionally put in place safeguards that would make certain that unique holdings, particularly in instances where an institution had taken HILC's backfile, would be continued. It was understood that willingness to accept and house a backfile carried with it the responsibility for continuing a current subscription.

Having thus closed the door on a jointly-owned center, the librarians set as their goal the pursuit of library cooperation through shared automation. Since 1978, HILC has been actively exploring the feasibility, costs and benefits of automated systems. While investigating a wide array of circulation systems that pretended they were on-line catalogs, we decided in 1979 to abandon the idea of automating circulation using any of the extant systems and to retrospectively convert as many of our bibliographic records as possible until technology had advanced far enough for us to contemplate an on-line catalog. Funds were sought for retrocon, not found and the proposal was delayed. In July of 1981, RMG Consultants, Inc. were retained to assist in the preparation of a Request for Proposal and a Requirements Report for "automated systems and services." Two proposals were received which the librarians felt did not meet the stated requirements. After due deliberation and negotiation, both proposals were rejected as not being in the best interests of the five college libraries. In early 1982 an agreement with OCLC to develop a multi-institution version of their local library system, since named LS/2000, was in place. A sizeable grant to support purchase of hardware and to support construction of a database was received in mid-year. HILC funds were used to support retrospective conversion by providing additional staff at each of the libraries. The cataloguers at our institutions agreed on a five college standard for cataloging. Hampshire College became the first installation of OCLC's LS/2000 system last year. This year all of our libraries are connected to our computer located at the University and all of us other than Hampshire are anxiously awaiting our turns to have our databases loaded.

HILC's governance was outlined in its by-laws at the time of incorporation in 1951 and has changed little since: a Board of Directors which consists of the directors of the five college libraries, a faculty representative from each of the five institutions, and the Five College Coordinator, are responsible for directing and managing HILC. The five library directors and the Five College Coordinator meet regularly as the Librarians Council and, for legal purposes, constitute a quorum for the transaction of HILC business between board meetings. The HILC budget is submitted to the Directors of Five Colleges, Inc., for approval, that group being the Chancellor of the University, the Presidents of the four colleges and the Five College Coordinator.

HILC's income is derived primarily from annual dues assessed each member library, but that income has been supplemented over the years by many grants from federal, state and private sources. Present grants include funds for "library cooperation," and a grant for a five college library automation system. The combination of four private institutions and one public institution has proven a fortuitous mix for federal and state funding. The umbrella of HILC, Inc., has made it possible for at least one major foundation which makes grants only to private institutions to consider not the members of HILC but the Incorporated HILC as the receiver of its grant. As a rule of thumb all HILC costs are divided by five unless there are compelling reasons not to. An example of a compelling reason is HILC's support of the Hampshire College Library as the five college center for cooperative film acquisition. Hampshire augments its own film funds with HILC funds and makes all of its film collection available to the other four institutions.

And how, you may ask, does this entity relate to coordinated collection development? When HILC had a staff and a collection, coordinating collection development was within the purview of the directors of the libraries who sat as the HILC Selection Committee. It was their purpose to determine which serials were of possible research value for the valley, and which serials were of such probable high use that they should be in one or more of the member libraries. Early on all agreed that a union catalog of serials would be of great benefit to the members. In 1966 the University began a printed list of its journal and serials holdings, which was expanded in 1969 to include the other three colleges (Hampshire not yet having been opened). In 1971 it was expanded to become the *Pioneer Valley Union List of Journal and Serial Holdings.* The present PVULS, as it is known, lists over 47,000 journal and serial titles, is no longer printed but on computer output microfiche and is updated quarterly. Subscriptions to the quarterly updates are sold by HILC to help recover costs.

The Five College Collection Development Committee developed a set of guidelines which have remained unchanged since their 1979 adoption. The Collection Development Committee was charged by the Librarians Council as follows: 1) to exchange information concerning proposed additions or deletions from the five periodical collections; 2) to be aware of the status of Five College academic programs; and 3) to develop guidelines for the ongoing exchange of information on collection activities, especially regarding expensive purchases. Procedures were set up whereby each member reports all new subscriptions to serials, standing orders and significant continuations to the other members. Cancellations are likewise reported as are the acquisition of major sets, extensive collections, major microfilm collections and relatively expensive foreign language material. The guidelines state that "The significance of the material cited will be determined by the judgment of each reporting member." It is noteworthy that the Committee's efforts relate only to serials: in the absence of a union catalog for the HILC libraries, it was thought that monographs should be excluded. However, all agreed that some coordination of monographs would be useful and to that end considered membership in a bibliographic utility as a means for obtaining machine readable cataloging records for a future union catalog. Amherst, Hampshire, Mount Holyoke and Smith joined NELINET (and therefore OCLC) in 1973 and 1974. The University became a NELINET member in 1979. Those OCLC records plus those added through retrospective conversion are the ones which are now becoming the initial database of the five college

LS/2000 system. Bibliographic records from Smith, Mount Holyoke, Amherst and the University (in that order) will be loaded during 1985-1986. Hampshire's file is being used as a training file by the rest of us, and is in place at the present time. Also in place is an Electronic Mail subsystem between the libraries.

The Collection Development Committee has been relatively inactive as the five college library system is being created. Our previous experience with coordinating our collections had shown us that we always lacked sufficient, reliable information to be able to make appropriate and timely decisions. A study of the probable overlap of our five collections took months to complete. We could not reconstruct usage patterns from the information available from our circulation systems. We could not determine which of us owned material unless it was in the OCLC database and unless it had been catalogued or published since we had begun using OCLC. We could only determine on order items by telephoning one another, seriatum, since our reporting mechanisms are after the fact and then only for serials. We firmly believe that there are instances where one or two of an item for the five of us will be sufficient. At Amherst, for example, the order request forms give the requestor the option of noting that items are needed at Amherst, or needed in the Valley by any of us. It is our belief that the system we are presently constructing will provide us with sufficient information to make appropriate collection development decisions. However, since each library is curriculum driven, we do not predict enormous savings. What is taught at our institutions will continue to determine the direction our collections will grow. The "total" system which we hope to have in place by the 1990's will include a shared on-line public catalog; a circulation and materials booking system which will display availability information for individual copies or volumes; and, an acquisition system which will record both bibliographic and fiscal information for materials being added to the libraries. Paradoxically, we believe that by totally integrating our bibliographic futures we will be able to retain each institution's identity best. While our institutions seek to build upon the strengths we found together in the 1970's, our libraries seek to respond to curricular changes with factual data about our collections. We hope, among many other important things, to be able to identify underutilized resources which will be considered for deaccessioning, storage, or, transfer to another of our libraries if that is more appropriate. We hope to identify parts of the files and sets in order to facilitate the rationalization of titles. We hope to be able to set up a mechanism for identification of the so-called "last copy in Valley" items where the owning library accepts the responsibility for keeping a last copy for the greater good as is now done with serials. And lastly, we hope to reduce the rate of increase of library costs but believe that in the long run the ease of access to information for our faculty and students and the possible reallocation of resources and staff time will be HILC's greatest achievement.

What we have learned in thirty-four years of library cooperation is best summed up as follows: we are better able to provide library services to our users through sharing of our resources than we are able to provide alone. Period. We have proven to ourselves that as a group we lacked the necessary critical mass to establish and run a center for jointly-held materials. We have found that the loss of a physical center did not stop the growth of library cooperation as suspected, but rather redirected our energies to a more fruitful agenda. We have found that all of our cooperative endeavors take longer than expected. (It has been said that "immediate" in consortial terms means within five to seven years.[4]) And finally, we have learned that patience, tolerance, understanding and flexibility are necessary for true cooperation. If we cannot share as partners we are doomed to fail.

There is little that could have been done differently given the budgetary restraints, the administrative turnover, and the changing perceptions of library cooperation in HILC's members. At times it was frustrating to have consultants say what the librarians had been saying all along and have only the consultants be heard. The mix of personalities and management styles within the five college libraries has led to some predictable clashes on procedural and policy issues. And, as is no doubt true of any cooperative endeavor, some are more willing than others to share. Though the dispersal of the HILC collection was traumatic for those intimately involved in building it, the trauma has been lived through. At this distance, no one questions the wisdom of the decision, nor the wisdom of the decision to pursue automation as a means for coordinating collection development. Much of what has occurred came about because we were able to agree (finally) on how to best achieve HILC's primary goal: to encourage and facilitate cooperation between its members.

We have achieved cooperative use by opening our doors to one another. We have achieved cooperative cataloging by having our catalogers hammer out an agreement for a Five College standard.

We have agreed that cooperative storage is not feasible at this time. And we have agreed that automation will provide us with the tools necessary to consider seriously cooperative acquisitions. Though certainly not in the way envisioned, we continue to pursue HILC's founders cooperative goals.

REFERENCES

1. Anne C. Edmonds and Willis E. Bridegam's "Perspectives on cooperation: the evaluation of a consortium" presented at the Association of College and Research Libraries National Conference in Boston, 1978, reviewed HILC's first twenty-five years.

2. Keyes D. Metcalf. *The Hampshire Inter-Library Center: a Survey of its Background and its Problems with Recommendations for the Future.* (South Hadley, Mass., Hampshire Inter-Library Center, 1957) 31p.

3. Richard Degennaro, Donald B. Engley, David Kaser and Louis Martin "A View of HILC and Its Future." Report submitted to Five Colleges, Inc. March 18, 1977. 17p.

4. Lorna M. Peterson. *Glancing Backward: Twenty-Five Years of Cooperation: a retrospective report on Five Colleges, Incorporated.* (Amherst, Five Colleges, Incorporated, 1984) p.8.

Response to the Paper HILC at Thirty-Four: A View from Within

Susan M. Maltese

Coordinator of Library Services
Oakton Community College
Des Plaines, Illinois

Since the Hampshire Inter-Library Center is in the middle of a shared automation project upon which so many plans hinge, it is difficult to access at this time. As Billie Bozone clearly states, there are many ways in which the Center (HILC) can make more realistic plans regarding projects once the automation is completed. The kinds of data that HILC hopes to be able to acquire (and reasonably so) correspond in many ways to what Illinois now has for those libraries on LCS.

One also assumes that given the scale of the project, and the relatively small size of four of the five institutions, records for all materials will be in the shared data base. All of this portends well for the future of HILC, including the chance for its advancement into the area of specific cooperative collection development. This move can complement other areas of sharing which have gone on over the years of the Center's existence.

However, if one is considering HILC in terms of offering insights for models for such planning, or in terms of meeting ALA, RTSD guidelines, important questions can be raised. The paper does not make clear the scope of the legal entity, Five Colleges, Inc., or how it relates to the success of HILC. One assumes that these five colleges are also cooperating in a number of other ways which have set powerful precedents and expectations for cooperation by the libraries. This may be true even if specific agreements are not involved. The fact that one of the five institutions, Hampshire College, was actually founded by the others also makes for a situation

© 1986 by The Haworth Press, Inc. All rights reserved.

which is probably unique. What role does this circumstance play in the attitudes of all participants, and especially Hampshire?

What part has the existence of Five Colleges, Inc., played in helping HILC to get financial support that might not otherwise have been possible? Ms. Bozone does point out how HILC itself has played a part in terms of providing a legal entity beyond the individual colleges, but the Five Colleges and its coordinator's role is not clear.

The other major set of questions is raised because HILC is a cooperative made up of one large public university and four small private liberal arts colleges. Obviously, very close physical proximity and a long tradition of sharing are valuable assets in these relationships. Certainly the special arrangements for using each other's collections have value in themselves. But Ms. Bozone raises questions about the extent to which serious cooperation in collection development will be possible, even with the best of statistics. She points out that at least for the private institutions there is much overlap in basic needs.

The University of Massachusetts no doubt has some different and specialized subject areas, but it is hard to see how these are likely to be complemented by what the other colleges would feel was appropriate to have in their collections.

In her paper, Ms. Bozone mentions that in the past consideration has been given to adding other institutions to HILC. In the specific area of cooperating on collection development, is it time to look at this issue again? There is no mention of how the different institutions are being affected by other state-wide plans in Massachusetts. Are any of these libraries, particularly the state institution, involved in any other projects which might offer different cooperative possibilities? In a relatively small state like Massachusetts, the logistics imposed by distances should not be too difficult. Inter-state considerations may even be needed to balance out types of institutions and variations in size.

How is the public library system related to the University? Was there consideration given to its being included in the automation plans? What are the concerns related to the University's service to this and other state institutions versus that to area private colleges? Will these issues become a problem as more specific cooperative planning begins?

Past informality seems to have worked for those projects which HILC members were committed to. Voluntary cooperation on an informal basis may not be enough for the future however. It would be interesting to know what the record is as far as the individual institutions having kept the agreements made as personnel changed and there were different pressures and priorities. Were current subscriptions maintained on those items obtained through the break-up of the HILC collection? "Last copies" kept? As the HILC librarians eagerly anticipate the rewards which automation will bring, some evaluation of past performance could be taking place. This, along with other considerations already raised, would help them to begin to work out the kinds of arrangements that will be needed if the "new" HILC is to succeed.

RESPONSE TO THE PAPER COOPERATIVE COLLECTION DEVELOPMENT IN THE TRIANGLE RESEARCH LIBRARIES NETWORK

The history of fifty years of successful, concrete cooperative collection development between the University of North Carolina, Chapel Hill, and Duke University is a pleasure to read. The valuable perceptions of Joe Hewitt on why the project has been so successful, along with his observations on its limited applicability as a model, also give us cause for pause. It appears that it has not been possible to introduce even one more institution into the process in a way that begins to approxiate the successful relationship of those first two.

The examples cited of regional subject divisions between Duke and the University are clear cut. It would have been helpful if Mr. Hewitt had given some of the specific cases where it has been possible to work out such arrangements with North Carolina State University. Presumably some of the statements about regional divisions apply, but that isn't clear. If not these types of arrangements, then what?

Are there significant areas where complementary materials available at North Carolina State have proved valuable? Have the formal arrangements with NCSU saved Duke and North Carolina from purchasing materials they might previously have purchased? Or merely provided quicker and more convenient access to materials that they would have borrowed through interlibrary loan? Why was NCSU brought into the arrangement? Did the state play a part either formally or informally in the establishment of a cooperative arrangement between these two major state universities?

In his paper, Mr. Hewitt mentions other unaffiliated institutions in the area for which the TRLN members also purchase materials. How has the acceptance of these three universities of their need to back subject areas for other local institutions been justified? Again, has the state played a part? Grants? What is the reciprocity involved? Is this part of a larger pattern of networking? While these concerns are not a part of the paper, Mr. Hewitt has opened the door to a broadened area of at least de facto cooperation that may be valuable to learn about. What are the formal or informal agreements to maintain these services, and at what level?

How does this, the admirable give and take of the TRLN libraries, fit in with state-wide plans for the university system? Is there an effort to interconnect with the public and community college libraries? As a private institution how does Duke fit into the picture as the "other" institution alongside the state's great research institution in terms of serving the public? Has Duke tied itself into a position through these years of intense cooperation with a state university that might place hard-to-bear demands on it as the move for cooperation between publically-supported institutions becomes stronger? Since important areas of these two collections have been built together, it seems that the line between them could be difficult to draw in terms of meeting state-wide library needs. Have these concerns been raised?

Mr. Hewitt believes that for cooperative collection agreements to be of significance on any scale, institutions must be developing indepth research collections. At the present time the University of Virginia is involved with TRLN in the area of Slavic Studies. It does seem reasonable that a possible next step would be inter-state arrangements, especially to provide for comprehensive collections. Bibliographic utilities are already providing data bases which could be used as a starting point in many parts of the country, including SOLINET in the southeast.

In an article in the February 1, 1985, *Library Journal*, colleagues of Mr. Hewitt's in the Triangle Research Libraries Network wrote about additional areas of cooperation involving the eventual implementation of an online catalog. It appeared from reading this article that incredible strains are being placed on all concerned as each of the institutions works out plans for getting needed funds for this project.[1]

What has been the role of those involved in cooperative collection development in these plans? Have the priorities of getting the system into place affected day-to-day concerns in collection development?

Or monies available to continue cooperation at the same level? How will additional libraries brought into the system (professional primarily) be involved? Are they already a part of cooperative efforts on their own? Has any planning been done with other state institutions in terms of expanding this system in a way which might further cooperative collection development (or at least analysis) beyond the Triangle?

Triangle members have had specific written agreements, and have built the support for their cooperation into their individual budgets, two important practical guidelines for success. In these and other ways indicated in the paper, the maintenance of these agreements so effectively for so long provides lessons of value for anyone involved in developing such plans today. How to apply these lessons to cooperative collection development in dissimilar institutions is the challenge faced by those of us trying to think in terms of a state-wide model.

NOTE

1. Gary D. Byrd, Jinnie Y. Davis, William A. Gosling, and L. Russell Herman, Jr., "The Evolution of a Cooperative Online Network." *Library Journal*, February 1, 1985, p.71-77.

Photograph by: Maurice C. Libbey and Gene W. Scholes, Eastern Illinois University.

Discussion #3

Discussion Leader, Susan Maltese

I would like for you, then, to have a chance to ask your questions. I know it has been as we've said, a long day, and you should get your chance to ask the questions you have for these two projects.

* * *

Joe, did I understand you to suggest, at least by implication, that one solution to our deliberation at this conference would be to give the money to two or three large research libraries—representing (even though not the libraries, but) the Library School at the University of Illinois, admittedly, I have some interest—and not worry about the medium sized libraries because, by default, they're going to come up with fairly unique collections anyway?

Is that a fair conclusion to draw from your statement?

* * *

No, I think it would be fair to say, "Give the *responsibility* to the large research libraries." Our programs (except for grant funding) have operated, more or less, with our own institutional funding. I expect that grant funding, over a period of years, does not exceed $1,000,000 or $1,200,000, but I think with the kinds of coordinated collection development that we do you're going to find it very difficult to accomplish in small and medium sized research libraries. There may be another type [of library that is able] that I'm not familiar with—maybe the client centered, for example, that was mentioned this morning.

* * *

I'm with the University of Illinois, also, but not the Library School. Actually, Terry, if you'd remember, one of your own dissertations (Mr. Potter's) shows that the same patterns of nonduplication appear with large and small libraries, as does those studies at Wisconsin (which were neglected) and New York. I think, Joe, that those same patterns will arise wherever you are.

It's quite true that the specificity of Egyptology in one place and Hawaiian Poetry in the other may not be appropriate for two libraries of varying size, but nevertheless, there are fairly significant patterns of borrowing which, I think, you can satisfy with cooperative collection development agreements with all kinds of institutions.

Not all library use—as we know, in large academic libraries—is for the purist of pure research. A fair amount is for pleasure or miscellaneous use. I was just recently a volunteer at the Urbana Free Public Library Friends Book Sale. I noticed a number of my colleagues purchasing (for 75 cents) books on how to make bird houses, romances of the worst sort, and a whole series of those.

I think that, indeed, gives us some indication that small engine repair might well be appropriate for Parkland Community College in a cooperative collection development arrangement with the University of Illinois. I would not be so firm as you are with size.

* * *

I think that we could see happening with the development of the bibliographic access systems is that some of this could be distance insensitive, so to speak. It really doesn't matter where (in which collections) certain materials reside, just the fact that you have bibliographic and physical access to them in some way. You need to look at the total resource available and not so much what is in one library or the other. I think, in that sense, libraries of all sizes can indeed cooperate, but in terms of getting UNC-Asheville, for example, to enter our East European agreements or something like that, it just doesn't make any sense to them or for us.

They can collect romances or something like that on our behalf.

* * *

Joe, just stay where you are, please. Joe and I come from the same part of the country, so this is really a friendly question. Susan raised this [question] about the cooperation of Duke with Chapel Hill. I have seen a recent report from the State Universities of North Carolina—I think there are sixteen of them—of a cooperative plan for collection development or resource sharing, but it does not involve (in a financial way, at least) Duke.

I asked that question, simply because Susan has raised that question previously. Could you speak to that?

* * *

I don't know just what plan you're speaking to, it may be it has to do with the funding for library materials within the university system which is done as a system. It's the only budget line in the general universities budget that is done in that way; everything else comes up through the campuses.

Do you see what I mean? The university libraries' budget for the total system comes directly to the libraries. That is for materials, without passing through the bureaucracy on the local campus. The operating budgets have to go through the local campus budget request system.

I think that's what you're talking about. Because of that, all library material within the State system are considered a state-wide resource, but we do not have cooperative programs in terms of collection development with the other institutions.

* * *

My name is Jay Whaley, I'm from Virginia Commonwealth University and my question is to Joe, again.

I can't tell you how delighted I am to hear that there really is a coordinated cooperative collection development program some where. I think that, obviously, there are some unusual factors that operate in your situation. You've mentioned geographical proximity as one, but I'd be interested in hearing what the other institutional arrangements are; for example, between faculty. It seems to me that the collaboration that you enjoy has to depend upon something greater than that between the libraries themselves.

* * *

I didn't mention some of the background, here, related to how these programs originated. In the thirties, the library programs originated under an organization—a university level cooperative organization—called the Committee on Intellectual Cooperation. It involved the Provosts, the Chancellors, and so on. Of the programs that were started in the thirties under that umbrella, the library programs are just one that remains today.

That committee, itself, hasn't existed for thirty-five or forty years. The others have to do with some institutes that have joint membership among the faculties—Latin American Studies, for one. We find that we facilitate a lot of our work with faculty through the fact that faculty at Duke and North Carolina belong to a single Institute for Latin American Studies. Our Latin American bibliographer also belongs to that Institute, so does Duke's. They work with the faculties as a group. The Far Eastern scholars on the two campuses don't have quite as formal a group, but they meet as a group every quarter or so. Our bibliographers attend. We use those groups to facilitate cooperation. Duke has a Canadian Studies Institute. We have a few faculty who are interested in Canadian Studies, and they are fellows of that Institute. We coordinate through faculty in that way.

There are some areas, that are not covered by those kinds of institutes, where we do have problems. The Polish Agreement, for example, is one. At the moment, Duke has high interest in Polish materials, but they are mostly for recent political science and economic materials. Our interest on the Carolina campus is more for eighteenth and nineteenth century historical materials. Duke's bibliographer is not a specialist in Polish, therefore, there is a faculty person doing the selection. We have to negotiate there when we send our requests over. They sometimes don't want to order them and we put a little pressure on them by saying, "Well, we won't order your Chinese materials," for example. There is a great interest at Duke in Chinese Studies, but they don't want to collect. They'd rather stick with the Japanese which is a division that we've had for many years.

It doesn't always work perfectly. The faculty's main interests seems to be in physical access problems rather than who owns what. For example, Duke's faculty in their own library can check out materials for one year. Our faculty wants to check out materials from Duke library for one year. Duke doesn't allow that. We made a special agreement with them so that, for materials bought under our programs, our faculty check out the materials for six months (which is what they get in our own library).

In general, the faculty is quite pleased with these programs. I've heard it said any number of times to possible faculty recruits that, "Our library is only 3,200,000 volumes, yet Duke library across the road is much larger and you can use it too, and there's only 15 percent duplication,'' and that sort of thing. It is a drawing thing, an attraction to faculty as well as being (in some cases) an inconvenience.

* * *

I'd like to ask one more related question, please. That has to do with to what extent have accreditation agencies accepted the concept of access versus ownership when you get into these cooperative arrangements?

* * *

I don't remember that ever being an issue because accrediting agencies focus mainly on your curriculum support, your teaching function. The areas where we have cooperative programs have not conflicted, as far as I know, in terms of any general accrediting agency.

In fact, we just this year completed the ten year Southern Association Study. We were allowed to do a non-traditional self-study on the research mission of the university. The university-wide committee which wrote that report highlighted the cooperative collection development agreements as one creative way that we were supporting the research mission on campus.

In terms of specific, or professional accrediting agencies, we don't really have any agreements that correspond with those I've discussed. In education, for example, we don't have any collection development agreements. We both collect what we need in those fields for the faculty and students in our programs.

We've never had any problem with any accrediting agency, that I'm aware of, because of lack of library materials. I think the general strength of the libraries tends to diminish the possibility that you would have any specific criticisms by accrediting agencies. Even though we are definitely weak in some areas, I think, they tend to overlook it.

* * *

In concluding, I do just want to mention—or to stress—one thing. That is, that both of these groups are now in the process of automation projects. Ms. Bozone talked about theirs rather extensively. It wasn't mentioned particularly by Mr. Hewitt, but for your interest, there is an article in the February 1 issue of *LJ* (if you haven't seen it) that was done by some colleagues of Mr. Hewitt's. It does talk about their project for an on-line catalog for the different libraries.

I would just like to clarify this because, I think, it's of interest in the article that they imply that others would be on that system. Was that correct for other area institutions? The on-line catalog is not just the three we're talking about today?

* * *

The others will have access to the system, but they won't be loading their records into it.

* * *

Okay, it is just an access kind of thing, so it won't significantly affect the kind of direction that you've been going.

A Stitch in Time: The Alaska Cooperative Collection Development Project

Dennis Stephens

Associate Professor of Library Science
Collection Development Officer
Rasmuson Library

ABSTRACT. The project, begun in 1982, involves academic, public, special, and school libraries in devising systems for optimizing collection development in a resource-poor state at a crucial point in its library growth. It seeks to establish a system of distributed, shared holdings and services that will most effectively provide for long-range knowledge and information needs. Supported by grants from the State Library, the work is coordinated by a Steering Committee representing all types of libraries. It currently concentrates on training librarians and library staff for collection development policy formulation and collection assessment, on liaison with cooperative collection development efforts outside Alaska, and on the establishment of the Alaska Conspectus. The Conspectus is intended to map collection strengths and serve as a basic step to coordinated statewide collection development.

The familiar arguments in favor of coordinated, cooperative collection development carry particular weight in a state characterized by relatively new and underdeveloped library resources, unstable funding for materials, and a population of just over 400,000 souls in a land mass one-fifth the size of the 48 contiguous states.

The Alaska library environment is one of small to very-small libraries, by lower-48 standards. All of Alaska's collections together might give a reasonable medium-sized university research collection. We are weak in foreign language materials, serials, and older materials except, as one might expect, for significant

---

The author wishes to thank the Statewide Collection Development Steering Committee and the Alaska State Library for having made this project possible.

© 1986 by The Haworth Press, Inc. All rights reserved.

Alaskana and Polar Regions collections. We have few subject or special collections bibliographers. There is one advantage in this. A stitch in time can form cooperative collection development structures and protocols *before* we have the opportunity to build too much redundancy and unnecessary duplication into our collections, and too much hidebound tradition into our collectors.

The University of Alaska was established in 1917, and the university system now consists of three four-year campuses, of which the largest library has some 550,000 book volumes and the smallest 65,000. Affiliated with the university system are 11 community colleges scattered over the state with libraries ranging from 2500 to 40,000 book volumes.[1] Several of these form consortia with local public libraries. In addition to widely dispersed community libraries, there are three public library systems, the largest with nine branches and some 330,000 book volumes and the smallest with two branches and 60,000 book volumes.[2] The state's largest school library system serves about 45,000 students and processes about 100,000 items per year. We also have village schools with perhaps 1000 items serving 10 students.[3]

We have a number of special libraries dealing, for example, with natural resources, geophysical research, atmospheric and space sciences, and high-latitude oriented studies.

Alaskans do tend to be library users. While the national public library median circulation per capita was 5.4 in 1983,[4] the Fairbanks North Star Borough Library, as an example, calculates theirs at just over 7 in fiscal year 1983-84.[5]

Alaska librarians share a traditional commitment to resource sharing across type-of-library lines that has been a particular strength of this and other projects. The Alaska Library Network includes each Washington Library Network-member library in the state, and the fiche catalog of their holdings is distributed to virtually every library in Alaska, down to the tiniest. The Anchorage School District is the first school library system anywhere to become a full member of the Washington Library Network, and two other school districts are now adding their holdings. While the Alaska cooperative collection development project is still in its infancy, librarians are coming to view it as another powerful tool in the resource-sharing bag. There has been a significant paradigm shift as we come to view our collections in a more systematic, analytical way, and see them in the context of the larger library that is all the state's library resources.

There is another imperative for this project. The Prudhoe Bay oil fields are expected to peak about 1990, and the state derives some 80% of its revenues from oil. Therefore, as deprived as we perceive

Photograph by: Maurice C. Libbey and Gene W. Scholes, Eastern Illinois University.

ourselves to be now, it was clearly not a candle to what the future could bring for library funding in Alaska. Experience elsewhere tells us that cooperative plans laid in "good" times have a better chance of surviving in lean times than the other way around. It seems a good idea to devise our own strategy to rationalize collection-building, before a program is imposed on us.

Obviously, this is an ideal time to be looking at cooperative collection development, at mapping resources and systemizing and coordinating the growth of the state's library resources. We want to be as sure as we can that we will collect the materials central to institutional missions, have detailed knowledge of the nature of collections elsewhere in the state and region, and have the ability to draw on them when needed. A basic assumption is that it's better to try to optimize what resources we have than to lament their limitations.

This is a strategic plan for the next 10 and 20 years. This paper is a progress report, not an account of an accomplished fact. The long-range goals of the project include the following:

1. Distinguish those knowledge and information resources that constitute the indispensable core collections of each library from the more detailed requirements of research/resource libraries that can be distributed and shared rather than duplicated at high cost to the state.
2. Devise a system of distributed, shared holdings, services, and conservation/preservation measures that will provide a greater capacity to respond to the knowledge and information needs of the state in a more adequate time frame, and at lower cost than would otherwise be possible.

Our short-term goals include:

1. Complete individual collection development policy statements by each of the Steering Committee libraries.
2. Provide advice and encouragement to other libraries as they complete their policy statements.
3. Compile and distribute these policy statements.
4. Proceed on, and make available, the Alaska Conspectus.
5. Complete and make available the Polar Regions conspectus division, to enable uniform survey of these geographically-oriented collections. These are essentially what we might have to offer in a regional and national collection development context.

6. Work with the Library and Information Resources for the Northwest program of the Fred Meyer Charitable Trust to encourage the building of standard collection survey tools and techniques in the Pacific Northwest.

The means to initiate a statewide project appeared in Spring 1982, when legislative funding became available through the State Library for "interlibrary cooperation and assistance" grants. A proposal was funded to bring a consultant to Alaska to help us define a cooperative collection development project in the light of similar work elsewhere.

Dr. Paul Mosher became our consultant, and his September 1982 report *A Plan for Cooperative Collection Development Among Alaska Libraries*,[6] and his subsequent visits, including one as keynote speaker at the Alaska Library Association conference last year, have provided the basis for a plan we have made our own.

Among Dr. Mosher's recommendations were the following. Some of them have been addressed, others are now being worked on, and others find themselves on our two, five, and 10-year plans. In spite of such excellent advice it sometimes seems that we follow Fletcher Byrom's rule, quoted in Peters and Waterman's *In Search of Excellence*: we use (planning) mainly to recognize change as it takes place.[7]

These were, as Robert Ludlum would perhaps have it, The Mosher Recommendations:

1. Each participating library should prepare or update its collection development policy statement, using a standard format.
2. In order to determine what it has to share, as well as to help relate its collection to its mission and goals, each participating library should survey its holdings and prepare a conspectus. These individual conspectae should then be compiled into a statewide map of library resources—an Alaska Conspectus.
3. The conspectus information should then be used to develop a statewide collection development program for a five and 10-year period to optimize the financial and human resources of the state in developing its information and knowledge resources.
4. The Statewide Collection Development Steering Committee should be continued and further organized as the central coordinating agency for the project.

5. A collection development institute should be offered for Alaska librarians.
6. A program of collection analysis should be developed providing uniform methodologies for use and user studies, collection evaluations, and verification and overlap studies.
7. Appropriate ways should be found to tie in the Alaska effort with those in the lower-48.
8. A cooperative purchase plan should be devised.
9. Staff support should be provided to the Steering Committee in the period involved with conspectus development and publication and collection development plan formulation.

The Statewide Collection Development Steering Committee provides the governance structure and coordinates the effort, sets priorities, and reports to the State Library at the conclusion of each funding year, then hopes for continued funding. One of the particular strengths of the project is that it involves all kinds of libraries—by extension, any library in the state which wishes to participate: college, university, community college, public, special, community college/public consortium, school, and the State Library. Each type of library has a representative on the Steering Committee, which now numbers 11.

Besides representing their type of library, the members also form regional groups across library type. For example, the school library/media coordinator from the State Library and the collection development librarian from our largest public library system gave a collection development workshop together with a Steering Committee member from a public/community college consortium. Subsequently, a community college librarian, a State Library member, and a member from a Dept. of the Interior library conducted a cooperative workshop for school, public, and community college librarians. The Steering Committee's services are available to any library or group of libraries in the state.

We have found that the local team approach to evaluating collections in each other's libraries, and collegial support in writing collection development policy statements, have been particularly positive approaches to cooperative collection development in Alaska. When the Steering Committee concludes a training workshop, local groups have continued the cooperative collection survey on their own, setting their own timetables, sometimes as a project of the local chapter of the state library association.

While the Statewide Collection Development Steering Committee bears responsibility for directing the project, the State Library grants have been to my library and I am principal investigator. The initial grant for the project was $7000 in Fiscal Year 1982, and the current year's grant amounts to some $17,000. These State Library grants have enabled the work to proceed by funding travel and other expenses of twice-yearly meetings (a not inconsequential cost; a coach roundtrip air ticket from Fairbanks to Juneau, for example, now runs about $420), consultant and professional services, materials, supplies, telephone, duplicating, and similar administrative costs. Very little, however, has been spent on staffing, amounting to a part-time clerk for several months. We do have access to the university system electronic mail facility and the statewide teleconference network, operated by the university and the department of education, which links communities throughout the state, for twice-monthly teleconferences at (so far) no cost to us. We have also made use of the pilot telefacsimile project serving libraries in the three population centers.

While we do have an OCLC library on the Steering Committee, Alaska is a charter member of the Washington Library Network and 24 libraries are now participants. Others are waiting in the wings. Access to a common bibliographic database is obviously an important step in coordinating collection development, particularly when that access includes acquisitions records, as is the case with those using a common acquisitions system.

As Scott Bennett of Northwestern University has said, "Cooperation cannot even begin until libraries are able to communicate with one another about their collections on both an item-by-item and categorical basis."[8] The Steering Committee has focused on the design and application of an Alaska Conspectus as a primary coordinating tool to provide information on collection strengths and collecting committments by subject categories. This tool is modeled after the Research Libraries Group Conspectus, now used in the North American Collections Inventory Project. One of the original tenets of our project was to assure conformity with cooperative collection development work outside Alaska, so the conspectus is a wheel we didn't reinvent. In order to make it work in libraries in size ranges significantly different from those in the Research Libraries Group, to say the least, we elaborated the scale of collection intensity indicators so that RLG level 1, the "minimal collection" level, is subdivided into 1a and 1b; level 2, the "basic information'' level, is likewise broken down into 2a and 2b; level 3, the "instructional support" level, is divided into three subcategories. We have found this Alaska scale seems to work even in school libraries with the addition of a readership level indicator. It maintains the integrity of the zero through 5 scale for standardization, and we're *not* embarrassed at having 1b's and 2a's if that's commensurate with the library mission.

The Alaska Conspectus is being designed around Condor software running on a Hewlett-Packard 150 microcomputer for the individual library conspectus. These individual library "conspectae" will be merged and sorted using the Image 3000 database manager on the HP-3000 that will host the university system-wide circulation, on-line patron access catalog, and indexing databases. Depending upon resources for development, we hope to have the Alaska Conspectus database on-line in the future. It is likely, however, that the Library and Information Resources for the Northwest collection assessment database will have significant effects on our future plans for the Alaska Conspectus.

It is the Steering Committee's intent to enable each library that wishes to participate to have its own conspectus, to whatever detail is suitable, and to include libraries when appropriate in the statewide conspectus or a local edition of it. Training was provided at an Alaska Collection Development Institute presented by the Steering Committee with Dr. Mosher in May 1983, at the Alaska Library Association conferences in 1984 and 1985, and by Steering Committee members at site visits. We look forward to further training under the auspices or the Library and Information Resources for the Northwest program through the University of Washington Graduate School of Library and Information Science. An orientation to cooperative collection development was published for the Alaska Library Network as part of *Alaska is a Library* in 1984.[9]

We have all had problems fitting in the time to do the collection survey work necessary to build our conspectus. Although supervisors and library directors have been uniformly supportive of this project, no additional staff has been available to any Steering Committee member to help in this effort. But it is rather like the story of the people of the town of Pisa who installed a clock in their famous Leaning Tower. They decided it was no use having the inclination, if they didn't have the time. So we're *making* time and writing it into our weekly calendars. We find it's important for libraries to "buy into" the project, to invest the time, so that they have a stake in the finished product. We've all missed our own deadlines, but that way we keep track of how far behind we are. This is, after all, an incremental process.

We plan to have our Alaska Conspectus completed by the end of 1986. Once we've got our conspectus, what are we going to do with it? I'm sure there are uses we've not even thought of yet. As collection patterns begin to emerge in the conspectus, we can begin making cooperative decisions on collecting responsibilities, based on collection strengths, collecting commitments, and on the missions of participating institutions. No one will need to relinquish or scale down any collecting activity unless they wish to do so, but where such decisions can be made we will be in a position to make them. We have agreed to consider this as conspectus data becomes available (the first statewide conspectus section, showing Steering Committee library holdings in U.S. History, has just been produced). We have agreed to discuss coordinated cataloging and conservation/preservation, in consultation with appropriate staff, as subsequent steps. It will form a basis for shared purchasing of pricey items. It will, we think, be useful to interlibrary loan staff to know where the stronger collections in a subject are located when they cannot trace a holding library for a specific title. We may finally solve the "what, where, when" problem of a last-copy depository by sending candidate items to the library reporting strongest holdings in this particular subject area. But the most important benefits will accrue to the individual library, which will be establishing its own collection policy in the course of developing its conspectus, and establishing the basis for cooperative, coordinated collection development work with other libraries. But all this will not happen automatically or spontaneously. It needs planning. It also needs, as Billie Bozone said yesterday, patience, tolerance, and mutual understanding.

Last Fall a serendipitous new element appeared on the southern horizon which holds great promise for a regional assessment of information resources. The Library and Information Resources for the Northwest program of the Fred Meyer Charitable Trust, mentioned earlier, has developed a plan for a Pacific Northwest region-wide resource mapping. It will draw on elements of the Alaska project, which has drawn on elements of other plans. The Library and Information Resources program is also addressing one of the thornier problems of our and similar projects involving both LC and Dewey libraries, by commissioning a conversion table. Alaska Dewey libraries have thus far used various versions of Dewey-LC tables but we anxiously look forward to Geri Schmidt's accomplishment. You will hear more about the Library and Information Resources for the Northwest Program in the next paper by Anne Haley.

A recent article by Bernard Holicky titled "Collection Development vs. Resource Sharing: the View from a Small Academic Library"[10] notes that "Small academic libraries are . . . now making the choice between collection development and resource sharing," and at the Purdue University Calumet library, "Only resource sharing combined with a substantial dose of collection management is the answer." We are finding that these two concepts are not mutually exclusive. Cooperative collection development recognizes that each participating library requires a well-defined core collection to support its well-defined fundamental mission. These materials may properly be duplicated in other libraries depending on missions and goals; overlap may be desirable. Core materials do circulate and are available to others through interlibrary loan. In addition, libraries require access to more peripheral materials for study and research, curriculum support, and recreational reading, more specialized materials which are less used than its core. This material may not need to be duplicated among libraries but can be part of the shared pool, located where it is most appropriate but accessible to all. This enhances the goals of all without damaging accessibility to materials by local users. In effect, cooperation creates a much larger pool of collectively available resources. Cooperative bibliographic access and document delivery make these collections available to all users. The process can be pictured as a series of concentric rings of distributed interdependence, or of shared dependence.

Document delivery is, of course, the stone in the shoe of resource sharing, and much needs to be done. The difficulties in Alaska are clear; for example, no roads link Juneau, the capital city, with the rest of the state. And there's no United Parcel Service. Again, we look to Library and Information Resources for the Northwest to address this vital issue.

We in Alaska have learned a great deal from others engaged in cooperative collection development work, and certainly from Illinois. Since one of the reasons for this symposium is to build a model of cooperative collection development, we hope we might have something to contribute as well. One of those contributions might be to suggest the appropriateness of multi-type library cooperation. In the Alaska library environment it has been a fine community-building approach. It is essential to emphasize, in any cooperative enterprise, those characteristics and goals the participants share in common.

The differences will be obvious enough. Please take care not to invent barriers where none have existed. I must say that listening to several papers at this symposium convinces me of an element of sheer contrariness in our profession. Building communities of enlightened self-interest has certainly worked in many other contexts, and it will work in this one.

An example of what can result from the multi-type approach to cooperative collection development is the Capital City Project in Juneau. The university and public libraries together with the State Library now have a common fiche catalog based on their Washington Library Network holdings. They are expecting the school district library system to join them. They are also preparing a verification and overlap study in their education collections, using a standard bibliography, to check their conspectus data. These steps are elemental blocks of coordinated collection development.

We have also found that funding agencies and parent bodies and other administrators are not blind to efforts to systemize and rationalize collection building. The conspectus and the policy statement can be effective tools for educating administrators. In two recent instances in Alaska school libraries, having appropriate information about available resources (or lack thereof) has meant modest but immediate budget increments. In the case of my library, having collection strength data on our economics and business collections is helping forge a new relationship of mutual self-interest with our friends in the School of Management, who are preparing their accreditation self-study.

There are some things we would do differently, if we had it to do again. We would try to avoid spending too much time on administrative housekeeping, and more time on thinking and planning. We would take the time earlier on to codify our goals and steps to achieving them.

What we have done well is to get a good consultant, and to stir the pot of enthusiasm for resource sharing ventures once again until cooperative collection development, like other resource sharing tools, becomes an established pattern of thinking.

As Dr. Mosher pointed out at the Alaska Library Association conference last year, everyone does collection development in one way or another. We want to do it better, and do it cooperatively. It stretches our budgets and gives us more options in our efforts to serve our library users better. After all, isn't this what it's all really about? The library resources of each library can become the resources of all, and the most substantial benefits accrue to the individual library and its users.

REFERENCES

1. Office of Institutional Planning, University of Alaska Statewide System of Higher Education, *U of A Today: Libraries, Fiscal Year 1984 and Fall 1984* (Fairbanks, Alaska: Office of Institutional Planning, University of Alaska Statewide System of Higher Education, 1984). Statistics updated by personal contact with appropriate staff.
2. *American Library Directory*, 37th ed. (New York: R. R. Bowker, 1984), pp. 27-33. Statistics updated through personal interviews with staff.
3. Interview with Ruth Jean Shaw, 3/5/85.
4. H. Goldhor, "University of Illinois annual survey: public library circulation holds; spending jumps 7%," *American Libraries* 15 (July 1984): 526.
5. Interview with Michael L. Herman, 3/4/85.
6. Paul H. Mosher, "A Plan for Cooperative Collection Development Among Alaska Libraries." Stanford University, September 29, 1982. Available from Dennis Stephens, Rasmuson Library, Univ. of Alaska-Fairbanks, Fairbanks AK 99701.
7. Thomas J. Peters and Robert H. Waterman, Jr., *In Search of Excellence* (New York: Warner Books, 1982), p. 40.
8. Library and Information Resources for the Northwest, "Mapping Information Resources in the Pacific Northwest: An Invitation to Participate." Portland, Oregon, January 1985. Available from Library and Information Resources for the Northwest, a Program of the Fred Meyer Charitable Trust, 2125 SW Fourth Ave., Suite 202, Portland OR 97201.
9. Nancy Lesh and B. Jo Morse, eds., *Alaska is a Library* (Anchorage: University of Alaska-Anchorage Library, 1984).
10. Bernard H. Holicky, "Collection Development vs. Resource Sharing: the view from a small academic library," *Journal of Academic Librarianship* 10 (July 1984): pp. 146-147.

The Pacific Northwest Collection Assessment Project

Anne Haley

Director of the Walla Walla Public Library
President of the Washington Library Association

Douglas K. Ferguson

Director of the Library and Information Resources
for the Northwest Program
of the Fred Meyer Charitable Trust

The Pacific Northwest Conspectus will be the outcome of a unique approach to information resource assessment initiated by a private foundation. The Fred Meyer Charitable Trust's Library and Information Resources for the Northwest Project is spearheading the design of a resource assessment process, training of library assessors, development of the database, production of a specialized collections survey, and encouragement of cooperative acquisition plans. The challenge to libraries in the Pacific Northwest will be continuing the resource assessment process beyond the Trust's initial commitment.

NEW WAYS OF MANAGING COLLECTIONS

The issue for the 1980s and 1990s is the development of new means of strategic planning and management of information resources that look beyond this year's budget and individual institutional resources. In this new regionalism, there are two assumptions: Any program of improved access must support a regional not just an institutional context for development of individual collections; any region-wide program must reach beyond the region and link it to key national information centers to supplement regional resources.

The Pacific Northwest is also developing a response to this challenge, although its form and structure may be somewhat different from regional resource sharing developments elsewhere.

THE REGIONAL CONTEXT

There are many conditions unique to the Pacific Northwest. The national resources based industries such as timber, fishing and agriculture have seen significant fluctuations in the past decade. They have been described as a roller coaster with no upswings. I can attest personally; my husband raises wheat. Seven years ago, the price for wheat was $5 per bushel; today it is $3.20 per bushel. These conditions affect the ability of communities, companies and educational institutions to maintain an adequate information infra-structure amid competing demands for a contracting pool of dollars.

The geography and demography, the land and people, of the Pacific Northwest are among its most distinctive assets. Yet, vast distances, widely dispersed populations and deregulation create real transportation and communication access problems, including access to information. For instance, a teacher in Billings, Montana, and a researcher in Anchorage, Alaska, have significantly less access to information than a student in Pullman, Washington, or even a citizen in Portland, Oregon.

While there are many fine schools and libraries in the Pacific Northwest, we have fewer large, central research collections and lower levels of per capita spending for public libraries than any set of states with similar demographics. Furthermore, strong disciplinary and subject collections are widely dispersed throughout the region. Despite progress with computer-based union catalog services, they are by and large invisible to individuals and information service professionals.

A FOUNDATION INITIATIVE

What can be done to deal with these problems short of the unending quest for more books, buildings, computers and people? This question was asked by the Fred Meyer Charitable Trust in deciding how to make an effective commitment with limited money, time and staff to improved information delivery among libraries in Alaska, Idaho, Montana, Oregon and Washington. This commitment is part of the Trust's efforts to assist educational institutions to respond successfully to the challenges of technological change.

In August 1983, the Fred Meyer Trustees approved the Library and Information Resources for the Northwest Program. An estimated $3.5 million was committed to this program which is intended to enhance access to information through assisting to improve collection management and resource sharing among libraries. Its goal will be achieved by promoting the design of new ways of cooperative information acquisition, coordination and delivery. Early attention will include academic and research libraries with involvement of special and public libraries. This was the Trust's first major program initiative and subsequently two others—aging and higher education—were approved.

The Director of the Library and Information Resources for the Northwest Program (shortened to LIRN Program), Douglas Ferguson, began work at the Trust in April 1984, one year ago. Kathleen Treb-Pollock serves as program assistant.

The LIRN Program has three components: The first is the establishment of a regional cooperative resource assessment process and has several parts: Cooperative assessments using a standard process that identifies subject patterns in the information resources of the region, development of a continuously maintained database for analyzing and displaying regional collection subject patterns, and a separate survey of specilized resources in libraries and other organizations.

The second component is the development of a regional approach to innovative, cost effective information delivery capabilities.

The third component is assisting with interinstitutional plans and agreements for ongoing resource development. The regional resource approach should reflect interinstitutional commitments in specific subject areas. It is expected that a regional framework for cooperative collection management and institutional agreements will emerge over a period of years.

The LIRN Program is utilizing a participatory, task force approach for planning the development, communication and promotion of these activities. Proposals then are used to select grantees who will develop specific elements of the components, such as the assessment training, the specialized collection survey and directory, and the collections database, (the "Pacific Northwest Conspectus").

The LIRN Advisory Committee was appointed in June 1984. It is composed of library administrators, officers of educational institutions, community leaders, library association leaders, state officials, and information technology specialists. The charges to the Advisory Committee were to anticipate regional information requirements for the 1990s, suggest how the LIRN Program could assist in providing a resource sharing structure to meet those requirements, and provide general policy advice.

The Resource Assessment Group was appointed in September 1984. It is composed of librarians from libraries in universities, community colleges, corporations, state colleges and public libraries. Its charges were to design, describe and communicate a process for assessing information resources in all types of libraries. Jutta Reed-Scott, who prepared the Draft Manual for the North American Collections Inventory Project, Geri Schmidt, Project Director for the Coordinated Cooperative Collection for Illinois Libraries project, and Dennis Stephens, Collection Development Officer, University of Alaska at Fairbanks, reviewed national and regional experiences to date. The group's deliberations were used to prepare a document for library administrators who decide on their institutions' participation in the assessment process. Several assumptions underlay the group's recommendations: The standard assessment process must be compatible with methodologies showing promise of widespread national use, the process must be useable by all sizes and types of libraries, existing processes should be borrowed and adapted rather than invented (our motto is: To steal from one person is plagiarism, but to steal from many is research), and the process must be flexible so that libraries can do the assessment at levels of detail appropriate to each library's collection and available staff.

DESIGNING THE ASSESSMENT

The resource assessment process identifies where specific types of information are located in the region. The difference between this approach and bibliographic utilities, such as WLN and OCLC, is that this resource assessment is subject oriented and the bibliographic utilities are title specific. The assessment process includes information in all forms—print, video, audio, digital, etc.—as well as library information that is not cataloged and public information resources not in libraries. The assessment process is based on the experiences of the Research Libraries Group, the North American Collections Inventory Project, the State of Illinois inventory project and the Alaska Statewide Collection Development Project.

Photograph by: Maurice C. Libbey and Gene W. Scholes, Eastern Illinois University.

During the assessment, library staffs will evaluate their collections using quantitative measures such as shelflist counts and qualitative measures such as professional judgement. The ECS, variously called the "existing collection strength" by RLG, the "existing collection level" by Alaska, and the "collection level" by the LIRN Program, and the CCI, variously called the "current collecting intensity" by RLG, the "committed collective intensity" by Alaska, and the "acquisition commitment" by the LIRN Program, will be reported in numerical ratings. Various terminologies for these measurements indicate that we are still searching for language which is meaningful both to resource assessment experts and working library staffs. The ratings will be entered into a database that will display collection levels at one or more libraries for any given subject division, field or topic.

The assessment approach is flexible to accommodate the wide range of libraries and information resources in the Pacific Northwest. Several levels of detail are possible and collections may be assessed at one or any combination of levels. Each level is an increasingly detailed breakdown of Library of Congress classifications (with Dewey conversions) for twenty-five major Divisions. For smaller libraries and general collections, the twenty-five Divisions may be most appropriate. For libraries with larger collections, the 500 Fields of the next level may be more useful. This level is compatible with the National Shelflist Count. Libraries with comprehensive or research orientations or special libraries may need the full 5,000 Topics of the ARL/RLG Conspectus Project. In some cases a combination of these levels may be best—using the detailed Topics for one or two strong subject areas and the more general Fields or Divisions for others. The first five areas to be assessed will be agriculture, economics, education, engineering and technology, and music. The second areas to be assessed will be biology, geography and earth sciences, health, law, sciences, physical science, and philosophy and religion. The intent of designating these first subjects for assessment is to quickly build a critical mass of information in the collections database. Geri Schmidt has been refining the assessment levels and preparing the Dewey conversion tables.

ASSESSMENT TRAINING

Assessment training will begin in the Spring of 1985. The Graduate School of Library and Information Science at the University of

Washington has been contracted to design, produce and deliver an innovative, effective training program for librarians in resource assessment techniques. The Director of the School, Margaret Chisholm, will serve as Principal Investigator. The Director of Continuing Education, Barbara Tolliver, will serve as Project Director. The training has two elements: A four-day workshop to train regional resource people as "instructors" will be used as a pilot for subsequent training workshops for library staffs; two-day training programs sited in each of the five states will train librarians to assess library collections for collection level and acquisition commitment. Workshop materials will be adapted from materials produced by the Alaska Statewide Collection Development Project, the Draft Manual for the North American Collections Inventory Project prepared by Jutta Reed-Scott, materials developed for the Indiana pilot project of the North American Collection Inventory Project, and RLG Conspectus worksheets and Supplementary Guidelines for Conspectus Divisions and related materials. The forms and worksheets will be the RLG/NCIP worksheets slightly revised for ease of recording information and keying it into the database. Workshop materials will include worksheets, forms, sample exercises, trainers' guides, and visual aids. A training manual will be produced and available for post-project training. These materials will be presented through diverse teaching and learning techniques which may include discussions, lectures, laboratory experiences and audiovisual presentations.

Thirty to forty instructors will be selected to represent geographic regions and diverse types and sizes of libraries. Teams of instructors will be responsible for conducting the two-day training sessions for library staffs. Librarians attending each training workshop will be selected from a somewhat limited geographic area so they will have access to instructors for subsequent consultation. Local peer support will be encouraged throughout the workshops. Provision will be made for follow-up meetings, such as scheduling them in conjunction with professional meetings or through site visits by the Project Director, a consultant or instructor. Major outcomes beyond assessment-trained librarians include: Adequate follow-up to assure communication among and support for staff engaged in the assessment; a train-the-trainer component so some librarians will be able to conduct any future training workshops needed in the region. An advisory group will be used to encourage the spirit of community involvement, which is critical, as well as provide concrete support and assistance in the resource assessment process by offering advice and recommendations at the local level. Members of this group will represent each state and all types and sizes of libraries.

THE PACIFIC NORTHWEST CONSPECTUS DATABASE

An assessment of collections produces management information about the state of collections and collecting activity. Following the pattern of the Research Libraries Group, the Pacific Northwest assessment data will be entered into a database, the Pacific Northwest Conspectus, and reports will be produced.

The database design process is just beginning and the pilot version of the database is expected to be available in the Fall of 1985 with a tested version available by the end of the year. The Trust will support the operation of the database throughout 1986.

The database will not necessarily be online during the period of the Trust's support. Printed reports will be produced and distributed to all participating libraries. Access via printed reports will assure the widest access to the database, since no one online cataloging service is available in all or even a majority of libraries in the region.

The database will produce a variety of reports some of which cannot be anticipated until there is experience using the data. The following reports have been identified: Reports on individual libraries showing a profile of that library's collection; reports on groups of libraries by type or proximity such as all community college libraries in a state or all libraries in a city or county area; reports of subject collections in all or a group of libraries such as all collections in literature at the Division and Field levels.

The database will be implemented and operated by a contractor in the region and that award will be made within the next two months. The data will belong to the participating libraries and not to the Trust and reports will be made available only to participating libraries. Continuation of the database either online or in batch access will depend on its usefulness and the willingness of libraries to support it beyond the end of 1986.

EXPECTING TIMING OF EVENTS

The elements of a regional approach include: Staff training, assessment data gathering, database building, producing reports, and using those reports for cooperative collection development.

Over the next two years, these elements are anticipated to begin and continue on the following timetable. The training will begin in April and will have two periods of intense activity, May through June and September through November, 1985. The database will be designed during the Summer and pilot tested in September and October, 1985, with full operation beginning in January, 1986, and continuing under Trust aegis through 1986.

Coordinated and cooperative collection development, based on the assessment data, will begin in 1986. Some arrangements may be new and some may be improvements. Collection coordination will be at the option of the participating libraries. The Trust will only assist with meetings or in other ways that create the conditions for coordination. It is likely that regional coordination will be "grown" from many agreements and it is not obvious that a central coordinating agency is necessary. Even if it were obvious, the Trust would not play that role.

ASSESSMENT PARTICIPATION

Among the 135 accredited institutions of higher education, 41 large public libraries, 25 large special libraries and over 700 public libraries in the Pacific Northwest, the number of libraries committed to participating in the assessment process stands at 210. The distribution is 35% academic libraries, 25% public libraries, 24% special libraries, and 6% branches and miscellaneous libraries. It is interesting that the distribution among types of libraries is quite balanced. Over 90% of the largest libraries in the region are participating in the assessment.

DIRECTORY OF SPECIAL COLLECTIONS

Another activity in the resource assessment component is a general survey of special collections in individual libraries and other organizations. Librarians will be asked on a simple, one page survey mailed during the Spring of 1985 to identify collections of books, microforms, newspapers, documents, technical reports, manuscripts, tapes, films, photographs, or other materials which are distinctive, rare or unusually important. Resources need not be classified but should be accessible for on-site use. The survey will be used to produce a directory in paper, microfiche and diskette forms.

INFORMATION DELIVERY DEMONSTRATION

Another of the LIRN Program's components is the exploration and encouragement of cost effective information delivery capabilities. This component has not had as much work committed to it as the resource assessment process. The Information Delivery Group was appointed in November, 1984. Its charges are to: Review technologies associated with electronic information delivery, suggest options and opportunities for developing cost effective information delivery, propose studies and demonstration projects, and recommend a document delivery demonstration. The LIRN Program is anticipating support for demonstration projects that will show cost effective ways for improving interlibrary information delivery.

COOPERATIVE ACQUISITION AGREEMENTS

A third component of the LIRN Program is the encouragement of interinstitutional plans or agreements for ongoing cooperative resources development. The LIRN Program does not anticipate utilizing a task force approach to create frameworks or organize libraries into agreements. Instead, it is hoped that the establishment of cooperative acquisition agreements will be spontaneous, based on the data emerging from the resource assessment process. Linkages could be formed in a local area among different types of libraries or on state or regional levels among or between libraries. It is hoped that cooperative acquisition agreements will be viewed as a tool for improved individual collection management and improved coordination between collections.

FINANCIAL OBLIGATIONS

The costs incurred during the resource assessment process will be shared by the LIRN Program and individual libraries. During 1985, the LIRN Program will support: Development of a comprehensive training program, design and development of training materials, scheduling and logistics of all training workshops, training of specialists and resource people, coordination and follow-up, travel and subsistence for one representative from each participating library to attend a two-day workshop, design, development and operation of the Pacific Northwest Conspectus database, and design, development and distribution of the directory of specialized collections. In 1986 and beyond, the LIRN Program will provide all materials and forms used in the training workshops, but the sponsorship, organization, scheduling and training itself will be the responsibility of libraries.

During 1985, libraries will be expected to support: Nominal administrative time, two days of library representatives' time for the training, some 25-75 hours of staff time to assess each Division depending on the level of detail, and nominal follow-up staff time for coordination and exchange of information on the work effort. There is a problem in providing an accurate estimate of the time involved in doing the resource assessment. The time required for a research library could be extensive, but for a smaller public library could be several hours per Division. Towards the end of 1985 when there is more experience in this and other collection assessment projects nationwide, there may be a better estimate of the time involved. In 1986 and beyond, libraries will continue to carry these costs, and through local and regional coordination, libraries will be expected to sponsor and schedule workshops as needed using resource people training in the LIRN Program.

OUTCOMES AND CONTINUATION

For many libraries in the Pacific Northwest, there is a high level of commitment to collection development and a willingness to risk with this new assessment process. Anticipated benefits to individual libraries include: A clearer profile of the collection's strengths and weaknesses that can be used for internal analysis of acquisition plans, priorities and strategies that adapt to changes in mission, programs, funding or user patterns; a better picture of resource patterns locally and regionally which may lead to better access to information for patrons and serve as a basis for cooperative collection arrangements with other libraries; and enhanced professional skills in systematic collection development and improved communication with other libraries also engaged in the assessment process.

The region will benefit from: The display of information patterns; identified subject collections nearer the inquiry point reducing burdens on large, distant collections; information on which to build cooperative acquisition plans; and the identification of special collections in corporations, governmental agencies, and special collections for individuals seeking information and professionals assisting them.

The Pacific Northwest resource assessment project is unique because its inception and motivation comes from outside the library profession, from a private foundation. This structure poses challenges for continuation. The Fred Meyer Charitable Trust does not want to create a coordinating agency to continue this activity, although it will assist or facilitate the planning for continuing the resource assessment process. In the area of assessment training, trained instructors and printed materials will be available for future training programs under the potential auspices of professional associations or continuing education providers. The Pacific Northwest Conspectus database will be maintained by the Trust as economically as possible through December 31, 1986. Responsibility for continuing the database could be assumed by a bibliographic utility or a computer center. The directory of specialized collections could be continued by the regional professional association. If no group is willing to take responsibility for any of these activities, then the priority need for them, the demand in the marketplace, is too low and the Trust feels that they should not otherwise be continued. The real challenge in this type of structure is the transference and assumption of responsibility from a private foundation to other organizations.

The Trust may continue to be involved in other activities which would help fulfill its primary mission, which is to assist in providing improved access to information in the Pacific Northwest. Based on the information generated through the resource assessment process, there may be some basis for the Trust to make investments in the form of challenge grants on a cost-sharing basis with local institutions to supplement local resources in correcting subject deficiencies. The Trust considers its investment to be risk capital for development and must be used to leverage additional funds.

CONCLUSION

In conclusion, the pattern of accelerating growth in the production of all forms of recorded knowledge continues in the 1980s. New means to organize, retrieve and deliver information are being developed continuously, but they are not enough. New methods of planning and managing information resources are needed if we are to cope with present information requirements, let alone future expectations and demands.

The collection assessment project in the Pacific Northwest poses challenges: The challenge for a private foundation to conceptualize a project that will assist libraries and improve educational and economic opportunities; the challenge for the LIRN Program to fulfill the Trust's expectations in this initial library program within a very short timeframe; the challenge of the profession to realize the potentialities of the foundation's resources and goals; and the challenge to perceive the long-term value of a new, pilot tool and to continue its development and promote its use.

Commentary on the Stephens and Haley Papers

Scott Bennett

Assistant University Librarian for Collection Management
Northwestern University
Evanston, Illinois

From where better than the far Northwest could we hear about the mapping efforts that are essential to the cooperative management of library collections? These are pioneering efforts, especially as they reach beyond research libraries, and I listen with interest and respect to what our colleagues from the Northwest tell us about this frontier in library cooperation.

Mapping, whether of land or of library collections, is a tricky business. Much of what we have just heard centers on technical issues in mapping, issues that merit considerable attention. Only if we come to agreement on these issues will the maps we draw be widely intelligible. We must all use the same benchmarks and the same descriptive conventions in mapping our collections if we are to be able to communicate effectively about the cooperative use of our collections. And just as important, this common language and the shared values it embodies are essential to whatever mechanisms we will in time build for holding libraries accountable for their cooperative undertakings. What we see in the Northwest is an important and welcome effort to amplify the use and the usefulness of the conspectus as an instrument of cooperative action.

It might be added that one of the primary values of the conspectus work both in Alaska and elsewhere has little direct connection with cooperative action. Ann Haley especially has emphasized that working on the conspectus produces enhanced professional skills in collection development and assessment. We are becoming better collection managers simply by accepting the challenge of describing our collections systematically.

© 1986 by The Haworth Press, Inc. All rights reserved.

Important as the conspectus is to expanding the frontiers of cooperation, I sometimes think we forget that pioneering efforts require something more than maps. We need canoes and blankets as well, and—most important—a willingness to run risks. Describing our collections is unquestionably a prerequisite to cooperative action, but we should not confuse the prerequisite with the thing itself.

Mapping our collections is not in itself a significant cooperative activity.

Believing that, I have carefully reviewed the two papers we have just heard looking for canoes and blankets. What did I find? What specific cooperative actions are in fact proposed? In Alaska, we are told, a cooperative purchase plan should be devised and the conspectus data should be used to develop a state-wide collection development program. Specifically how the conspectus will figure in the first, or how it will be used in the second is not clear to me. If we are left guessing about these two key matters in Alaska, the prospect for action beyond mapping is far dimmer elsewhere in the Northwest. We are told that the development of cooperative acquisition agreements is one of the principal objectives of the LIRN Program. Curiously, a task force approach to meeting this objective is disavowed, and we are left with nothing but the hope—hope, mind you—that the establishment of these agreements will be spontaneous. What a remarkable hope! Can anyone looking at the failure of hard times in the 1970s to drive libraries into cooperative collection arrangements, or can anyone familiar with the limited success of RLG in this area believe that cooperation on collection matters will come about spontaneously?

Both of these papers challenge us to think about what we will do once we have completed our maps. Perhaps it will be useful for me to list some seven questions about that future which these papers suggest to me.

—Does knowing what other libraries collect automatically or spontaneously lead to cooperative collection management? If not, what will lead us there? Do we in fact know where we want to go? Has anyone advanced a specific set of goals for cooperative collection management in a specific library network?

—Is there a difference between resource sharing and cooperative collection management? If so, what is the difference?

—Exactly how will maps of our collections be used to differentiate core collections from collections that can be distributed and shared, rather than duplicated? Precisely what data are we recording in the conspectus to identify this difference? Take a hypothetical example: if we know there are eleven Level 4 collections in forestry in the Northwest, do we then know whether these collections are core collections or are sharable ones?

—Both the Alaska plan and the LIRN Program stress voluntary participation on the part of libraries. Will that in fact work? If the essence of cooperative collection management is the agreement of Library A to do something because Library B is doing something else, how will Library A hold Library B accountable for the maintenance of the agreement? Do we need a permanent governance structure for cooperative action? What muscle do we need to give this structure?

—Do we expect, or even wish, the present allocation of book or staff resources in our libraries to change because of cooperative collection management? If so, change how and by how much? Do we expect resources already in our budgets to change, or do we expect only to set aside some new resources for cooperative decision making?

—The success of cooperative collection management is likely to hinge on costly improvements in document delivery systems. Are we confident that meeting these costs, and copyright charges, and other administrative or overhead costs is the most effective way to improve access to material needed by our library users? Do we really know when borrowing is less expensive than owning?

—How will we know when we have succeeded in cooperative collection management? What are the specific measures of that success? How much effort should we spend getting ready for success—by mapping our collections, for instance—before we have defined, and defined in terms on which we can act, what success will be?

There are many other questions that should be asked and, more importantly, talked about at this meeting. Let me stop by asking you to start. Please ask your questions and make your comments about the pioneering work of our colleagues from the Northwest.

202 COORDINATING COOPERATIVE COLLECTION DEVELOPMENT

Photograph by: Maurice C. Libbey and Gene W. Scholes, Eastern Illinois University.

Discussion #4

Discussion Leader, Scott Bennett

There are many other questions that should be asked and, more importantly, talked about at this meeting. Let me stop by asking you to start. Please, ask your questions and make your comments about the pioneering work of our colleagues from the Northwest.

* * *

I'm Hugh Atkinson from the University of Illinois, Urbana. I have some comments—not just of the papers of my friends from the Northwest, but about all of the papers. One of the themes that runs through all of the presentations which concerned me is a sense of too great a commitment to neatness. While as librarians we do believe that neatness is important (or we wouldn't have invented the Dewey Decimal Classification or LC scheme, although the latter is somewhat less neat). We still believe that there is an order to the world that we try to impose upon it—at least that portion that we administer. However, neatness for its own sake strikes me as being one of the dangers for cooperative collection development. Insisting that early Celtic literature is collected by someone because nobody else is [collecting it], and nineteenth century Osteopathic medicine is collected somewhere else because no one else has it. Maybe there's no reason to collect some areas.

I would suggest, as Scott just did, that there should be a reason behind the analysis of the collection which is to form a cooperative collection program. I would suggest further that the cooperative collection program itself has a reason, also. It is the same reason that we have for local collection programs. That is to buy, beg, or steal materials to put in our libraries so that our patrons can get materials into their hands and, hopefully, the contents of those materials into their heads. That's what the libraries are about.

Given that, we can see that you can start to quantify. Just as we quantify the goals for an acquisition department. I think those same kinds of quantifiable goals for cooperative collection development can occur. Let me give you a couple. Scott, I'll answer one of your seven questions and that is the question of: "Is borrowing more expensive than owning?" The answer is: "Owning is cheaper than borrowing when there's a lot of it, the question is not 'owning vs borrowing,' it's 'the amount of activity.'"

If I look at our experience, and I have set some goals for our libraries, quantitatively, for resource sharing. One of the reasons I'm such an enthusiast is that those goals are being met. To do that, one has to recognize (as I think I do) that all libraries fail to some extent. Even a truly world class library like the University of Illinois fails, I think, approximately one third of the time. That is, about 30 percent of the time, my colleagues and I, come away from using the library missing something, missing one third. That range of success will run from 40 percent to some 65 percent in most academic libraries. In most public libraries the range of success may be broader because their success is not measured in known item retrieval. That vote may range from 20 or 30 percent success to as high as in the mid-eighties.

Nevertheless, when one should start to think in such terms and think of one's goals for cooperative activity. The goal that I've stated, as many of you have heard, is that one third of our failures should be recovered from a system of inter library cooperation and resource sharing system. It has nothing to do with cooperative collection. Since we circulate some 2,000,000 items, that goal is 200,000 items a year to be borrowed from the system. We're better than halfway there so, I'm absolutely convinced that within the next two years we will be borrowing in excess of 200,000 items a year.

I would propose as a goal for cooperative collection development that another third of our failures be met. Similar goals can be applied to public libraries, the smaller academic libraries, of *any* size. In our case, I would expect (this will take five to ten years, it seems to me) that anybody developing cooperative collection development for our library should have a goal to arrange for other libraries in the State to own materials so that we can borrow another 200,000 items a year. It is silly to put the effort and time into small, small amounts; for us it has to be the recovery of two thirds of our failures—that is one third by the system, and one third by the planning of collections. After all, if we get to those (and I think we can) we will then be borrowing some 400,000 items a year (given that our circulation internally doesn't go up any more than it has).

If that is the case, that is still only 20 percent of our circulation. That is not an unreasonable goal if you truly believe that we are interdependent institutions.

* * *

I'm Terry Weech of the University of Illinois Graduate School of Library and Information Science. I sort of had the feeling that Hugh may have answered more than one of your questions, but I'm going to give a stab at answering, or at least giving my response, to one or two.

Scott, when you asked whether knowing what libraries collect will lead to CCCD, maybe it's too self-evident to the rest of us to respond. It seems to me that the answer is that it may not be a sufficient cause or motivation for giving us CCCD, but it is certainly a necessary one and a step toward that process. Another step leading to sufficiency may be the element you raised in your second question, namely, "Is there a difference between resource sharing and CCCD?" I'm not sure I'm ready to tackle the fine points of the differences at this time, but it seems to me that resource sharing is one of those additional elements (along with mapping) that will eventually lead to sufficient causes to result in CCCD.

I do have some questions to ask Dennis and Anne. Specifically, Dennis, when you were referring to "supplemental" collections, is that a synonym for "non-core collections" or what was your reference to "supplemental?"

* * *

It is material that's not central to the institution's mission, but which could be expected to be required of them.

* * *

Both Dennis and Anne referred to the fact that, being multi-type cooperative collection development projects, they depended heavily on the strengths of non-research collections in their areas. I detected in Anne's explanation a certain element of almost an apology because of the fact that there were not that many strong research collections in the Pacific Northwest.

I'm wondering, in light of Paul Mosher's statements yesterday on the importance of working all types and sizes of libraries into a national research collection whether, Dennis, you are quite as apologetic as I seem to perceive Anne to be in the inclusion of the various types of libraries?

* * *

Well, it's certainly clear that the smaller libraries will not have as much to contribute in terms of unique items, except in the case of pleasant little surprises that we are finding in Alaska which are little caches of Alaskania materials. For example, old-timers and sourdoughs have given their local public library some quite valuable materials that, really, no one else knows about. Beyond research of things, it's quite clear that a small public library (particularly small in an Alaskan sense) won't have a lot to add, but it's still worth doing for the spirit that it generates and for the things, the pleasant, serendipitous things that you will find.

One of my favorite stories about this is from members of our steering committee who worked in Washington school libraries on this for the State Library. In Alaska, a school librarian (maybe a coordinator) indicated that a large university system in Washington deigned to have nothing to do with a certain school library collection until, by happenstance, they found them a nice pocket of unique materials and thereafter became rather heavy borrowers of that material.

* * *

I think your analysis of apology is, perhaps, misplaced. It's not an apology that there are fewer large major resource collections in the Pacific Northwest. It is simply a fact of life. It's a different library demographic situation than what you may have in the Midwest where you may, in fact, have the same number of large research collections, but in a much smaller geographic area. One of the reasons that we've included multi-type libraries is to help relieve some of those large identifiable collections in a problem that we're now facing in the State of Washington which we are calling, "the balance of trade in the interlibrary loan traffic."

Another philosophy that undergirds the LIRT program is that we have a philosophy of inclusion rather than exclusion. If a small genealogical or historical library in the Yakima Valley in the town of Grandview wants to participate—wonderful. It may be, however, that the small public library collections account for 5 percent of the actions, but that's okay. We are looking at this program of not only contributing to the national scene secondarily, but the primary focus is the regional, or the state-wide, or the local collection development agreements that can be drawn.

* * *

I have just one last comment, and that is I hope that others would tackle some of the questions that Scott raised because I think they are excellent questions and deserve our consideration.

* * *

I'm Beverly Lynch from the University of Illinois at Chicago and I think that we should ask Hugh not to use the word "failure" when he talks about what he's done in Illinois, but "success." Sixty-six percent success rate is not bad.

I do hope that, perhaps, later this morning there will be some explorations of the basic assumptions underlying each of the important programs that we've heard about. I do think assumptions are varied here and some exploration or, perhaps, explication of those in the proceedings would be very useful.

Joe Hewitt mentioned a little bit yesterday about differences in purpose in terms of the historical programs, really looking at enhancement of collections to serve a research clientele. More recently we are looking at cost containment. It's not clear to me whether we are talking about cost containment at an institutional level, at a regional level, or at a state level. I think each of those are important objectives, but we should be very specific about those objectives as we talk about these kinds of programs.

I think if you were coming at a cooperative collection development program from a circulation librarian's viewpoint, then the circulation of library materials is a measure of success. It may be that one of the measures people would want to begin to incorporate is a percentage of circulation to non-primary clientele as a measure of resource sharing. We don't see that percentage really displayed. As your institutional circulation goes from 500,000 to 600,000 and your non-primary clientele circulation goes from 60,000 to 80,000, what difference is that in a circulation statistic? How does that impact upon things other than collection such as the staff resources, etc., etc. Those are all important considerations and, I hope, as we look ahead they're brought into there.

* * *

I'd like to address Scott's seven issues just a little bit, for fun. I guess it's inherent in pioneering efforts to not know for sure exactly what you're going to find when you set out to get there. It's very hard to get there unless you have a map to help you along the way. In a way, what we've heard a lot about is, really, the results of the mapping process (or the nature of the mapping process) some hope for goals, but many of the efforts we've heard from have not yet really been there—like the Duke-North Carolina Project—for 40 years to talk about what they've really achieved in the new world when they've arrived there.

Secondly, clearly, the Conspectus effort—the mapping effort—isn't an end in itself any more than any mapping effort is. It's merely a way of trying to discover what you're really dealing with and understanding what's there. It's something that's been missing in the past and it may have had something to do with the lack of success of some previous efforts at collaboration.

Third, it's in the nature of collaborative efforts to collaborate. I guess I'm not as suspicious, as Scott can be a little bit, about the process of communities collaborating in their own interest in the fact that they have to discover how to do it. In the past, at least, if they sit down and try to draw out too clearly exactly what they will do in the process of discovery, they discover that they never set out in the ship at all because they can't really agree on the ship, where they're going to go, or what the new world will be that they're trying to find. They end up only with all of the hypotheses or the plans and not really the actions. I guess one of the exciting things is to hear people setting out on their voyage, beginning to talk about what they'll do and, certainly, beginning to agree on how they'll get there.

I agree, also, with Hugh and Dick Dougherty, that one way of trying to measure or determine what the benefits of all of this may be, or even deciding how you'll use the map in getting to the new world, rests in the area of resource sharing. That is, you look at your interlibrary lending arrangements or your borrowing arrangements (whether they're direct borrowing, interlibrary loan, or whatever), and you say, "What are we doing well? What are the failures? What would we like to do?'' You use some of these new tools to achieve it, and then you use your lending arrangements, as Beverly has suggested, as measurements of success along the way to determining whether what you're doing is worth the candle or not.

* * *

I'm not sure if committee members' responses should come later, but since this is an answer or fits in with one of Scott's questions it seems appropriate now. It seems to me that, in answer to Scott's question about "have we heard real examples of cooperative collection development?" that (it's already been mentioned at least twice in the last few minutes) the response is the Duke-University of North Carolina situation. If you think in those terms it's discouraging at first because we can all see how that situation is not going to apply to most of us especially in a multi-type situation. However, I think that we get too bogged down thinking of only the value of great in-depth research collections for borrowing.

I think there are at least two levels in which the borrowing can be very valuable, even when it's not at that level unless something can begin to be done with cooperation in different sorts of ways.

One is the famous example, which everybody I've worked with in Illinois has heard of, when all of the copies at the U of I in Urbana of Huckleberry Finn are out they can borrow them from my community college. That's one level.

The other level, though, maybe lends itself to more what we think of as cooperative collection development as opposed to what might be termed resource sharing. That's the fact that when a community college, for instance, such as the one I'm at which is in the Chicago area, has 200 volumes in Chicago history (because we have an Illinois History course) that's nothing compared to a comprehensive collection. I'm sure it wouldn't even fit into the deeper levels of the national inventory projects, but in terms of borrowing on a state level, that can be very valuable.

We have bought OP copies of some things, and that kind of thing. Chicago Historical Society doesn't lend, at Chicago Public Library it might be checked out (to use a gracious word), and so it's actually more valuable in larger state-wide terms than it is, perhaps, for the Chicago area or for our systems. People in our system, if they want to, can make that trip down to the Chicago Historical Society and it's a truly marvelous, and of course extensive, intensive collection.

But if you're 200 miles downstate, you're using a data base which shows what we have, and you know because of the mapping which has been done (which is available to everybody) that we have strength in that area, and it can be quite a valuable collection to someone.

I really think that while for those doing in-depth graduate level or publishable research that the great research libraries are, of course, the only answer. For all kinds of other people wanting all kinds of other information these small, minor collections have a great deal of value. I think that's something that really hasn't been explored much, and from my work in the past in Illinois I think it's something that we should think about.

* * *

Kenneth Peterson from Southern Illinois University. I think the conference has been extremely helpful in identifying a lot of issues, perhaps alleviating some anxieties, and creating some new ones. I don't think that Scott intended to close us in an air of pessimism in the last seven questions. I think that we can cope with those particular issues.

There are three issues, and I don't add these as pessimistic questions or as pitfalls, but rather as issues that I think we need to make sure are incorporated in any plans within Illinois for a comprehensive collection development program. I think they've been touched on by the various speakers, but it seems to me rather thinly. We will need to be sure that we don't lose track of them.

First of all, how can we assure the people on our campuses and the people who are guardians of the stewardship of our collections that the integrity of collections which have been developed over long years with specific purposes in mind are going to be maintained. I think this is extremely important. I think that we need to be very careful that we're not dealing with numbers, that we're not making our assessments based upon numbers, but that in the qualitative review we do respect and make plans to maintain the integrity of collections that are needed by scholars.

Secondly, one area that has been touched on, but I think needs far more working on is: how do we involve our faculties in this whole process? This is not just a librarian's activity or venture. We are doing this for our faculties so that the resources of the State can be more effectively developed. I think we're all aware of the fact that we're going to meet a certain amount of resistance by our faculties, and in a very positive way we're going to have to show them the benefits of cooperative collection development. I think that we need, in the early stages, to think of, "how do we bring our faculty along and win their support?" because their weight and influence will be very necessary as we make decisions.

Finally, it seems to me that while we have been talking about the Conspectus, evaluating the strengths of the existing collections, and so on, we haven't said very much about the shifting of programs and the development of academic programs in the institutions of Illinois. I hope very much that we do not lose track of that. Our collections, after all, are not built in isolation. They are built to meet the needs of academic programs that are parts of our institutions. Some of these programs are complimentary, some of them are unique at certain institutions, some of them will be growing at some institutions, some of them will be moving from one institution, perhaps, in its strength to other institutions. I think any program for cooperative collection development is going to have to respect the changes and the trends that we can experience in the future in terms of our academic programs.

* * *

I think it's interesting that all of us from Illinois have to say something. It's very clear that we're dealing with a subjective kind of situation right now. What we will obviously need, as Beverly Lynch has suggested, is some more objective kind of data to know what the costs and the trade-offs are as we move into a new era or new approach—a new operational mechanism.

I would like to bring our thinking around to what Bob Wallhaus mentioned at the opening of this conference yesterday. That is, to think about this as an inventory problem. It is a problem that takes into consideration the total inventory of all of our libraries, and as Hugh Atkinson has mentioned, we all cannot do all things to all people for all people. We need each other. There just will be different mechanisms that will have to be put into place to address that particular kind of problem. There are fixed costs and there are variable costs. As we try to implement new mechanisms in that process we will have to make trade-offs.

* * *

While the next person is deciding to come to the microphone, let me turn the tables and ask Hugh a question. It follows up on Mary Alice's last comment.

Hugh, I'm very much attracted by what you said because it gives us a sense of direction. I wonder, in thinking about your proposal that you want to see cooperative collection management account for another two hundred thousand transactions at your library, whether you have given much thought as to how much you're willing to pay to achieve that end and how those costs would compare with other costs that you are already bearing.

* * *

What I'd be willing to pay and what the institution would be willing to pay, remember, are two different things. Let me give you a way of looking at that. We spend, more or less, $4 million a year to buy materials in our library. For that, some 80 percent of our circulation is on some 20 percent (as it is in all academic libraries) of our collection. Applying that to the acquisition dollar, because I still think of these things in terms of trade-offs for that, that means that some 1,600,000 circulations are because of some $800,000 (or 50 cents each). Yet, another group—the lower-use items—come to about $8 an item.

It's also our experience, by the way, that it's because about half of the items we borrow are items we already own, but are unavailable to the patron at the time that I sure don't want cooperative collection development to say, "You can only have one copy in the State." Half of the things are 50 cent items and half of them are $8 items. If we're looking for 200,000 more items, that's 100,000 at 50 cents ($50,000) and 100,000 at $8. That $850,000 is the cost target.

If that's the price then I can do it myself, so I don't want to spend all of that money, of course. I don't know whether it's 10 percent of that (which strikes me as not too illogical) or 20 percent, or 50 percent, or 70 percent. Any of those numbers would, in fact, be a payoff, but at the moment politically unobtainable. The reason I'm for the question that Ken asked about faculty involvement is, in fact, when we look upon these as devices to serve that faculty and demonstrate that often enough and long enough, I think we'll have the faculty support to continue to develop the cooperative programs. I do think that as we move forward that, in fact, we will be moving towards numbers similar to that.

* * *

I don't want this to be a song and dance team, but (in response to your question, Scott,) there is another very important program in Illinois that has to be folded into the discussion: That's the Historical Program of the R&R Centers and the payment of monies in the State of Illinois to circulate materials. If indeed, we are talking about a real change in resource sharing in the State of Illinois based on circulation then, I think, that entire program must be reviewed as well, and that involves State law.

A Model Criterion for a Statewide Plan/Process/System

Carl W. Deal

Director of Library Collections
University Library
University of Illinois at Urbana-Champaign

INTRODUCTION

As the moderator of this final panel, I have two responsibilities. The first is to synthesize for you in a few moments the best and most appropriate advice, encouragement, and ideas which have been presented by our invited conference speakers. This presentation will be formatted into a set of criteria or guidelines which I hope will have some lasting and beneficial impact on coordinating cooperative collection development undertakings in this and other states.

My second responsibility is to invite all of you here to offer new ideas, cast your doubts, ask further questions and otherwise participate in our final discussion of this very important topic. Your questions will be directed to one of the four panel leaders or to the appropriate conference speaker.

Let me begin by pointing out that the need for this conference became apparent to its planners who discovered, upon being faced with the problem of planning and coordinating cooperative collection development especially among academic libraries in the State of Illinois, that the literature offered very little guidance based upon the experience of other states or regional groups which had undertaken programs of cooperative collection development. The planners I refer to are members of the Subcommittee on Cooperative Collection Development of the Illinois Association of College and Research Libraries Liaison Committee to the Illinois Board of Higher Education. This subcommittee, of which four members are discussants for the panels at this conference, is composed of a diverse group of university and library administrators representing community colleges, four year colleges and universities, regional library networks in the State of Illinois, private and public universities, the Illinois State Library and the Illinois Board of Higher Education. Cooperative collection development has been viewed by this subcommittee as not being restricted to the participation of only a selected few libraries, but as having broad impact on the entire state which is interconnected by eighteen regional networks sharing the same resource base. Our ambition results from the obvious need to cooperate on a grander scale.

Resource sharing is central to cooperative collection development, and coordinating that development today is much more feasible since automation has made it possible to identify and share resources in a way that would not have been possible a decade ago. Perhaps that is why others and I believe libraries have entered a new era in which cooperative collection development may become the centerpiece to improved access to library resources. Yet, as David Farrell has pointed out, coordination is very difficult to bring off, and we don't yet know enough to determine how costly or beneficial it might be. The extent to which cooperative collection development can be successfully carried out, the way in which it can be most effectively implemented, and the funding requirements, be they less in some cases for savings in duplication of materials and efforts, or more in other instances due to improved access to more materials, are the unanswered questions which have most interested this subcommittee. Those same questions are not answered or widely discussed in the library literature, and one goal of this conference is to produce with these proceedings some guidance which will be useful to other committees or groups of concerned librarians and funding agencies which I know in other states are dealing with the same problems.

This is also an opportunity for me to commend our speakers for the quality of their advice and guidance. Dr. Paul Mosher and Marcia Pankake have produced the model guidelines, "A Guide to Coordinated and Cooperative Collection Development," which is intended to suggest possible contexts, goals, methods, organizations, effects, and processes which should be investigated for their advantages and disadvantages while planning for establishing such programs. Our conference speakers have provided a series of practical seminars for us on just how cooperation has been atempted and achieved across the country. I shall attempt to tie together these practical experiences into a set of model criteria/procedures.

The model criteria which follow are extracted from the papers presented at this conference. They are based on practical experience rather than assumption. They corroborate completely the guidelines developed by Mosher and Pankake for the profession, but they cannot be considered complete. Coordinating cooperative collection development is still in a formative stage, and criteria require the flexibility necessary to cope with new formats of information which will require new techniques for resource sharing. With these views in mind, the criteria which we can gain from present experience shared at this conference have focussed on six very specific areas which are: administration and funding, access and delivery of materials and information, planning, requirements of participation, activities most appropriate for cooperative collection development, and assessment of resources. They are presented here within a framework based on these specific areas.

MODEL CRITERIA FOR COORDINATING COOPERATIVE COLLECTION DEVELOPMENT AMONG ACADEMIC LIBRARIES

I. Administration

A. General

1. A governing authority should be established to coordinate efforts and respond to or set priorities. This central authority receives annual and periodic reports from participating institutions, organizations, and committees.
2. A mechanism should be devised to insure the continuous interaction of collection development administrators, selection officers and bibliographers in formal and informal meetings to provide a current environment for developing new opportunities for cooperative collection development.
3. Task forces and appointed committees may be required to create frameworks or organize libraries into agreements. Whenever cooperative resource sharing is already well established, cooperative collection development agreements may be designed through both planned and spontaneously conceived programs. For smaller local client-centered systems written agreements are useful, but there may be no need for separate governance.

4. Building on an established system or network can give leverage in achieving greater cooperation from less interested libraries. However, libraries agreeing to undertake certain activities as part of a plan should participate in their own self-interest and in meeting the needs of their primary clientele.
5. Funding and staff support are required for the administration of any large and formalized program of cooperative collection development. Experience where formal programs are underway in Colorado and New York suggests that even when programs are building on preexisting systems, there are administrative costs which require funding.
6. Constant promotion of programs among faculty and other constituents is a feature which enables users to perceive the benefits of cooperation.

B. Funding

1. Proper funding is the stimulus which will most attract the participation of libraries.
2. Funding is an incentive and should not be used as a threat. Libraries should not be penalized for not participating, nor should they be funded for participating if they do not wish to be a member or cannot participate on an equitable basis.
3. Funds for planning proposals and to support training for preparation of collection assessment tools and developing those tools are required.
4. Activities to be supported should be considered and prioritized so that excessive funding of a single program does not jeopardize the needs of other programs.
5. Formulae for funding must be carefully drawn to avoid inequity in funding for participating institutions. This has most occurred to the initial disadvantage of the larger research libraries or regional state systems with the highest user populations.
6. The long-term maintenance of programs of cooperative collection development depends upon incorporating their support into ongoing budget allocations.
7. Cooperative collection development should be funded for a sufficient period of years to become ingrained in a library's budget process. Such programs can become remarkably persistent once they are so established.

8. When outside grant money is secured for cooperative collection development, it should be used as seed money continued by state funding ideally for three or more years in order that patterns of cooperation in a given activity or area can become firmly established.

II. Access

A. General

1. Activities essential to cooperative collection development include the development of a network base linking members through a compatible online circulation system, as well as an automated public access catalog.
2. Central to the success of a program in coordinating cooperative collection development is the ability to incorporate online access and data retrieval mechanisms into cooperative collection management strategies. At the core of the most efficient system is a commonly accessed data base kept online or available in batch access.
3. Reliable information and data on collections must be shared and analyzed in order to make forceful and timely decisions. Collection overlap, interlibrary loan patterns, and pre-acquisitions order information are part of the reliable information referred to.
4. Cooperative collection development requires access to supplementary collections for study and research and to specialized materials which are less used than core collections. This material can be part of the shared pool where it is most appropriate but accessible to all.
5. Access to material is improved whenever actual ownership of materials may be freely transferred to another more appropriate location.

B. Delivery

1. An effective information delivery program is a component of cooperative collection development.
2. Direct access and/or delivery through interlibrary loan are essential to cooperative collection development.

3. Regional state-supported systems encourage resource sharing not only by facilitating location and delivery but through interlibrary loan agreements. Through negotiation the system works to increase access; through its interlibrary loan procedures it seeks to equalize the burden of requests.
4. To insure up-to-date and efficient delivery of information to the user, careful consideration and review should be given to technologies associated with information delivery in planning for the most cost effective and efficient information delivery system.

III. Planning

A. While coordinating collection development might work best with systems of academic libraries, the benefits of cooperative collection development reach out to other types of libraries. The inclusion of the needs of other libraries and of representatives of those libraries in the planning of a statewide system is advisable.
B. There must be a certain degree of parity if cooperative collection development is to work as a mutually beneficial enterprise. Smaller nonspecialized libraries cannot collect systematically at a level that would be useful to the research libraries without seriously overbalancing the collections of the smaller libraries.
C. In the case of collection development planning, a common vocabulary and set of descriptors is paramount. Those descriptors are well presented in the Mosher, Pankake "Guide to Coordinated and Cooperative Collection Development" and in the American Library Association's *Guidelines for Collection Development.*
D. States wishing to undertake collection development on a widespread basis should conduct surveys throughout the area of participation to determine the status of collection development at each participating institution.
E. A description of resources on a systemwide basis should describe the needs and a plan to meet those needs. Basic tools for planning are the Mosher, Pankake guide and ALA guidelines.

F. A standard list of collection subject areas will make the planning process easier. The National Shelf List Count, which is reproduced in the ALA *Guidelines for Collection Development*, and RLG conspectus are useful models from which standard lists may be compiled.
G. Decisions on collecting responsibilities are based on collecting strengths, collecting commitments and on the core missions of participating libraries. Cooperative collection development recognizes that each participating library requires a well-defined core collection to support its primary mission.
H. Funding for the measuring of collections quantitatively and qualitatively will yield more uniform collection depth descriptions.
I. Collection development workshops or seminars should be offered to insure greater uniformity and compatibility of collection development statements and provide for a more systematic program of building collections and sharing resources.

IV. Participation

A. Access by interlibrary loan and/or extension of direct borrowing privileges are requirements for participation in programs of cooperative collection development.
B. Consortia which have cooperative collection development as their enterprise should not restrict membership to all private or all state funded institutions. Participation should rather be based on how to best serve the public receiving the services and sharing the resources.
C. Participation in cooperative collection development is appropriate for multi-type library cooperation.
D. Members participating in cooperative collection development should be encouraged to form regional groups across library types. The building blocks of cooperative collection development at the system or state level must be effective local collections.
E. Cooperative collection development at the local level prepares us well for participation in national and regional programs. The areas of specialized collections depth developed under local programs are more likely to make a useful contri-

bution to the goals of national and regional programs than are areas of collections which have been developed in a vacuum.

V. Activities

A. General

1. Collection development is an important trend in librarianship which has grown into a philosophy of management reaching beyond the boundaries of basic selection and deselection. Therefore, funding for collection development should provide for a variety of activities among which are funding for the formulation of bibliographic databases, retrospective conversion of member's records, conservation and preservation objectives, and planning grants for outside funding and program improvement. All of these activities are important to the sharing of resources which is the most compelling reason to cooperate.
2. Cooperative collection development activities should not be limited to a single effort like shared purchasing. In spite of the fact that this might be the most saleable item to legislators, it may have less impact on cooperative collection development at different stages in a state's development of programs.
3. Accessing of many unanalyzed collections is a problem. Support of the proper cataloging and analyzing of these collections is a proper cooperative collection development activity.
4. Preservation in all of its facets of activity is a component of coordinated cooperative collection development.
5. The preparation of up-to-date union lists of serials is a useful activity.
6. A program of collection analysis should be developed providing uniform methodologies for use and user studies, collection evaluations, and verification and overview studies.
7. An analysis of special strengths of a region or state will be facilitated by a directory of special collections.

B. Cooperative or Shared Purchasing

1. A program of cooperative acquisitions is a goal of cooperative collection development.
2. Cooperative purchasing imposes specific administrative burdens if utilized extensively. To maximize the effectiveness

in cooperative purchasing, the following factors should be examined in developing a policy.
   a. Adequate administrative support is required for selection of proposals, setting of priorities within the limitation of the funding allocated and for maintaining a high interest and high level of participation. Such support will vary from a committee representing participating institutions to a part-time or full-time staff member for more extensive programs.
   b. Purchasing cooperatively should have clearly defined goals which take into consideration the availability of materials through interlibrary loan and the accessibility of the materials from other repositories outside of the cooperating system.
   c. Periodic evaluation of cooperative or shared purchasing should be undertaken and a methodology of evaluating the use of cooperative purchases should be agreed upon by the participants.
3. Adequate bibliographic and physical access must be available or provided to permit effective sharing of resources.
4. In shared purchase programs, form and format are unimportant. Eligible materials should include but not be limited to computer based services, machine readable data files, newspapers and other serials, archival and manuscript collections, and large microform collections.
5. The emphasis on cooperative or shared purchases of little used serials material is a common product of cooperative collection development. However, in a time of retrenchment this may not be a valid use of resources, if only limited funds are available for this purpose.
6. Choice of location may be dictated by various factors such as academic programs, strength of collections, projected use, and reasonable consideration of equity in distribution of materials among participating libraries.
7. Material may be puchased for the system as opposed to being purchased for a single library. This accompanies a philosophy also whereby material may be transferred freely to another library and become a part of its permanent collection.
8. There are limits to shared purchasing as a coordinated collection development activity. Funding levels should be adjusted to not exceed those limits.

VI. Assessment

A. General

1. Coordinated collection development cannot operate within its widest range of possible activities until a collections inventory and database is completed. Assessment is the means to build a critical mass of information in order to establish a collections database.
2. The assessment process should be usable for all sizes and types of libraries, although the time involved in the assessing of major collections of research libraries is much greater than required for smaller collections.
3. The standard assessment profiles must be compatible with methodologies showing promise of widespread national use.
4. Uniformity in definitions and methodology allow a more rational approach to collection comparison between institutions, enable more effective cooperative purchasing, and provide a mechanism that justifies collection development on a state-wide basis.
5. In assessing their collections, library staffs should evaluate their collections using quantitative measures such as shelflist counts and qualitative measures such as professional judgment.
6. Assignments of collection responsibilities must be based on specific levels of collecting intensity.
7. Formal agreements which impose lasting responsibility accompanied by signed agreements are advised as subject and area assignments of collecting are assumed or assigned, particularly at the research level. Elaborate and finely drawn agreements assigning specialized areas of responsibility may very quickly reach a point of diminishing returns when applied below the level of research libraries.
8. The regional resource approach should reflect interinstitutional commitments in specific subject areas.

B. Collection Development Statements

1. The development of collection assessment tools requires in the planning process provision for developing workshops and the proper materials and guides for instructing participants. Training manuals as a post training product are recommended.

2. Library holdings should be assessed through the medium of updated collection development statements using a standard format.
3. An online maintenance system permitting in-house adjustments to all sections of the statement, including the narratives, is essential to maintaining a current, efficient and reliable online database of collection development statements.

C. *Conspectus Preparation*

1. Cooperation cannot begin until libraries are able to communicate with one another about their collections on an item by item basis and categorical basis. The best tool for that communication is an online catalog for sharing resources and a conspectus of collection strengths which is developed around standards that insure conformity with cooperative collection development in other areas outside of the state and which is compatible also with a national database built around the RLG conspectus and the North American Collections Inventory Project of the Association of Research Libraries.
2. Each participating library should survey its holdings and prepare a conspectus. These individual conspectuses should then be compiled into a statewide map of library resources.
3. Conspectus information should be used to develop a statewide collection development program for a five and ten-year period to optimize the financial and human resources of the state in developing its information and knowledge resources.
4. Staff support should be made available in the period involved with conspectus development and publication and with collection development plan formulation.

In summary, coordinating cooperative collection development is time consuming and hard to analyze. While it may not save dollars, it allows libraries to utilize their resources more effectively in making available greater resources to their users. Many librarians today are committed at least to the ideal that cooperative collection development is a desirable library enterprise. Speakers at this conference have acclaimed various benefits and identified problems from different perspectives and experiences.

Paul Mosher asks we "keep the future in mind, while working in the present, to think of the whole and not just the parts." For the Triangle Research Libraries Network, cooperative collection development increases the availability of more materials to library users and avoids unnecessary duplication. Long range benefits are massive once they begin to appear, and cooperative collection development at the local level prepares libraries well for participating in national and regional programs. In Alaska and the Pacific Northwest, sharing resources through cooperative collection development is the most appropriate way to utilize limited resources in the face of an accelerated growth in the production of all forms of recorded knowledge. In Indiana, testing for participation in the North American Collections Inventory Project is completed and suggests that NCIP is a desirable and feasible project. In California, Colorado and New York, the need to better support and share library resources in the face of rising costs and greater demands by library users has attracted state funding. In Illinois, funding from the State Library has produced a manual on cooperative collection development for a multi-type cooperative library system, and in New England, a consortium of academic libraries from both private and state universities is developing a model system which through automation will provide better service through resource sharing.

All of these programs have the same final objective: to serve the needs of library users as completely, efficiently, and economically as possible. Unless greater experience with coordinated cooperative collection development in the future produces different and negative advice, it appears coordinating this activity warrants the most serious consideration of academic libraries and the systems they serve.

REFERENCES

American Library Association, Collection Development Committee. *Guidelines for Collection Development.* (Chicago, The Association, 1979)

Association of Research Libraries, Office of Management Studies. *Manual for the North American Inventory of Research Library Collections*, January 1985 ed. (Washington, D.C.: The Association, 1985)

Colorado Commission on Higher Education, Colorado Academic Master Plan Committee. *Colorado Library Academic Library Master Plan.* (Denver: The Commission, 1982)

Kruger, Karen. *Coordinated Cooperative Collection Development for Illinois Libraries*, 3 vols. (Springfield, IL.: Illinois State Library, 1983)

LC/DEWEY CLASSIFICATION Conversion Tables, [for the National Shelflist Count] Draft 1983. Prepared by Geri Schmidt. 1985.

Mosher, Paul H. and Pankake, Marcia. "A Guide to Coordinated and Cooperative Collection Development." *Library Resources and Technical Services*, 27. (October/December 1983): 417-431.

Research Libraries Group. *RLG Collection Development Manual*, 2nd ed. (Stanford, Calif: Research Libraries Group, 1980-81)

Photograph by: Maurice C. Libbey and Gene W. Scholes, Eastern Illinois University.

APPENDIX

Model Criteria for Coordinating Cooperative Collection Development among Academic Libraries

I. ADMINISTRATION

A. General

Neuman/Rutstein	1. A governing authority should be established.
Hewitt	2. A mechanism should be devised to insure the continuous interaction of collection development administrators, selection officers and bibliographers.
Krueger/Haley	3. Task forces, and special appointed committees may be required to create frameworks or organize libraries into agreements.
Krueger/Neuman	4. Building on an established system or network can achieve greater cooperation, but libraries should participate in their own self-interest.
Rutstein/Neuman	5. Administration of large programs requires funding and staff support.
Hewitt	6. Promotion of programs among faculty and other constituents should be undertaken.

B. Funding

Buzzard	1. Proper funding is a stimulus and should not be used as a threat.
Buzzard	2. Libraries should not be penalized for not participating.
Haley	3. Funds for planning proposals and to support training for preparation of collection assessment tools and developing those tools are required.
Buzzard	4. Funding of a single program should not jeopardize the needs of other programs.
Neuman	5. Formulae for funding must be carefully drafted.
Hewitt	6. The long term maintenance of programs of CCCD depends upon incorporating their support into ongoing budget allocations.
Hewitt	7. CCD should be funded for a sufficient period of years to become ingrained in a library's budget process.
Hewitt	8. Outside grant money is secured for CCCD should be used as seed money.

APPENDIX (continued)

II. ACCESS

A. General

Rutstein	1. Activities essential to CCCD include the develpment of a network base with an online circulation system and an automated public access catalog.
Haley/Stephens	2. The incorporation of online access and data retrieval mechanisms into cooperative collection management strategies is useful.
Krueger/Hewitt	3. Information and data on collections must be shared and analyzed.
Stephens	4. CCCD requires access to supplementary collections.
Bozone	5. Access to material is improved whenever actual ownership of materials may be freely transferred.

B. Delivery

Haley	1. An effective information delivery program is a component of CCCD.
Bozone/Buzzard	2. Direct access and/or delivery through interlibrary loan are essential.
Neuman	3. Regional state-supported systems encourage resource sharing.
Haley	4. Consideration should be given to information delivery technologies.

III. PLANNING

Neuman	A. While CCCD might work best with systems of academic libraries, benefits reach out to other types of libraries.
Hewitt	B. There must be parity if CCCD is to work as a mutually beneficial enterprise.
Neuman	C. A common vocabulary and set of descriptors is paramount.
Rutstein	D. States undertaking collection development should conduct surveys to determine the status of collection development at each institution.
Neuman	E. A description of resources on a system-wide basis should describe the needs and a plan to meet those needs.
Neuman	F. A standard list of collection subject areas makes planning easier.
Stephens	G. Decisions on collecting responsibilities are based

APPENDIX (continued)

	on collecting strengths, collecting commitments, and on core missions of participants.
Neuman	H. Funding for the measuring of collections quantitatively and qualitatively will yield more uniform collection depth descriptions.
Stephens	I. Collection development workshops or seminars should be offered.

IV. PARTICIPATION

Hewitt	A. Access by interlibrary loan and/or extension of direct borrowing privileges are requirements for participation.
Bozone/ Buzzard	B. Consortia should not restrict membership to all private or all state-funded institutions.
Neuman	C. Participation in CCD is appropriate for multi-type library cooperation.
Krueger/ Stephens	D. Libraries participating in CCD should be encouraged to form regional groups across library type.
Hewitt	E. CCD at the local level prepared libraries well for participation in national and regional programs.

V. ACTIVITIES

A. General

Neuman/ Stephens	1. CCCD funding should provide for a variety of activities.
Buzzard	2. CCCD should not be limited to a single effort like shared purchasing.
Buzzard	3. The proper cataloging and analyzing of unanalyzed collections is a proper activity.
Buzzard	4. Preservation is a component of CCCD.
Rutstein	5. Preparation of up-to-date union lists of serials is useful.
Stephens	6. Collection analysis should provide uniform methodologies.
Haley	7. An analysis of special strengths of a region or state will be facilitated by a directory of special collections.

B. Cooperative or Shared Purchasing

Stephens	1. Cooperative acquisitions is one goal of CCCD.
Rutstein	2. Cooperative purchasing imposes specific administrative burdens.

APPENDIX (continued)

        a. Adequate administrative support is required.
        b. Purchasing cooperatively should have clearly defined goals.
        c. Periodic evaluation of cooperative purchasing should be undertaken.

Buzzard   3. Adequate bibliographic and physical access must be available to permit effective sharing of resources.

Buzzard   4. In shared purchase programs, form and format is unimportant.

Bozone   5. Shared purchases of little used serials material in a time of retrenchment may not be a valid use of resources.

Buzzard   6. Location may be dictated by various factors.

Hewitt   7. Material may be purchased for the system as opposed to being purchased for a single library.

Buzzard   8. There are limits to shared purchasing as a CCCD activity.

VI. ASSESSMENTS

A. General

Haley   1. CCCD cannot operate without a collections inventory and database.

Haley   2. Assessment should be usable for all sizes and types of libraries.

         3. Standard assessment profiles must be compatible with methodologies showing promise of national use.

Rutstein   4. Uniformity in definitions and methodology allow a more rational approach.

Haley   5. Library staffs should evaluate their collections using quantitative measures and qualitative measures.

Hewitt   6. Assignments of collection responsibilities must be based on specific levels of collecting intensity.

Hewitt   7. Formal agreements are advised as subject and area assignments of collecting are assumed particularly at the research level.

Haley   8. The regional resource approach should reflect inter-institutional commitments in specific subject areas.

APPENDIX (continued)

B. Collection Development Statements

Neuman/Haley	1. Development of collection assessment tools requires workshops and the proper materials and guides for instructing participants.
Stephens/ Rutstein	2. Library holdings should be assessed using a standard format.
Rutstein	3. An online maintenance system is essential.

C. Conspectus Preparation

Stephens	1. Cooperation cannot begin until libraries are able to communicate with one another about their collections.
Stephens	2. Each participating library should survey its holdings and prepare a conspectus.
Stephens	3. Conspectus information should be used to develop a state-wide collection development program.
Stephens	4. Support should be made available in the period involved with conspectus development.

Panel Discussion

Moderator, Carl W. Deal

EDITOR'S NOTE: Highlights of the Conference are framed within the model criteria presented and reviewed in this final session. This discussion provides the opportunity to compare operating plans with each other and with the practical and philosophical aspects of coordinating cooperative collection development.

* * *

I'm not sure if this is a question or an avid pronouncement, but I'll make it. I'm the Director of the Urbana Free Library. My academic library is the University of Illinois, which [makes it] very nice to run a public library a mile away from seven million books. It simplifies the procedures, but there are some things we can't get from them. Once in a while we have something they need which is what I want to talk about, because we've only touched briefly on public libraries and their place in CCD arrangements. One thing, obviously, several people have touched upon is local history. I think, this is the one area that, actually, collections do exist.

What has bothered me in looking at collections in public libraries is the degree to which there are virtually no in-depth collections in areas that are of no interest whatsoever to academic institutions. There are many fun areas, such as, if you want to get at a really massive collection of materials on gerbils—good luck. You know, people laugh because nobody in the academic world really has a big interest in gerbils these days, but there are people out there [who do]. If you want to see the annual (I'm making things up off the top of my head) national baton twirling championship final performance programs for the 1930's, where are you going to find these? There are a lot of fascinating areas; my favorite is model trains which I hate to mention because everybody laughs at me again, but there are huge ranges of areas for which materials exist, are not very expensive, and virtually no collections exist.

The problems seems to be that the libraries that think in scholarly ways don't collect them. The libraries that think in terms of these subjects are not academic libraries. As a result, a great many subjects simply fall through the cracks in the floorboards. None of them are terribly expensive to collect. You could set out to build, I'm sure, a gerbil collection (I should pick a less silly example) but, what would a subscription to "Act on Gerbilliana" cost?—not a great deal.

In almost any area, an expenditure of a few thousand dollars a year would provide a genuine scholarly collection. It seems to me that what we have to do eventually is that public libraries have to nail down narrow, specific areas that are within their ability to afford and simply buy everything available. Not buy slightly better collections, which has been one way that public libraries have tended to have gone with purchase agreements where we go from spending $3,000 a year in business books to $5,000 a year in business books, but to (literally) buying everything in a special narrow area we can afford. Because many public libraries have tiny book budgets compared to academic institutions, I don't think we're blocked from it. It's always possible to redefine the areas of specialty even more narrowly. For instance, if a public library devotes 2 percent of its book budget to a topic, it can buy a topic sufficiently small so it can still own everything. This is one way, I suspect, of overcoming the problem. Most of the academic libraries I know that buy pop materials don't really maintain the collections. A huge collection is given and the collection sits there, but it isn't continued.

Owning a few interesting cases, the University of Illinois has massive continuing funding for the purchase of books in the occult. I'm not sure that Hugh [Atkinson, University Librarian] would buy them, all other things being equal and that money not being earmarked. He'd find a different and more academic use for it. Am I putting you in a bad light, Hugh?

* * *

(Hugh Atkinson: You're absolutely correct.)

* * *

I think this is almost a different kind of planning and I don't think it will work simply by cooperation. I think we almost have to go ahead and once the agreement is made, cudgel each other into doing it.

To respond to one of Scott (Bennett's) questions, I don't think public libraries easily and naturally will fall into saying, "Okay, I'm going to spend 2 percent of my budget for the next 50 years buying books on model airplanes," because they keep falling back on the ultimate argument: "What do our users need?" The users, once in a long time, need that kind of material and then they simply can't find it.

It's all made more complex by the fact these things are unindexed, uncataloged, unanythinged. Trying to even find your way through to the fact the materials exist is difficult. One of the things that I remain convinced of in looking at patrons requests is that people don't request things they don't know about. Unlike a scholar to the academic admissions, it has never occured to them that this magazine title may exist and it has exactly what they want.

I think, ideally, in this kind of situation these collections that function (like Illinois' R&R Centers where the staff, in addition to simply owning the materials which might literally be a dozen shelves), would also be prepared to answer questions dealing with them simply because nobody else collects in enough depth to know how to cope with them.

* * *

I have a lot of practice not laughing at Fred [Schlipf], so I think I'll respond. One of the concerns that I've had yesterday and today as we've heard the various presentations is a theme that has been brought out several times and then seemed to be dropped. It relates to what Fred has expressed as a concern over popular material sometimes not defined as 'scholarly.' It also relates to the call that Beverly Lynch put forth to consider the assumptions that are behind the planning and not just in the area of financial support, but also in the area of some of the definitions of terms such as research, scholarly, and popular, and what those eventual definitions that are arrived at mean for the type of cooperation plan and format that might eventually evolve.

We've had several speakers that have described multi-type cooperative collection development efforts and several other speakers that confirmed a philosophical commitment to that type of cooperation. Yet, there seems to be (in many of the responses and considerations in the discussion) a locking in on 'scholarly' or 'research' as a presumption or assumption of what we're talking about when we're talking about cooperating and collection development. I would like to encourage others, if others have a concern, to follow up on Fred's comments. Also, as a result of this conference, I know it's a very difficult job and Carl (Deal) did a great job of trying to match ideas and concepts on the list that was distributed to you, but it seems to me that one of the things that are missing (though it's referred to in several sub-units) something to the effect of the recognition that there *may* be a need of multi-type or variety involvement. At least three or four of the speakers of the conference have referred to that, and it seems to me, it at least deserves further consideration in trying to come up with the general principles behind the cooperation.

Does anyone else have any other thoughts in that area?

* * *

Ken Sertic from the Illinois Valley Library System. I crossed out—not being sacreligious or anything—"Development Among Academic Libraries" and put down "Model Criteria for Coordinating Cooperative Collection Development Among All Types of Libraries" because as a administrator of a multi-type library system, I think that's one of the challenges that, at least, I'm going to be taking back to see what can be done in terms of a multi-type library environment to encourage resource sharing, collection development, and collection management. For example, one of our smaller libraries which happens to be a high school library was asked by means of an OCLC terminal to lend something to a library in the Soviet Union. I would think that the librarian who received the material could care less whether it came from their core collection or the collection to support the other side of the collection that was referred to.

I also hope that the challenge after this meeting is not to go back and talk, but rather to try and implement. I think that we do a good job in many cases of planning and talking. I think it's encouraging to hear that things are happening in a multi-type library environment, so that if nothing else, which I think is a big thing for me to take away from here, the challenge of seeing how it will work in a multi-type library environment.

* * *

I would like to raise one other point under assessment, item number VI on Carl's list (and again not just in Karen Krueger's presentation, but it was referred to in Joel's discussion of Colorado and, I believe, in some of the other papers): the concern over client centered or user centered assessment. Maybe I'm misreading or not seeing it coming through, but it seems to me that it's something which deserves more attention and consideration than we've given it.

I'm not saying it's right or wrong or the proper way to go, but are we really just dismissing it at this point without further discussion since it hasn't seemed to be something that is coming up in the discussions that we've had so far. Is it too difficult, too complex, or impossible to verify? What are the problems and concerns some people see?

* * *

Bev Miller from Suburban Library System. I guess it takes an ex-public librarian to talk about that because you're constantly justifying your cost to your taxpayer. I think that's why you have to go back to the user.

I think what Fred was referring to is existing out there in the public libraries. We need to identify it, but a lot of those model airplane collections, or I think of a play collection, has come because of the local user. They may have a very significant local amateur theater production company, etc., so that play collection is there because there are local users.

I just want to underscore what he said, but it has to go back to the client. Any kind of multi-type cooperation with the public library has to be very user oriented. That's where you justify your tax dollars.

* * *

Let me follow up pretty quickly, I think sometimes it simply doesn't exist. I think some of these collections, it's not a matter of sharing resources, because in some of the areas the collections simply don't exist at all. I think we'll have to, in some cases, simply create them and it's a matter of convincing our tax payers that the end result is worth it; the fact that we are dropping several thousand [dollars] a year in an area that they would rather see a little less spent on, is an absolutely essential criteria. There's no way that adequately in-depth collections and pop areas can be built simply on the strength of local enthusiasm. I may be overly cynical about it, but I really don't think it can happen.

Since I'm standing here, I think, just in reaction to a couple of things that were said: There is no equation between non-academic and non-scholarly. A lot of people have incredible scholarly interest in non-academic areas. I think we have to keep that in mind. I notice that in these pop culture areas all the time. The depth of knowledge and research that somebody fascinated with the history of the Rock Island Railroad as a rail fan will dig into is of, certainly, sometimes even greater depth than that pursued by a doctoral student working on a thesis. It can be really incredible.

I think another thing that happens in pop areas is that the local demand is extremely elastic for materials. It's very hard to measure the demand because, in a large part, demand results from what actually is there. As the provision changes the demand changes. I'm convinced, and it's too late to do a study now, but 10 years ago we started really building our local history collection. Today, I think, it's one of the biggest in down state Illinois. Demand has skyrocketed, and I'm sure, if we'd gone around the community 10 years ago and said, "Do you expect a good local history collection in a public library?" vastly fewer people would have said yes than would say so in response to the same question today because they expect from the library what they come to find at the library. I think this is much more true in public libraries than it is in academic libraries, where the curriculum comes much closer to driving the demand on the library, but in public libraries people come to look because they know it's there. Given that, it's very, very hard to go out and evaluate what the demand actually is because we simply don't know until we provide it. It's an awkward circular kind of situation. I don't see any easy planning solution to.

One other thing, I think, is really critical in pop culture areas is that many of the best collections are out there, but they are in the hands of non-loaning institutions. This is a major problem. If I want (to come back to my favorite example) to access to a major collection on model trains, but they won't loan. They are in a mixture of private hands and in the hands of associations that maintain research libraries in their headquarters and tell non-members to look elsewhere. One of the most critical things, I think, that has to come is the formation of these collections in areas in institutions that are willing to let the books go out of the library.

* * *

I was really excited when this conference started because Robert Wallhaus started with what, I thought, was a terrific talk. The very first think I wrote down in my notebook was a statement and I think this is a pretty accurate quote, "We need to continually analyze data to see if customers demands are being met."

I've become more discouraged as the conference has gone on because I feel that we aren't looking at the customer. I think, doing an analysis of collections is essential. I think the Conspectus is one way to do that, I think there are many others. There's tons of materials out there about analyzing one's collection and we've talked a lot about how different people do that, but what we really haven't discussed is, "Are we building those collections for the sake of building collections?"

I remember being taught in library school that we needed to build balanced collections. You evaluated your collections based on where you were weak and where you were strong. In my definition of strength and weakness, it does not mean you're strong because you have 'x' number of materials, or particular kinds of materials, or a depth in that subject. You have a strong collection if that collection meets the needs of the people that come into your library who want materials on that subject. I have to say that I hope somewhere in all of this we can come to some approach that looks at the user and the client and whether, as Robert Wallhaus says, we are really meeting their demands.

* * *

Saying that I pay taxes in the City of Urbana and so I'm one of the users that uses the Urbana Free Library, and I have always been immensely pleased with the direction that it gets from someone who says to the citizens of Urbana, "We need to think about the unique possibilities for collecting at that library." We have, in other context at this conference talked about our need in academic libraries to talk with the faculty; convince them that what we're trying to do in cooperative collection management is in their best interest.

I think Fred's been trying to do the same thing in Urbana. In fact, it is the same enterprise. It's only because we're engaged in the same enterprise that, I think, there is much hope in talking about multi-type cooperation. I really do welcome it, I think that we face the same job. The key here, (in talking about client centered activities in libraries) is to remember how much the active, vigorous, intelligent, systematic development of collections is at the heart of our ability to serve users.

* * *

I have to make my comment about pop culture in academic libraries. I've always believed very strongly in academic libraries as a community, as far as that we're supporting a community of users, not just for research purposes. I've always believed in building that way and certainly taking into account user/client related assessments of collections.

I wish to remind our public library friends of this, too. We're very much involved in building popular collections for our users. We have a very good browsing current awareness collection at my university library and I'm kind of proud of it. We get a lot of use out of it. It doesn't cost that much money to maintain. Perhaps, the most important thing is it brings a lot of people into the library. I think anything that brings people into the library, just like with the public library, is extremely crucial. I'm all in favor of that, believe me, for academic libraries.

* * *

To try to tie back to academic libraries; at the break, Hugh Atkinson was telling me, if I remember correctly, that about 50 percent of the materials borrowed on LCS at the University of Illinois are for items the University of Illinois already owns. I think, that is something we need to think about when we're talking about what constitutes a core collection, what constitutes a research collection, what constitutes resource sharing, and what the relationship of resource sharing is to cooperative collection development. As he said, he's interested in what other core collections are being developed. Yet, I detected in some of the papers that were put forth, an attempt to distinguish between core collections which were, in a sense, noncirculating collections to meet local needs, and supplemental collections or (as someone said) the shared collections—collections that you could borrow from.

The tradition established in Illinois, (particularly in LCS as well as, in many ways, in ILLINET) is that the important thing is getting the material to the user and sharing resources. That connection to cooperative collection development and is, perhaps, the point we're at to try to reconcile what may be initially perceived by some people as a difficult dilemma of matching the needs with the primary clientele in a given library situation.

* * *

Since my paper mentioned core collections and supplementary collections, I hope I haven't created a miscomprehension. By core collections, *I* did not mean non-circulating materials. It seems that, perhaps, some people have misunderstood that the core collection that an individual library builds to fulfill its mission does not circulate; that is not true, at least, insofar as my paper was concerned. Those materials, also, are available for circulation in interlibrary loan.

* * *

I think, to try and put it back on a level that crosses all kinds of libraries, again, from the most major research institution to a smaller public library, [that] part of the reason we would be willing to collect in an area is because we, also then, want to be able to borrow from somebody else that collects in an area. I appreciate Karen's points and her concern for the local use and the local patron, but if some patrons in that library want to borrow from somebody else that's built a collection, then there's a reciprocity there.

I think, that comes back to some kind of public relations (in the highest sense of the word,) whether it be at a large research institution or a small public library. The reciprocity is being built by building something special in your collection so that you can borrow something special from somebody else's collection.

To bring some of our speakers back in again; I had a good number of other questions yesterday, but it was late in the day so I really didn't go ahead and ask them. In relation to that, I'd like to ask Joe Hewitt a question or clarification from his paper. He mentioned the fact that, not only do they buy requests from their other institutions that are in the area they're to cover, but they also buy from area libraries when it's . . . (I wasn't quite clear whether it's in the subjects area they cover or other areas). I'd like to ask him a little more about what that kind of arrangement is, what the trade-offs and benefits are, and how it started. I thought, that was an interesting supplement to the main type of cooperation he was talking about in his paper, and something that could right some other additional insights we didn't get.

* * *

Did you say, "buy *for* other libraries?"

* * *

Right, yes.

* * *

We do, mainly for other agencies, not necessarily libraries. The National Humanities Center, located in the Research Triangle Park, is an organization that sponsors 50 scholars a year who come and live there, have private offices, secretarial help, free food, and work on their scholarly work. They're supposed to spend their time there in their very pleasant commons area and not go out and work in the libraries. One reason they're there is because of the library collections and we are supposed to support their needs. Some of those scholars have as many as five-hundred books checked out at one time, we've found. Any time they need materials they submit their request to the librarian on sight who operates a reference service, who in turn screens them and directs them to one of the three libraries according to where it will best fit and we purchase those materials. We do that, to a certain extent, for other companies and agencies in the Research Triangle Park. We don't get any payment from them, but we do get moral support and letters of support when we go out for grants and that sort of thing.

It seems to me that certain questions may have been directed at my comments yesterday relating to the possibility that the effort at coordinated collection development ought to be focused on the research libraries. That was just a suggestion that I brought up from my experience in North Carolina and what I meant, really, is that I believe there is a difference in the nature of cooperative collection development as it would take place at that level and in other types of libraries. It certainly doesn't mean that you should not have it in both types of libraries.

I know that it relates a little bit to the question of, "what is resource sharing versus cooperative collection development?" If a faculty member walks into Duke with a stack of Australian materials to be ordered and the librarian says, "We don't collect in Australia, but there's a possibility that some other library might so we're not buying these," that's one thing; that's resource sharing. If, on the other hand, the faculty member comes in and is told that, "We don't collect in Australia, but North Carolina does and we'll send these orders over there for them to buy on your behalf;" that's cooperative collection development. I think, there are very few cases where a large research library could participate in that way with much smaller libraries. There are cases in North Carolina where it can be done. Appalachian State University has the best collection in the State on materials relating to the Appalachian region. On that focused level, they certainly would participate with us in cooperative collection development.

I think that what I'm saying is that there might be several levels where the character of the coordination is somewhat different. The small and medium sized libraries contribute greatly to materials available for resource sharing, but very few of them are in a permanent responsibility to collect systematically in areas of interest to researchers and major research institutions. What they have out there is going to help greatly in satisfying the incidental requests that the research librarians couldn't, in any way, anticipate in their collection development processes.

Our users use a lot of materials that are not related to their research. These are things that we can not expect to fill, yet we want to assist them in fulfilling through whatever resource mechanisms exist. There's a great deal that can be accomplished through cooperation, but whether or not this should be done through the great effort that goes into coordinated collection development may be questionable in my mind.

* * *

Doris Brown, DePaul University in Chicago. One area that hasn't been covered at all in our discussion of academic, research, and public libraries is the special libraries. Those of us who are in an urban area where we have a heavy reliance on special libraries and the informal agreements that we've worked out with the special libraries for their research materials are especially interested in this.

There are some people, various subject groups, etc., that are meeting, again, informally or under the aegis of, sort of, floundering groups.

I'd like some comment from the people on the Illinois committee, from the people from the other states, or from members of the audience of what discussions have taken place about the incorporation of special libraries. What plans are there? Is there a role for special libraries? There's been discussions about the confidentiality of a lot of their materials. What kinds of talks have you had on that area? What plans do you see? Is there a role for special libraries?

* * *

I'm Marge Dorigan, and I'm from the Standard Oil Library Information Center and probably one of the very few people here from a corporate library. I'm here because I'm the chairman of a task force to establish a collection development policy for the eight libraries in our company. There is also some one here who I've just met from 3-M and we're probably 'it'.

I just wanted to mention that our policy as far as making our materials available and opening our library to individuals, and so forth, is that we allow anyone who has a reason to come to use materials that we have rather uniquely—in other words related to the petroleum, petrochemical, or chemical industry—to use our materials. Some people seem to be rather surprised at this, but we've done it and we do it extensively. By the way, we borrow from you at DePaul a lot. I don't know that you ever borrow from us. I wish you would because we feel we'd like to reciprocate. We are very open to anyone using our materials.

As far as what we are doing, other than this person from 3-M, we're kind of just beginning as far as this collection development area is concerned and it's primarily within our own company. We do all have on-line catalogs. We do communicate via electronic mail for interlibrary loans, photocopies and that kind of thing, but it's all inter-company.

As far as doing anything for the outside, we'll do anything that's asked of us, but we don't, for instance, participate in OCLC because we don't have any of our material cataloged. We have everything indexed, and so we really couldn't contribute our material as far as adding it to OCLC so that people are going to see that we have it, but if anyone calls us because they think we're the kind of library that has or is likely to have something, we're very happy to lend. I can tell you I spend a very great deal of my time in this function: giving tours, 'dialoging' with people who are interested in what we have and what we do, we're always hosting special library groups from various universities and we lend a great deal. Even more than that, we have people coming in to use our materials because a lot of them are things like *Platt's Oilgram Price Service, Petroleum Intelligence Weekly*, and things like that which are bibles to us and we can't really let out, but we will let people use. I don't know if that answers your question.

I appreciate the fact that you brought it up. One of the reasons I'm here is because I have not known of any forum where this topic is being discussed. We're just getting started in it and as I said, the people from 3-M are already into it, but I'd be very happy to know if anyone knows of anyone else who is because I wish I could take advantage of their expertise.

* * *

I'm Anne Lee from the Connecticut State Library, and I'm sorry that my colleague from the Connecticut had to leave a little earlier. One of our regions in Connecticut is involved, now, in a coordinated collection development program using Karen Krueger's example and it does include several special libraries including insurance companies. I'd be glad to give you some more information about that.

* * *

Howard Dillon, University of Chicago. I appreciated Joe's coming back to resource sharing and coordinated collection development. What he said sort of clicked for me and put some things into a perspective. It was interesting that his comment was followed by the special library example because, I think, that fits into what fell into place for me.

I was associated with the Illinois Regional Library Council for a long time during its history. That, I think, was an important resource sharing mechanism. I think, in terms of a state or a region, resource sharing can involve libraries of all types because you're dealing with the known and how to make it available to others, or making what's there known.

It seems to me in the coordinated collection development, one is looking also at institutional commitments over a very long haul and over an attitude that exists within that institution. While the attitude of a public library may be to take on documenting (for the long haul), the history of its community it is not necessarily, in my experience, the case that public libraries would make such long term commitments to other areas because I do believe, (as has been pointed out by a few speakers) those libraries have to address the changing interests of their community. A continual assessment of needs would, perhaps, move them away over time from some particular areas of interest.

Coordinated collection development or collection management, I think, carries with it also, the responsibility for preservation. It's not something that's been talked about here, but I think that that becomes, again, a very long term commitment.

To Joe's point, which I was thinking about yesterday when he made it: what are the obligations, then, of research institutions where the notion is that a lot of materials are collected, not because they are in use now or not because somebody has identified that as an area of interest, but because somehow we believe our society—our intellectual life—will need that information at some point. Perhaps, need it in ways that we don't anticipate now.

I think there is, therefore, something in that rather provocative remark that Joe made yesterday afternoon that has to be thought about as we think about a program here in Illinois, and whether there are some differences between resource sharing for the things we have in our collections now; and collection development, which means what we're prepared to commit to buy over a very long haul, preserve as it deteriorates, and justify its expense whether there is a client driven use or not.

* * *

Howard, just to comment on the preservation—it wasn't mentioned at this conference, but the State of New York does provide $1 million a year for preservation activities. I think about $800,000 of that goes to nine large research libraries who are using it for that purpose.

* * *

I think there is a distinction here in terms of a definition of coordinated cooperative collection development; certainly, collecting, having primary responsibility for the collecting on a subject is the traditional. It's the one that most of you here, I think, are interested in; but when we looked at collections, the use patterns, and acquisition patterns in some of our libraries—one of the subjects, for instance, that was highly in demand was in the field of medicine. That's why I used it as an example. There are lots of people and this crossed school library, and academic library, and public libraries—it wasn't just public libraries. A lot of people in those constituents were interested in current, up-to-date information on cancer, on all kinds of medical related information. It seems to me, it's very appropriate for all types of libraries to be doing coordinated cooperative collection development to acquire materials that are not of primary collecting responsibility where they need to commit to those for 50 years, because those materials go out of date in 5 years. They're gone. There are a lot of subjects like that. We had the same thing happen with Literary Criticism. We have students who go to the public library. We have college students who go across library bounds. Those materials need to be purchased in a coordinated way, and once that coordinated collection development is done they need to be shared with the resource sharing mechanisms we have in place.

I think, we really have two divisions of definitions of coordinated cooperative collection development. Mine may be more of a currentness, not a long, lasting, in-depth primary collection responsibility, but I would stand by the view that coordinated cooperative collection development is appropriate for every size and type of library.

* * *

I want to react very quickly to something Howard said, and then I promise to sit down and not say any more. One of the things that he was talking about preservation in public libraries and long term commitment. I think, public libraries have really failed in some of these areas, but to the extent that a public library is maintaining a long term history collection, for example, on the local community, either it learns preservations or it has a terrible collection. It has to somehow keep the thing going. So even though we may not meet all the standards we'd like to meet, at least we have to struggle.

The other thing has to do with general acquisition policies. Public libraries have a very strange history in this area. For one thing, if you read the acquisition policies of public libraries they never tell you what they buy. All they do is reaffirm the right to read and the right of the staff to buy books. When we set out to write one on local history, we scoured the whole country and then wrote our own. We even went to historical society collections and couldn't find a good example of a local history acquisitions policy for long term collection development.

I think what's happened in public libraries is they began with a kind of politely humanistic collection development aim. They were going to buy good books for literate, sober readers. Then sometime in the last generation we've shifted to something which is completely reactive, which is we simply buy whatever we think people want today. I'm not sure that is the optimal solution either. It seems to me, that sooner or later public libraries have to say, "There's more to it than either buying elegant literature for nice people, and more to it than buying whatever it is that we think the market calls for this afternoon," because at that point, then we end up (I'm not trying to twist Karen's words), but we end up simply buying nothing but books we intend to throw away in 5 years.

* * *

I'm Ann Schaffner from the Boston Library Consortium. I wanted to follow up on the question of commitment which has just been raised and ask if anyone has more detailed comments on some of the political aspects of bringing a cooperative collection development program into being. Specifically, how do we encourage this voluntary participation which we all agree is so important? What are some of the kinds of resistance that we might meet, and how can we answer that kind of resistance?

I think these are issues that were raised in the beginning, but not really explored in any detail.

* * *

That's a good question. I just have, I guess, a very brief response and that is you get people to cooperate willingly by showing that it's in their own self-interest to do so.

* * *

It's not all commitment. Once they get started it becomes a practical matter. For example, in our case of our two catalogers in the East Asian area, neither can catalog in Japanese. If we wanted to break our commitment and start collecting in Japanese we would be in real trouble. Our whole staff, over a period of time, has tended to be oriented to the commitments that we have. Once that happens you no longer have a moral commitment, but a very practical one to continue your obligations under these programs.

* * *

I'm actually only reiterating what I said yesterday about the funding stimulus. Yes, once people are doing things they become habitual, they see how valuable they are, they think, "Gee whiz, we should have been doing this all along," but how do they get started? We feel that the funding built into the program in New York State has gotten people started. It's still new, it certainly hasn't reached a point that everybody thinks, "Gee whiz, we should've been doing this all along." It's something that's going to take time to get to that, but they will stay with it because there's reason to stay with it.

If we can get it expanded to other types of libraries, it will open up some of those things. For instance, with the public libraries—if they were getting, comparable funding to what the academics are now getting in New York, and it probably wouldn't be set up exactly that way, but say it were—a public library might be getting $4,000-$5,000 for cooperative acquisitions of one sort or another. Maybe they could invest half of that money, whatever they got in, into building one of those specialized collections that were for the good of the whole (in addition to whatever users they happen to have that sparked it). Probably, in choosing among all those kinds of special things (like "Why gerbils and not parrots?"—I would much rather have parrots) somebody started your interest in that, and they kept asking for all this stuff.

All right, why not build in that one? Nobody else obviously had it, but if you had some 'income source' that stimulated it that wasn't taking it out of the monies coming out of your local tax money that the user wants to see something that's specifically for his or her purpose. With the special libraries there may not be a way to use those funds in exactly that way, but there may be ways to put into the system mechanisms for having a better idea of what are in those special libraries that are able to share.

We have that problem—a great willingness to share, but we don't know what they have in detail. We know that they collect in the area of population. We've got a number of special libraries (Population Council, Planned Parenthood, some of these), but knowing that we've got three or four libraries that collect in this area doesn't tell us where any specific item might be. We might be able to take it a little further if there were some pooled funds that did that, even if we couldn't hand over the money to them. Maybe we could if we thought it through because we are handing over money to private institutions that happen to be academic libraries.

There's a lot of things that could be done to facilitate. They may not be the same for all types of libraries, but you will have a richer pool of materials if you include them all. I think, the stimulus of the money is going to make it more possible to do that if you look in those directions.

I was a little bit frightened by what had been suggested, at least what I think is suggested, in the outline I was given of what your criteria would be. It sounded to me like you were talking about some funding stimulus that was going to go away. Received money is marvelous, but how many of us know about programs that got a little bit of money and they were just dandy while they were getting that money. Then when the money wasn't there, the program wasn't there. Maybe it didn't go on long enough to get established so that people knew it really was that dandy and they wanted to keep it going, or maybe there are so many other pressures on money. Just think of all those programs that were good programs that aren't there anymore because that outside funding source isn't there, on at least a minimal level, to keep it going. Remember, I said, for the academic libraries "the funding that's coming in is only 2 percent of their acquisitions budgets." That's not really big money and yet, it's enough of a carrot, so keep that one in mind.

* * *

I would just follow up to what Joan has said in my review of both the New York and the California situation that an external force was the initiator for the programs in those two states. I think it took that external force to actually set a mandated direction or goal backed up, of course, by the funding mechanism.

I think another major point that has been brought out in the discussion of all the papers is the need for information. Information is a powerful tool. Once we know what you have in your collections and where those collections are located, you can then begin the process of exchanging making enlightened decisions about what you purchase on your local level; what we might be able to purchase, weed out, manage, preserve, store, and work on a system-wide level. I think the information is a key to that whole process.

* * *

I'm Barbara Tolliver from the Graduate School of Library and Information Science at the University of Washington. Certainly, in reply to the gentleman from the University of Chicago on justification: justification by faith is surely not enough. We do need data. If I were on the City Council of Urbana, Iowa City, or wherever, of course, *I* would want that quantitative information.

I also think that in defense of popular materials if we in any way (before those funding bodies) seem that our materials are irrelevant or trivial, we're dead in the water. Also, some of the selection implications that this gentleman raised certainly, for library schools in educating people who are excellent selectors, is an issue facing library education. In the criteria—it's not really a criteria, but I hope that it's something that we really pay paramount attention to—is our professional self-image. That kind of assessing, the real knowledge of our collections, will give us a confidence that, I think, is something we need very much.

We talk about the need to remotivate and restimulate. In many cases, for people in the profession, this is a marvelous way to do it. (Not to be too academic about it, but that phrase "Professional Librarian" to me, personally, is galling. That's a redundancy as far as I'm concerned.) Real assessment tools are one of the measures we have of affirming that.

Finally, at risk of the sanctity of local autonomy we're implying that there is a choice. In fact, with those funding bodies there may not be a choice about cooperative coordinated collection development.

* * *

We have time for one more question.

* * *

The point I want to address was addressed earlier by several people in the audience. That was the existence of many fine excellent research collections in special libraries and museums which need to be coordinated or integrated into this whole concept. I have personal experience with using many of them in the Chicago area and their existence, outside of a few librarians or people in the area, is minimal.

Photograph by: Maurice C. Libbey and Gene W. Scholes, Eastern Illinois University.

For Product Safety Concerns and Information please contact our EU representative GPSR@taylorandfrancis.com
Taylor & Francis Verlag GmbH, Kaufingerstraße 24, 80331 München, Germany

www.ingramcontent.com/pod-product-compliance
Lightning Source LLC
Chambersburg PA
CBHW071818300426
44116CB00009B/1357